17 <u>95</u>

Poetics
of Imagining

PROBLEMS OF
MODERN EUROPEAN THOUGHT

Series editors
Alan Montefiore
Jonathan Rée
Jean-Jacques Lecercle

POETICS
OF IMAGINING

From Husserl to Lyotard

RICHARD KEARNEY

HarperCollins*Academic*

An imprint of HarperCollins*Publishers*

Published by
HarperCollinsAcademic
77–85 Fulham Palace Road
Hammersmith
London W6 8JB

First published in 1991

British Library Cataloguing in Publication Data

Kearney, Richard
Poetics of imagining : from Husserl to Lyotard. –
(Problems of modern European thought).
1. Imagination. Philosophical perspectives
I. Title   II. Series
128.3

ISBN 0-04-445450-3
ISBN 0-04-445451-1 pbk

Library of Congress Cataloging in Publication Data

Kearney, Richard
Poetics of imagining : from Husserl to Lyotard / Richard Kearney
p.   cm. – (Problems of modern European thought)
Includes bibliographical references and index.
ISBN 0-04-445450-3. – ISBN 0-04-445451-1 (pbk.)
1. Imagination (Philosophy) – History – 20th century.
I. Title   II. Series
B105.149K42   1991
111'.85–dc20
90-21234
CIP

Typeset in 10 on 12 point Garamond
Printed in Great Britain by Billing and Sons Ltd, London and Worcester

For
Anne, Simone and Sarah

In Wahrheit singen, ist ein andrer Hauch.
Ein Hauch um nichts. Ein Wehn im gott. Ein Wind.
RAINER MARIA RILKE, *The Sonnets to Orpheus*

Contents

Editors' foreword

During most of the twentieth century, philosophers in the English-speaking world have had only partial and fleeting glimpses of the work of their counterparts in continental Europe. In the main, English-language philosophy has been dominated by the exacting ideals of conceptual analysis and even of formal logic, while 'Continental philosophy' has ventured into extensive substantive discussions of literary, historical, psycho-analytic and political themes. With relatively few exceptions, the relations between the two traditions have been largely uncomprehending and hostile.

In recent years, however, Continental writers such as Heidegger, Adorno, Sartre, de Beauvoir, Habermas, Foucault, Althusser, Lacan and Derrida have been widely read in English translation, setting the terms of theoretical debate in such fields as literature, social theory, cultural studies, Marxism and feminism. The suspicions of the analytical philosophers have not, however, been pacified; and the import of such Continental philosophy has mostly been isolated from original philosophical work in English.

The PROBLEMS OF MODERN EUROPEAN THOUGHT series is intended to help break down this isolation. The books in the series will be original philosophical essays in their own right, from authors familiar with the procedures of analytical philosophy. Each book will present a well-defined range of themes from Continental philosophy, and will presuppose little, if any, formal philosophical training of its readers.

Alan Montefiore
Jonathan Rée
Jean-Jacques Lecercle

Acknowledgements

Acknowledgement is due to the following for permission to reproduce material appearing in this work: extracts from *Imagination* by Jean-Paul Sartre reproduced by permission of Gallimard and the University of Michigan Press; extracts from *Ideas* by Edmund Husserl reproduced by permission of Collier; extracts from *Husserl* by Paul Ricouer reproduced by permission of Northwestern University Press; extracts from *The Psychology of Imagination* by Jean-Paul Sartre reproduced by permission of Gallimard and Citadel Press; extracts from *Eye and Mind* by Maurice Merleau-Ponty reproduced by permission of Northwestern University Press; extracts from *Time and Narrative* by Paul Ricouer reproduced by permission of University of Chicago Press; extracts from *Soleil Noir* by Julia Kristeva reproduced by permission of Gallimard; extracts from *In the Beginning was Love* by Julia Kristeva, copyright 1987, used by permission of Columbia University Press, New York.

My thanks to all those who helped me write this book, in particular my students and colleagues at University College Dublin and Boston College.

Poetics
of Imagining

Introduction

Why philosophize about imagination? Why turn one of the great gifts of human existence into an object of intellectual interrogation? After all, is it not obvious what imagining is? Are we not doing it every day, every night, every time we dream, pretend, play, fantasize, invent, lapse into reverie, remember times past or project better times to come? So why not just let it be? Why analyse? Why, in the poet's words, murder to dissect?

It is true that imagination lies at the very heart of our existence. So much so, as we shall see, that we would not be human without it. But precisely because imagining is such an immediate and inextricable feature of our experience it is easy to take it for granted, to assume it as given. As a result, we may lapse into an attitude of inattentiveness, ceasing to worry about the everyday ins and outs of imagination, forgetting to ask about its origins and ends.

Might we not say of imagination what Augustine once said of time – we think we know what it is but when asked we realize we don't? Of course we all know – each one of us – *something* about imagination. It is the wager of philosophy, however, that we may come to know *more* about it by asking questions of it. Not that knowing is everything. But it can, at best, heighten our appreciation. And better to appreciate what it means to imagine is, as I will argue, better to appreciate what it means to be.

Since the beginning, imagination has been acknowledged as one of the most fundamental, if concealed, powers of humankind. Its elusive presence is accurately conjured up in Kant's famous words about 'an art hidden in the depths of nature . . . a blind but indispensable faculty of the human soul without which we would have no knowledge whatsoever'. This formulation represents a telling transition between ancient and modern accounts of imagination. And by way of introducing our present study it may be helpful to take a cursory glance at some key moments in the historical genesis of such accounts.

1

Whether one follows the Greek version which traces the imaginative power of making (*techné demiourgiké*) back to the Promethean theft of fire, or the biblical version of the origin of the creative drive (*yetser*) in the transgression of Adam and Eve, it is striking how the origins of humankind and of imagination coincide.[1] In both these founding narratives of Western culture, the power to imagine is considered a property unique to human beings. Neither gods nor animals possess imagination. Only mortals are blessed with it. And it is a mixed blessing.

The biblical tradition of commentary identifies imagination with the knowledge of opposites. Such knowledge is inextricably linked, at root, to the human potentiality for good and evil – a potentiality fatefully activated with the Fall of the First Man (*Adameth*) into history. This loss of paradise in turn signalled the birth of time. It corresponded to the specifically human experience of temporal transcendence as an imaginative capacity to recollect a past and project a future – that is, the capacity to convert the given confines of the here and now into an open horizon of possibilities. Once east of Eden, imagination was free to spread its wings beyond the timeless now into the nether regions of no-longer and not-yet. And, henceforth, the creative power of imagining would be seen as inseparable from the power to transmute nature into culture, to transform the widerness into a habitat where human beings might dwell. Or to put it in the specific terms of rabbinical exegesis: the *yetser* is the freedom to prospect a future of good and evil possibilities where we may choose to complete the Seventh Day of Creation (*Yetsirah*); or choose, for that matter, to lapse into an idolatry of false images by locking ourselves up in our own idle fantasies. As one biblical commentator put it:

> Imagination is good and evil, for in the midst of it man can master the vortex of possibilities and realize the human figure proposed in creation, as he could not do prior to the knowledge of good and evil . . . Greatest danger and greatest opportunity at once . . . To unite the two urges of the imagination implies to equip the absolute potency of passion with the one direction that renders it capable of great love and great service. Thus and not otherwise can man become whole.[2]

The Greeks also recognized the dual tendencies of image-making. Plato notes its association with error and transgression – dating back to the Promethean theft of fire as recounted in Greek mythology – and he acknowledges that the human ability to 'erect images of the gods' means that mortals can set themselves up as rivals to the divine demiurge. Accordingly, in the *Republic* Plato cautions against the making of images (*eidōla demiourgia*) as a mere *imitation* of truth whereby artist and sophist alike – and for Plato they are really two of a kind – fabricate fake copies of reality. Imagination, named alternatively *eikasia* and *phantasia* by Plato and the Greek thinkers, is roundly condemned as a pernicious strategy of simulation: one which tempts mortals to take themselves for omniscient gods, whereas in fact they are merely playing with reflections in a mirror. And, if it is true that Aristotle is more lenient in allowing *phantasia* a certain legitimacy as an aid to practical reason (by recalling past experiences and anticipating future ones it can mobilize our present behaviour in a particular direction), even he is reluctant to permit *phantasia* any freedom in its own right (*De anima*, 428–9). Aristotle was prepared to admit there could be no thinking 'without images' (*De anima*, 432a), but he still holds to the view that 'imagination is for the most part false' (*De anima* 428a). Moreover, the Latin authors, who generally translated *phantasia* as *imaginatio*, are no less suspicious of its pseudo pretensions, with Pliny remarking that 'nothing could be more foolish than a man ruled by imagination'.

The conflation of classical and biblical cultures extended the litany of accusations against imagination. Christian thinkers like Augustine, Aquinas and Bonaventure all warned against its susceptibility to irrational passion (even demonic possession), while granting that in certain pedagogical circumstances it could be used, under the strict supervision of reason and revelation, to instruct the faithful. As one rather pragmatic prince of the early Church put it, if one had the Holy Scriptures in one hand. one needed Holy Pictures in the other.

The most compelling reason for the censure of imagination in the mainstream tradition of Western philosophy was the suspicion that it threatened the natural order of being. Most classical and medieval thinkers considered imagination an unreliable, unpredictable and irreverent faculty which could juggle impiously with the accredited distinctions between being and non-being, turning things into their opposites, making absent things present, impossibilities possible. Or, as Thomas Aquinas observed in a resonant phrase, imagination makes 'everything other than it is'.

Modern philosophies developed the basic understanding of imagination as *presence-in-absence* – the act of making what is present absent and what is absent present – while generally reversing the negative verdict it had received in the tribunal of tradition. For Kant and German idealists such as Schelling and Fichte the imagination (termed *Phantasie* or *Einbildungskraft*) is celebrated as a creative transforming of the real into the ideal. Fichte even goes so far as to claim that 'all reality is brought forth solely by imagination . . . this act which forms the basis for the possibility of our consciousness, our life' (*Grundlage*, 59). Moreover, Kant's description of it as the 'common root' of all our knowledge and Schelling's identification of it with the 'unconscious poetry of being' were to have a momentous impact on the entire Romantic movement. Samuel Taylor Coleridge, writing directly under their philosophical influence, was to set the agenda for Romantic poetry when he defined the 'primary imagination' in the following quasi-divine terms: 'It is the repetition in the finite mind of the eternal act of creation in the infinite I AM' (*Biographia Literaria*, XIII). But it was no doubt the French poet Baudelaire who delivered the crowning accolade of Romanticism when he nominated imagination 'the queen of the faculties . . . which decomposes all creation and creates a new world, the sensation of novelty'. It is a short step from finite thrones to infinite ones. 'Since it has created the world, it is fit that it should govern it,' concludes the author of *Paradis artificiels*; adding that since 'the possible is one of the provinces of truth, [imagination] is positively related to the infinite'. Plato would not have been pleased. Though he would probably have claimed the rueful satisfaction of 'I told you so'.

The plurality of terms for imagination mentioned in our above summary – *yetser*, *phantasia*, *eikasia*, *imaginatio*, *Einbildungskraft*, *fantasy*, *imagination* – have at least one basic trait in common: they all refer, in their diverse ways, to the human power to convert absence into presence, actuality into possibility, what-is into something-other-than-it-is. In short, they all designate our ability to transform the time and space of our environment into a specifically human mode of existence (*Dasein*). This is the miracle of imagining which has so fascinated and confounded those philosophers who throughout the centuries have sought to explore and explain it. The present work is just one further tentative footstep on this path of inquiry.

This work differs from my previous studies on imagination, in particular *Poétique du possible* and *The Wake of Imagination*, by focusing on a

4

single movement of modern philosophy rather than attempting an over-all genealogy or ontology of imagination. The single movement I speak of is that which comprises the broad *phenomenological* project which extends from the writings of Husserl and Heidegger in the early decades of this century, through the *existentialism* of Sartre and Merleau-Ponty to the ulterior assessments of *poetics* (Bachelard), *deconstruction* (Derrida, Lyotard) and *hermeneutics* (Ricoeur, Vattimo).

The phenomenological movement, considered in this extended sense, embraces various critiques and surpassings of Husserl's initial formulation of the project. But all its variations share the virtue of inviting us to think again, to go back to beginnings, to question anew. This has the methodological advantage of enabling us to ask what things *mean* – as if we were asking for the first time. We no longer take 'things themselves' for granted. We enter an attitude of methodic unknowing where things cease to be facts, data, objects, possessions, and become *questions*. So doing, we acquire what Paul Ricoeur has termed a 'second naïveté' capable of conducting old inquiries in new ways.

The history of philosophy is, of course, full of such new beginnings, from Socrates' *docta ignorantia* to Descartes' doubt, Hume's scepticism and Kant's critique of the conditions of possibility of knowing. Phenomenology does not presume to break with such critical precedents, merely to repeat them in a more radical and fundamental manner. Thus, if phenomenology offers the possibility of rethinking the age-old question of Being in a novel manner – as Heidegger, Sartre, Merleau-Ponty and Bachelard maintain – it also empowers us to rethink the question: What does it mean to imagine? Moreover, the *question of imagining* resembles the *question of being* in that both relate to something so obvious as to be overlooked and so elusive as to be unnameable. A paradoxical phenomenon, now here, now gone. Something, as the poet said, 'more distant than stars and nearer than the eye'.

Phenomenology solicits a radical shift of perspective (*Blickwendung*) whereby imaginative consciousness may reflect upon itself. So doing, imagination ceases to take itself for granted and comes reflexively to acknowledge its own pre-reflective engagement with everyday lived projects and preoccupations. In addition, therefore, to bringing the life of imagination to the light of reflection, phenomenology simultaneously reminds us that all radical questioning takes its point of departure in our pre-conceptual experience of the life-world (*Lebenswelt*). This means, in respect of our present concerns, that our investigation of imagining will take its measure from the particular cultural and historical conditions that prevail in our century. Clearly, imagining cannot be expected to mean exactly the same thing today as it did in the Middle Ages or in antiquity. For one thing, Aristotle and Aquinas never watched television.

Where the traditional theories generally placed the emphasis on the suspect role of imagination within the pre-given order of Being, the modern turn towards humanist models of subjectivity laid great stress on imagination's prowess to *fashion* truth rather than merely represent it. Thus we find phenomenology exploring imagination as an intentional act of consciousness which both intuits and constitutes essential meaning. It wagers that imagination is the very precondition of human freedom – arguing that to be free means to be able to surpass the empirical world as it is given here and now in order to project new *possibilities* of existence. It is because we can imagine that we are at liberty to anticipate how things *might be*; to envision the world *as if* it were otherwise; to make absent alternatives present to the mind's eye.

Three decisive claims made by phenomenology – as it emerges in Husserl and evolves through his existential and hermeneutic disciples – are: (1) imagining is a productive act of consciousness, not a mental reproduction in the mind; (2) imagining does not involve a courier service between body and mind but an original synthesis which precedes the age-old opposition between the sensible and the intelligible; and (3) imagining is not a luxury of idle fancy but an instrument of truth.

The relevance of such a philosophy of imagining in our own age is evident. At a time when transcendent value is increasingly experienced as inaccessible, if not inexistent, it is entirely logical that the imaginative powers of the human subject should be so highly prized. Anguish, alienation, absurdity, nothingness – these are the operative terms of modern philosophy. They testify to the abstention of accredited meaning, to the sentiment that value is elsewhere – in some golden age of the past, some utopia of the future, or simply nowhere at all. In this historical context, imagination promises to present 'absent' value in the immediate here and now. It encourages consciousness to defy the historical postponement of meaning. Imagination resolves to create its own meaning, out of nothing, even if it has to invent an unreal world in which to do so.

It is small wonder, then, to find the role of imagination being celebrated by the phenomenological movement in a century when humanity feels bereft of objective foundations of truth, ghosted by a *deus absconditus* and devoid of any compelling sense of real presence. This contemporary experience of residing in a world 'too late for the gods and too early for Being' (Heidegger) certainly heightens the urgency to philosophize about imagination. And it is precisely because the mediating structures of the old traditions and authorities have lost much credibility that the poetic manifesto of a thinker like Bachelard commands such ready attention: 'A phenomenology of imagination must do away with all intermediaries . . . it is not a question of observing but of experiencing being in its *immediacy*' (*Poetics of Space*, 1957).

From this ontological function of imagining the phenomenologists frequently extrapolate an ethical one: as when Bachelard argues that imagination's freedom from the imitation of reality and commitment to its perpetual transformation represents the ethical task of 'establishing imagination in its living role as the guide to human life'.[3] For 'the moral life', he explains, 'is like the life of imagination a cosmic life: the world in its entirety seeks to be renovated'.[4] This ethical role of imagining will serve as one of the guiding threads of the present work.

Because of its attentiveness to the contemporary happenings of the life-world, phenomenology has been the first to recognize that the modern experience of homelessness in the given order of things is what propels us to construct a new house for ourselves in imagination. But phenomenology also bears witness, as we shall see, to the attendant danger of solipsism. It registers how imagination's desperate efforts to set itself up as its own promised land can fall victim to self-inflation, that is, presume to reduce the world to its own image and likeness. The modern imagination, in short, risks becoming a one-eyed king in the valley of the blind.

But the story is not yet over. Or, if it is, another is already beginning. I refer to the emergence in recent years of a post-modern account of images and imagining. This account is epitomized by the paradigm of parody. Parody assumes that images no longer refer to some transcendental signified, be it outside the human subject as in Platonism, or inside the human subject as in modern idealism from Kant to Sartre. Images, we are now told, refer to other images. There is no *origin* of meaning which images can be said to present or represent. Dispensing altogether with the established notions of origin, original, originality, the post-modern imaginary seems to circulate in an endless play of simulation.

One particularly dramatic instance of this is the role played by images in the electronic media of cinema, television and video. The phenomenal impact of the communications revolution in our century has meant a crisis of identity for imagination. This is most graphically expressed in the fact that one can no longer be sure who or what is actually making our images – a creative human subject or some anonymous system of reproduction. This *crisis of identity* is compounded, in turn, by a *crisis of faith* in the modern aesthetic of the productive imagination. The triumphal rise to supremacy, since the Enlightenment, of technological reason dwarfed the status of Romantic imagination to such a degree that the subsequent post-modern subversion of its claims to 'originality' and 'genius' was greatly facilitated. Our Civilization of the Image, as Roland Barthes describes mass-media culture, finds it more and more difficult to credit the Romantic concept of an original human imagination producing original human images. Hence the paradox that it is precisely in a culture where the image reigns supreme that the notion of a creative human imagination appears most imperilled.

The erosion of belief in authentic images is characterized by the predominance of technologically reproducible images in the contemporary media. And so we find both the classical metaphor of the *mirror* reflecting the sun (Plato's *Republic*, book 10) and the modern metaphor of the *lamp* projecting its own light from within human subjectivity (Kant's *Critique of Pure Reason*) being subsumed into the post-modern metaphor of *circular looking glasses* – each reflecting the surface images of the other in a play of infinite multiplication (Derrida's *Dissemination*, II). This paradigm of a self-proliferating and self-parodying imagination has already been analysed in some detail in the third part of *The Wake of Imagination* and is taken up again in the conclusion to the present work. Suffice it to say here – to sustain my paradigmatic metaphor – that the 'sun' of the post-modern imagination appears to rotate around a void. Samuel Beckett exemplifies this cleverly in *Imagination Dead Imagine* when he illustrates the life-and-death of imagining in our contemporary world in terms of solar vacillations between light and darkness, heat and cold, day and night. And Andy Warhol gives the metaphor a further twist when he compares his role as the Pope of pop art to a mirror looking into a mirror and seeing nothing. While Raymond Roussel, so admired by Foucault, offers an even more alarming gloss on the post-modern imaginary as the blank mirroring of an eclipsed sun: 'This void is paradoxically the sun . . . But what can the solar hollow be except the negation of madness by the

8

work? And of the work by madness?...the absence through which work and madness communicate with and exclude each other'.[5]

Some philosophers have reacted to this contemporary crisis of imagination by declaring it an anachronistic illusion – an ideological leftover of bourgeois idealism. This response issues largely from thinkers of structuralist or post-structuralist persuasion. In sharp contrast, thinkers of the phenomenological and hermeneutic movement have responded to the crisis as a clarion-call to elaborate new accounts of the imaginative enterprise – accounts more faithful to its creative resources and more attentive to the positive potential of our contemporary 'social imaginary'. A salient preoccupation of this response is the re-creation of imagining in a cultural era often described as the 'end of modernity': an era of trauma and transition suspended between the alarming extremes of instrumental rationalism and apocalyptic irrationalism. This affirmative hermeneutic stance may be said to comprise a 'poetics' in the broad sense of that term – an exploration of the human powers to make (*poiesis*) a world in which we may poetically dwell.[6]

A critical poetics of imagination transcending both the empire of reason and the asylum of un-reason has become an urgent concern for a number of thinkers in our century. These pathfinders of a new hermeneutic comprise a movement of inquiry which stretches from Husserl's affirmation of the philosophical centrality of imagination, through the radical revisionings of Heidegger, Sartre, Merleau-Ponty, Bachelard and Ricoeur, down to the more recent adumbrations of a post-modern hermeneutic of imagining in the writings of Vattimo, Kristeva and Lyotard.[7]

The spark for this contemporary current of thought first came, we will argue, from Edmund Husserl who initiated the phenomenological project with the publication of his two-volume *Logical Investigations* in 1900–1; and who was later to declare the act of imagining to be the very life-source of essential truth. But the decisive ignition was started by Martin Heidegger whose hermeneutic rereading of transcendental imagination as our most originary mode of temporal existence in *Kant and the Problem of Metaphysics* (1929) exerted a considerable, if generally ignored, influence on all subsequent phenomenologies of imagining. Even though I do not devote a separate chapter to Heidegger in this work – I have already dealt with his interpretation of the Kantian imagination at some length in other works[8] – the significance of his contribution is remarked in almost every study below and special mention of it made in my study of 'The hermeneutic imagination'. But if most of this book is devoted to radical variations on the phenomenological theme of imagination – existential, dialectical, poetical, hermeneutic and deconstructive – it is undoubtedly the case that these trails were first blazed by Husserl and Heidegger, the two founders of twentieth-century phenomenology.

The present work is intended as a critical response to the paradoxes and challenges raised by the phenomenological project. It proposes to *supplement* this project in the dual sense, observed by Derrida, of adding to work already done and identifying gaps not yet addressed. The proposal does not pretend to the status of terminal synthesis. It sees itself as work in progress gravitating towards that controversial point of exchange between a) hermeneutic thinkers who hold that imagining is a mode of being-in-the-world which makes and remakes our *Lebenswelt* by disclosing new possibilities of meaning, and b) those deconstructionists who dismiss creative imagination as an outdated mirage of modernity. Our concluding discussion focuses accordingly on thinkers such as Ricoeur, Vattimo and Lyotard whose work on imagination is, in my view, positively engaging the crucial debate between hermeneutics and post-modernity.

Finally, I would like to identify three main questions which guide my inquiry throughout; (1) how does imagination relate to *truth* – the epistemological question; (2) how does imagination relate to *being* – the ontological question; and (3) how does imagination relate to the *other* – the ethical question. In seeking to respond to these three questions of imagination, I hope to shed light on the more general question of what it means to exist in this world at the present point of time and space. That is my ultimate, and overriding, hermeneutic wager.

Notes

1 See my *The Wake of Imagination*, (London/Minneapolis: Hutchinson/Minnesota University Press, 1988), chs 1 and 2 on the 'Hebraic' and 'Hellenic' Imagination, pp. 37–114.

2 Martin Buber, 'The good and evil imagination', in *Good and Evil* (New York: Scribner, 1952), pp. 93–7.

3 G. Bachelard, *L'Air et les songes* (Paris: Corti, 1943), p. 209 (my trans.).

4 G. Bachelard, *L'Eau et les rêves* (Paris: Gallimard, 1938), p. 202 (my trans.).

5 The post-modern character of the works of Beckett and Warhol – amongst others – is analysed in *The Wake of Imagination*, pt 3. For a more detailed discussion of Roussel, see Michel Foucault's *Raymond Roussel*

(Paris: Gallimard, 1963, pp. 207 ff., trans. Charles Ruas as *Death and the Labyrinth* (New York: Doubleday, 1986); and also David Carroll, *Paraesthetics, Foucault, Lyotard, Derrida* (London: Methuen, 1987), p. 75.

6 It is in this extended sense of 'poetics', which covers both theory and practice, that we can agree with the post-modern thinker Richard Rorty when he claims that 'poetic' moments occur in many different areas of culture – 'science, philosophy, painting and politics as well as the lyric and drama' ('Deconstruction and circumvention', *Critical Inquiry*, vol. 2, no. 1, pp. 1–23). See also Linda Hutcheon's definition of a post-modern poetics as an 'open, ever-changing theoretical structure by which to order both our cultural knowledge and our critical procedures. This would not be a poetics in the structuralist sense of the word, but would go beyond the study of literary discourse to the study of cultural practice and theory': *A Poetics of Postmodernism* (London: Routledge, 1988), p. 14.

7 A crucial trait shared by all these phenomenological accounts of imagination is a common debt to the Heideggerean–Kantian disclosure of the intimate, indeed inseparable link between imagination and temporality (that is, intentional recollection of the past and projection of the future). Perhaps our opening analogy between the elusive character of the *question of time* and the *question of imagining* is not, therefore, accidental.

8 See in particular my section 'Heidegger's interpretation of the Kantian imagination' in *The Wake of Imagination*, pp. 189–96; and my *Poétique du possible* (Paris: Beauchesne, 1984), pt 1. *Poétique du Possible* offered a reinterpretation of the poetic power of imagination which would embrace all of the 'figurative/transfigurative' activities of human existence (from perceiving and acting to thinking and speaking) and ultimately disclose this power of creative 'figuration' as the basis for a new hermeneutics of the 'possible' – ontological or eschatological. *The Wake of Imagination*, by contrast, sought to explore the genealogical development of the various concepts of 'imagining' (*yetser, phantasia, eikasia, imaginatio, Einbildungskraft, Phantasie*) from the classical and medieval philosophies through to the modern and post-modern critiques. The present work is a sequel to both texts, supplementing their respective emphases on the hermeneutics of possibility and on the cultural history of ideas, with a more concentrated study of new hermeneutic approaches to our contemporary understanding of the imaginative activity itself.

1

The phenomenological imagination (Husserl)

What does phenomenology do for imagination?

The phenomenological movement elucidates potentialities of imagination which Edmund Husserl, its inaugurator, believed were neglected in most previous philosophies. Whereas phenomenology discloses and celebrates imagination's creative power of intentionality, as we shall see below, traditional theories tended to stigmatize it under three main headings: (1) *dualism* – images were generally considered allies of the lower corporeal order and thus inimical to the elevated pursuits of the intellect; (2) *representationalism* – images were construed as mere copies of our sensible experience; and (3) *reification* – images were treated as quasi-material things (*res*) *in* the mind rather than acts *of* living consciousness.

Despite the strenuous efforts of certain modern thinkers such as Kant and the German Idealists to restore a productive role to imagination, it was not until phenomenology formally disclosed its function as a dynamic and constitutive act of intentionality that imagining was fully freed from its inherited conceptual constraints. Only at this point could what Sartre identifies as the classical 'illusion of immanence' be definitively overcome:

> By revealing the image to be an intentional structure, Husserl frees it from the condition of an inert content of consciousness. At one stroke vanish, along with the immanentist metaphysics of images, all the difficulties concerning the relationship of the simulacrum to its real object, and of pure thought to the simulacrum ... Husserl

freed the psychic world of a weighty burden and eliminated almost all the difficulties that clouded the classical problem of the relations of images to thoughts.[1]

The main aspect of this classical problem was the tendency to confuse images with thoughts and perceptions.[2]. Such confusion made it virtually impossible to distinguish the essential characteristics of the image itself.[3] Against the erroneous identification of images with faded copies of sensation, the phenomenologists strove to reinstate imagining as a *sui generis* activity of human consciousness. For phenomenology, any genuine account of imagination must satisfy at least two requirements:

It must account for the spontaneous discriminations made by the mind between its images and its perceptions. And it must explain the role that images play in the operations of thought. Whatever form it took, the classical conception of images was unable to fulfil these two essential functions. To endow an image with a sensory content is to make it a thing obeying the laws of things, not the laws of consciousness. The mind is thus deprived of all hope of distinguishing images from the other things belonging in the world and by the same token there is no way at all to conceive the relation of this thing to thought.[4]

As long as the image is conceived after the classical fashion as a *thing in* consciousness rather than after the phenomenological fashion as an *act of* consciousness, imagination can never be fully recognized for what it really is.[5] It was not until Husserl and other phenomenologists acknowledged imagination as a free and creative intentionality that the 'illusion of immanence' could be finally surpassed. Simply stated, imagination needs phenomenology; for without it, it cannot be understood as it is in itself.

In *Ideas* (1913), Husserl makes several suggestions as to how phenomenology might give rise to a novel conception of imagining. He rejects what he considers the traditional methodological extremes of induction and deduction. Induction, he maintains, can only construe the imagination from within the 'natural attitude' as an object of empirical experimentation. It reduces the vital 'experience' of this mode of consciousness to a collection of merely probable sense-data.[6]

14

Deduction, on the other hand, is equally limited in its attempt to establish the nature of imagination from certain logical presuppositions. The phenomenological method, in contrast to both, operates on the conviction that there are certain unique modes of consciousness, imagination being one of the most central, which can be 'experienced' in a unique mode of 'reflection', free from empiricist and rationalist premisses.

Husserl strove for a theory of consciousness erected on a foundation as rigorous and certain as that of the sciences. Contrary to natural assumptions, he held that such a foundation could not be reached by simple observation of the empirically given. Before one can observe something one must know *what* that something is. Before understanding *how* something exists one must understand the fundamental essence of the existent.[7]

And so Husserl insisted that the disclosure of the essential structure of imagination cannot be accomplished by either a pure mathematics of extension or empirical induction. It requires a phenomenological method reflectively alert to the constitutive process of consciousness. Such a method does not deny the validity of the other approaches. It does suggest, however, that it is only *after* such an eidetic investigation has taken place that experimental and existential evidence can be legitimately adduced. It is in this light that phenomenology proclaims itself the only method adequate to a pure and presuppositionless description of the essence of imagining.[8]

Referring to the imagining of a centaur, Husserl writes that 'in the very essence of the experience lies determined not only *that* but also *whereof* it is a consciousness'.[9] This definition rests upon his claim that there is an essential distinction between the act of imagining and the object – the centaur – which it is intentionally conscious of by means of this act. Husserl thus endeavours to resolve the classical conundrum of whether to construe the image as a thing internal to consciousness (the fallacy of immanentism) or a thing external to consciousness (the fallacy of positivism), by arguing that it is not a *thing* at all. Phenomenology redefines the image as a *relation* – an act of consciousness directed to an object beyond consciousness. Imagination cannot reduce the world to a myriad of faded inner sensations, as Hume maintained. The world remains at all times transcendent of the consciousness which intends it.[10] Under no circumstances can the object intended be translated into an image-copy within the mind. Indeed, it was precisely the conception of the image as an internalized quasi-thing which prejudiced most preceding theories of imagination. The phenomenological method redresses this error by disclosing the essence of the image to be an intentional *actus*.[11]

We have already noted how the classical conception of the image as something internal to consciousness led to a misunderstanding of the process of imagining. Conceived as different from perception only on a quantitative basis, the image was considered 'true' when it faithfully represented its external original and 'false' when it failed to do so. This understanding of the image-as-representation was, Husserl argues, primarily due to a confounding of the role of imagination with that of perception. The subsequent problem of distinguishing the image from the percept was thus rendered absurd and insoluble. For once one begins by stating the qualitative sameness of two things it is of course impossible later to establish the difference between them.

Phenomenology reveals the intentional nature of imaginative con-sciousness by demonstrating how its very mode of constitution distinguishes it from both the things of the world and from the other modes of consciousness – in particular perception.[12] As different modes of intentionality, image and percept are aware, reflectively or pre-reflectively, of their difference.[13] This is so since, as phenomenology shows, all modes of intentionality are conscious that they exist to the extent that they are purposive determinations of a conscious ego.[14] Consequently, *qua* intentions of consciousness, images prove to be spontaneous acts which can no longer be mistaken for mere residues of sensation serving as a background support for thought. Nor can they be mistaken for unconscious pulsional drives – which could be said to 'cause' our intentional acts – for the simple reason that they are themselves intentions. Images do not determine consciousness; they are determining acts of consciousness.[15]

Phenomenology dispenses accordingly with the old metaphysical worry about the 'reality' or otherwise of images and accepts the mode of being of the image as its mode of appearing to consciousness.[16] To be sure, the image as an act of presenting something to consciousness is not to be confused with the *something* thus presented. Returning to his example of the centaur, Husserl writes:

> The flute-playing centaur which we freely imagine is certainly a presentation we have ourselves constructed ... but the centaur itself is not psychic. It exists neither in the soul nor in consciousness, nor anywhere else, it is in fact 'nothing', mere 'imagination', or, to be

more precise, the living experience of imagination is the imagining of a centaur. To this extent, indeed, 'the centaur as intended', the centaur as imagined, belongs to the experience itself as lived. But we must also beware of confusing this lived experience of imagination with that in the experience which is imagined qua object imagined.[17]

In this passage Husserl is suggesting that the fact that the centaur does not actually exist does not entitle us to dismiss it as a mere psychic entity. The object of the centaur image-intention is, quite obviously, an 'irreality'; but *qua* irreality it can, Husserl will argue, still maintain a transcendence *vis-à-vis* the mind.[18] We shall return to this enigmatic claim below.

To *perceive* my brother and to imagine my brother are two different ways of intending the same transcendent object. The intentional percept refers to the same object – my brother – as the intentional image; but the crucial difference is that the first intends him as *real*, the latter as *unreal*. In this way, phenomenology rescues imagination from its 'naturalistic' confusion with perception, and restores it to its essential role as a power capable of intending the unreal *as if* it were real, the absent *as if* it were present, the possible *as if* it were actual. Husserl thus strives to reverse the classical neglect of the unique character of imagination by describing it not as an intermediary storehouse of image-impressions but as a *sui generis* activity of our intentional relation to the world.

'Between perception, on the one hand, and on the other, presentation in the form of an image, there is an unbridgeable and essential difference.'[19] Throughout his many writings on the relationship of image and percept, Husserl is adamant on this point.

In the *Logical Investigations* (1900–1) Husserl first outlines a basis for a distinction between imagination and perception. In a refutation of the traditional 'imagery theory' which confounded the mode of presentation with the object presented, Husserl retorts that the image and the percept are different modes of presentation, even though they may be intending the same object. Furthermore, since the object imagined is not itself the image, then it is of no real importance whether this object really exists or not.[20] At this early stage, however, Husserl does not deal with the possible objection that if the image is an intention *of* something (as every intention must be) how can the image be of *nothing*, or at least *nothing that exists*.

17

In these investigations Husserl regards imagination and perception as homologous in so far as they are both *intuitive* rather than *signitive* modes of intentionality. Signs and what is signified 'have nothing to do with one another' (for example, the sign 'red' has nothing to do with the action of stopping). Images and percepts, by contrast, are intrinsically connected with the object intended (for example, the percept or image of a horse must resemble a horse). This means, in effect, that, while the sign intends an object without intuiting it, the image and the percept both 'present' the object intended in some sort of 'fulfilling' intuition. But, while similar in their difference from signs, images and percepts differ radically from each other in so far as the object of perception is intuited in its presence, whereas the object of imagination is intuited in its absence.[21]

It must also be said that in the *Logical Investigations*, as in many of his writings, Husserl seems to privilege the perceptual mode of intentionality precisely because of this direct access to the flesh-and-blood *presentness* of things. This preference does not prevent him, however, from also celebrating the indispensable powers of imagining in liberating us from the here-and-now limits of perception. It is this latter, if often neglected, aspect of Husserl's thought which I am concentrating on in this study.

In the first volume of *Ideas* (1913) Husserl provides his most comprehensive treatment of the whole perception/imagination problematic. One of the most crucial passages is Husserl's classic contrast between the different modes of intending Dürer's engraving 'The Knight, Death and the Devil':

> We distinguish here in the first place the normal perception of which the correlate is the 'engraved print' as a thing, this print in the portfolio. We distinguish in the second place the consciousness within which in the black lines of the picture there appear to us the small colourless figures, 'Knight on horseback', 'death', and 'devil'. In aesthetic observation ... we have our attention fixed on what is portrayed 'in the picture', more precisely on the depicted realities (*Algebildet*) – the knight of flesh and blood, and so forth.[22]

We see in this example how both perception and imagination, while referring to the same drawing of lines, shades and shapes, intend it in entirely different ways. In the aesthetic or imaginative attitude, consciousness undergoes what Husserl calls 'a neutrality-modification' whereby all attitudes regarding the existence or non-existence of the things imagined are 'bracketed'.[23] But Husserl is quick to remind us that this does not in any way mean a 'privation' of all existence, only a 'neutralization' of the problem thereof.

Here again imagination is described as a *sui generis* mode of intentional consciousness. To imagine, as opposed merely to perceive, the Dürer engraving is to re-create the invisible intention which lies behind the visible lines on the paper. The matter upon which the percept and the image are formed is, of course, the same (a print on a page); it is in the *way* this matter is intended that the difference resides. The image, Husserl tells us, is always a 'spontaneous' way of intending its object, whereas the percept is directed to an already existing object which largely determines what we see.[24]

In perception the object must be given 'really' whereas in imagination the object can only be given 'irreally'. Nevertheless all 'irrealities' of imagination – such as the knight, death and the devil – are outside consciousness.[25] They cannot be contained in some mind box, as classical theories of imagination sometimes supposed. But, if Husserl succeeded in revealing the image to be an act of consciousness intending an 'irreality' transcendent of consciousness, he did not succeed in explaining what precisely is meant by this 'irreality'. This in turn prevented him from adequately explicating the ontological distinction between imaginary and perceptual worlds.[26]

What does imagination do for phenomenology?

The phenomenology of imagination as first outlined by Husserl is a response to two main questions: What does phenomenology mean for imagination? and What does imagination mean for phenomenology? Having dealt briefly with the former, we now turn to the latter.

(a)
In a curious passage in *Ideas* Husserl offers us the following riddle:

> If anyone loves a paradox, he can readily say, and say with strict truth if he will allow for ambiguity, that the element which makes up the life of phenomenology, as of all eidetical sciences, is 'fiction', that

fiction is the source whence the knowledge of eternal truths draws it sustenance.[27]

What does Husserl mean by this extraordinary statement? How can such a phenomenological privileging of the works of imagination be justified? The surest clue to the riddle is provided by Husserl himself in an adjoining footnote. 'This sentence', he warns, 'should be particularly appropriate for bringing ridicule from the naturalistic side on the eidetic (essential) way of knowledge.'[28] Clearly, phenomenology is on the side of the 'eidetic'; naturalism holding the opposing view that all modes of consciousness are reducible to the empirical standards of the natural sciences. If phenomenology is the champion of human imagination, naturalism is its chosen adversary.

Things are apprehended in their essence (*eidos*), Husserl claims, when they are grasped not only in their actuality but also in their possibility – the latter being the special preserve of imagination. It is because what is possible has priority over what is actual when it comes to revealing essences, and because phenomenology sees its primary task as the disclosure of essences, that the imaginative power of fiction is hailed as the life-force of 'the eidetic way of knowledge'. This claim draws the scorn of naturalists to the extent that they resist all attempts to go beyond an empirical understanding of our world as a 'fact' existing independently of human consciousness. But Husserl's view of consciousness as *intentional* – that is, as always conscious *of* a world – challenges the dualist model of an 'objective' world set over against a 'subjective' knower. Man is a being at all times related to a world. Man and world come into being through one another. Or, as Husserl puts it in his last work, the *Crisis* (1938), all essential meaning arises out of a human life-world (*Lebenswelt*).

The naturalist attitude, by contrast, upholds the traditional subject/object dichotomy, and thus ignores the essential relation between consciousness and world. Phenomenology rediscovers this relation by (1) suspending the naturalistic prejudice which reduces human experience to empirically observable data; and (2) by acknowledging imagination as an indispensable agency for the disclosure and intuition of meaning. The error of naturalism was to construe consciousness and world as two 'natural' entities mechanically conjoined by causal laws.[29] Phenomenology, by contrast, recognizes human consciousness as a primordially lived experience (*Erlebnis*) intentionally connected to the world – *before* any separation into subject and object.

It is in this shift of attention from the empirical existence of things, as objects among objects, to their intentional existence, as live phenomena of consciousness, that imagination is accredited as the surest means of grasping essences. In other words, imagination releases things from their contingent status as facts and grants them an ideal status as possibilities, possibilities of which each fact is but a single instance. 'The positing of the essence', he writes, 'does not imply any positing of individual existence whatsoever; pure essential truths do not make the slightest assertion concerning facts.'[30] And he goes on to assert that the veritable nature of 'immediate, intuitive essence apprehension' is assured more by pure essences 'exemplified intuitively in the data of imagination' than in the data of 'perception or memory'.[31] Husserl thus promotes a phenomenology of imagination as one of the most effective means of reaching necessary truths.

Unlike many of his existentialist and hermeneutical disciples, Husserl believed that truth could be reached by an intuition of ideal essences (*Wesensschau*). Since our 'natural attitude' is exclusively preoccupied with facts, some other mode of attention must be called upon. To conceive of an essence after the naturalistic mode is to misconceive it as a mere copy of things reached through a process of intellectual abstraction. By contrast, to conceive of essences after the phenomenological mode is to recognize them as idealities constitutive of the 'things themselves' – ideal possibilities to which the most direct access is provided by imagination.

It is for this reason that Husserl ventures the proposition that the 'intuitive content' of essences is 'imaginative'.[32] And he even goes so far, on one occasion, as to claim that '*every* intuitive presentation of something objective represents it according to the mode of imagination'.[33] This identification of pure essences as fictions of imagination seeks to overcome the habitual eclipse of essential meaning by empirical information. For Husserl, fictions are neither impressions of fact nor by-products of perception. They represent a thing's possible mode of existence as a free intention of consciousness which – paradoxically – grounds the necessity of truth. In short, free creations of imagination provide the basis for necessary evidence. Emancipating essences from the ball and chain of fact, imagination opens phenomenology to an ideal world of timeless truths. Phenomenology needs imagination, therefore, for two main reasons: (1) to sever our natural bondage

21

to empirical experience; and (2) to provide access to a realm of possibility whose very freedom is the token of a necessary (that is, apodictic and transcendental) science of essences.

(b)
We thus see how the requirements of the phenomenological method led Husserl to acknowledge imagination as one of the most vital factors in the intuition of essences. Though the heuristic nature of Husserl's interest in imagining made for a fragmentary rather than a systematic treatment of this activity, it is possible to discern a coherent thesis emerging through his works. To delineate this thesis better, we turn now to a more detailed examination of the precise role played by imagination in the phenomenological method.

Imagination is a prerequisite of all phenomenological inquiry in so far as it reveals the life of human consciousness to itself. How is this achieved? First, by bracketing or neutralizing our normal 'perceptual' relation to things we enter an imaginative perspective from which the teeming flux of consciousness may be apprehended in all its possible permutations. Instead of viewing consciousness as the cause of an effect, or the premiss of a conclusion, we now grasp it as an intentional activity constantly directed towards the things of its life-world. By reaching back into this deeper layer of our conscious experience we locate a path to essential intuition inaccessible at the surface level of everyday accidents. 'In phenomenology', Husserl explains, 'images assume a privileged position over perception' because they afford a 'freedom which opens for the first time an entry into the spacious realms of essential possibility with their infinite horizons of essential knowledge'.[34]

Husserl maintains, as we noted above, that the image is the consequence of the 'neutralization of the positional act of representation'.[35] As such, it permits us to contemplate what is being performed in the intentional activity of representation.[36] It provides us with a dispositional (that is, neutralized) attitude with which to investigate the positional attitude of our normal consciousness. This dis-positional attitude of imagination views things as 'mere pictures' without imparting to them 'the stamp of being or not-being or the like'.[37] By using such images as tools for its self-investigations, consciousness frees itself from the tyranny of fact and discovers the intentional nature of its own life. These self-investigations are not, Husserl points out, 'analyses in the usual sense (analyses into really immanent parts), but *uncoverings of intentional implications*, advancing from a factual experience to the system of experiences that are delineated as possible'.[38] Without the 'ideal' depth and clarity furnished by the process of imaging, the intentionality of consciousness could not be adequately disclosed. Because the image is not a copy of the datum of being, but a pure creation of consciousness, it can best reveal the essence of consciousness to itself as a perpetual movement towards meaning.

In this way, the classical poles of consciousness as passive *tabula rasa* or active intellection are replaced by a more bi-polar notion of consciousness as a reciprocal rapport with what is other than itself. It is precisely because the imagination imparts nothing about 'being' that it is best capable of imparting something about consciousness as an attitude towards being.[39] In short, neutral with respect to the existence of facts, imagining is exemplary with respect to the meaning of essences.

(c)

It is for this reason that Husserl returns again and again to the distinction between imagination and perception.[40] While perception is bound by the ephemeral conditions of the here and now, imagination is free to prescind from given particulars and vary its intentional objects as unreal phenomena.[41] This liberty of variation – to which we will return below – allows imagination to detach itself from perceptual data and reflect upon them in the form of an *as if* mode of consciousness where they can be alternated and adjusted at will for the purposes of clarity and definition. This *as if* attitude of imagination is one of the central acquisitions of Husserl's famous phenomenological 'reduction'.[42]

By reduction Husserl does not understand a positivistic narrowing of meanings to facts but, on the contrary, a leading back to (*re-ducere*) the essential structures of phenomena. It is imagination which enables consciousness to emancipate itself from its immersion in the world of actuality (first phase of reduction) and to return to a realm of pure possibility (second phase of reduction) where its own essence as intentionality is given in an intuition of immediate certainty (third phase of reduction). This was the indispensable role which Husserl assigned to imagination in the phenomenological method. But imagination is not only indispensable for a disclosing of the essence of consciousness as an act of intending things. It is equally indispensable for disclosing the essence of the intended 'things themselves'. Or, to use Husserl's more technical terminology: the imagination is that which reveals not only the 'noetic' but also the 'noematic' essence of intentionality – that is,

23

the things intended by consciousness as well as the intending acts of consciousness.[43]

When Husserl first formulates this process of imagining essences in the *Logical Investigations* he calls it 'free variation' or 'ideation'.[44] It arises in the context of his refutation of Hume's notion of consciousness as a sum of discrete and contiguous impressions. Husserl wishes to show that consciousness is a continuous and constitutive activity operating according to certain universal and *a priori* 'laws of essences'. He proposes 'free variation' as the most effective method of discovering these laws. Because it is a process of imagination rather than of perception, Husserl believes that it allows us (1) to see beyond the actual mode of existence of a thing to variations of its other possible modes of being, and (2) to intuit thereby an ideal unvarying paradigm. Put in another way, the phenomenologist refashions the given data of an object – say, a table – by freely varying it in his imagination. He or she allows the data to move continuously from the actual appearance of the table to its 'real possibilities' (*Vermöglichkeiten*, that is, possibilities prevailing within our real world) and finally to its 'essential possibilities' (*Wesensmöglichkeiten* which may transcend this real world altogether).[45] In so doing, the imaginer becomes aware of all the possible variations which the identical phenomenon of the table may be subjected to; and such an awareness culminates in the intuition of a general essence of tableness. By defining imagination as the portal leading from the natural to the eidetic realm, Husserl bound imagination and phenomenology in a Gordian knot.[46]

(d)

Imagination leads to an intuition of essences, which Husserl designates as 'universals not conditioned by any fact'.[47] Moreover, their free and flexible nature proves infinitely more apt to the process of uninhibited ideation.[48] This would seem to be the basis for Husserl's dictum that 'the science of pure possibilities precedes the science of actualities and alone makes it possible as a science'.[49] And it is no doubt this same phenomenological maxim that Heidegger had in mind when he affirmed in his introduction to *Being and Time* that 'for phenomenology possibility stands higher than actuality'.

By suspending a thing's actual or empirical existence and allowing it to float freely as an 'imaginary irreality' (*phantasiemässige Unwirklichkeit*) amidst an infinitely open series of possibilities, ideation discloses the essences of the 'things themselves'. But ideation is not just a stage in a philosophical method. It also operates, Husserl insists, at a pre-philosophical level of lived experience – albeit in an informal and inchoate fashion. Whenever this imaginative function is lacking, human consciousness loses its freedom and falls victim to surrounding circumstances. No longer able to envision alternative modes of experience transcending our present state of affairs, we despair – we fall back into unfreedom.[50] Imagination's power to suspend the natural attitude in favour of the phenomenological attitude of free variation is, for Husserl, the surest guarantee against the classical confusion of facts and essences. And, by extension, it acts as the surest guarantor of human freedom.

Imagination can afford an ease in our apprehension of things, impossible in empirical experience and indispensable to the intuition of essences. Such ease is attainable, Husserl holds, only when consciousness enters into the unrestricted realms of *essential* possibility.[51] In *Ideas* Husserl gives us the instructive example of the geometer:

> The geometer when he thinks geometrically operates with imagery vastly more than he does with percepts of figures and models ... Whereas in actual drawing and modelling he is restricted; in imagination he has perfect freedom in the arbitrary recasting of the figures he has imagined, in running over continuous series of possible shapes, in the production there of an infinite number of new creations; a freedom which opens up to him for the first time an entry into the spacious realms of essential possibility with their infinite horizons of essential knowledge.[52]

Husserl seems to be suggesting here that geometrical imagining prefigures geometrical knowledge. Geometrical images adumbrate the geometrical essences of things, while geometrical models merely write these images large. Here we find a good example of the way in which a *fiction* (as a possibility) serves to incarnate an *essence* (as a truth of geometry) in a *fact* (as an experimental datum-model of science).

This leads to the view that 'the freedom of research in the region of the essence necessarily demands that one should operate with the help of imagination'[53] Fictions are here regarded as the prerequisite of free research in so far as they enable us to explore the thing in its essential evidence – after the natural attitude has searched its 'apparent' evidence. This essential evidence applies, as we have seen, not merely to things but to consciousness itself; for fiction, as Husserl understands it, is nothing other than a certain type of consciousness at play with possibilities. This point is forcefully reiterated by Donald Kuspit who argues that, because phenomenology recognizes fiction as the liberty to investigate both self and world in their essences, it recognizes the priority of art over science: 'In art ... the thing's features stand out with fictitious clarity, because the thing's factuality – obscuring insight into it – has been taken from it. In fiction the thing's essential features are no longer unclear as they are in the factual things.'[54]

Fiction, as deployed by phenomenologists and artists alike, reveals not only that things have unexpected essences but also that consciousness is an unexpected activity – a process of free fancy.[55] Husserl makes this quite clear, moreover, in a crucial passage in *Ideas* where he states: '... it is naturally important to make rich use of fiction for the free transformation of data ... and we can draw extraordinary profit from what art and particularly poetry have to offer us in this regard.'[56]

(e)

Imagination allows essences to present themselves through multiple rather than merely single instances. To be sure, the *a priori* essence is present in every single instance of its actual experience. But it is present in a partial and implicit way, as but one moment of its total horizon. Free variation allows this essence to present itself in a full and explicit way, by filling out the total horizon with fictional instances. This filling-out process is what Husserl calls 'constitution'. The essence does not actually exist *prior* to our constitution of it. Rather, it comes to be through the process of free variation. As Husserl puts it: 'The being of the universal in its different levels is essentially a being-constituted in this process.'[57]

Essences may be acquired by imagination in both a positive and negative fashion. Positively, essences are reached by an intuition of the invariant paradigm emerging through a variety of individual instances. But there is also a negative mode of free variation based on the principle that removal or addition of certain moments in a variant destroy it as an instance of the *eidos* we are trying to identity.[58] If we try to imagine a material thing without extension, or a melody without time, for example, we no longer have a material thing or a melody. Extension and temporality are thus shown 'negatively' to be of the essence of thinghood and music respectively. Husserl concludes accordingly that disclosure of the *eidos* takes place in imagination not because a pure essence must be free from the contingency of perceptual experience, but because if our variation stayed within perception it could never reach beyond empirical generality to eidetic necessity. From perception alone we could never conclude that extension is integral to thinghood as an eidetic necessity. For if we were confined to our immediate perception we could not imagine instances where this might not be so, and thereby (by a process of negation) discover that it must be so. In perception, we could not present the test variations that turn out to be impossible and so mark the essential limits of an object. An *eidos* is not an *eidos* until we have confirmed the impossibility of eliminating any of its parts without eliminating the whole. Hence the paradox that freedom of fiction can secure the necessity of things.[59]

But could not signification or conceptualization suffice here? Husserl is inclined to think not. In contrast to concepts or signs which are empty intentions, imaginative variants provide an *intuition* of the object. Imagination allows us to look to the things themselves, not just to our words or thoughts about them. It permits us to *see* things as if they were present. To define time and tone abstractly as integral to music is not sufficient. We must begin with instances of music and then freely vary these in the imagination until we can register the impossibility of it being what it is unless such attributes belong to it.

To cause the datum of consciousness to vary imaginatively is to discover not only the *eidos* of the experienced thing but also the *eidos* of my consciousness as an *a priori* possibility. The *eidos* of consciousness – what Husserl calls the *eidos-ego* – is intentionality. But it is *my* intentionality. For it is the purity of my consciousness reached through imaginings of my own life. Here, however, Husserl finds himself confronted with the vexed problem of solipsism.[60]

No matter how liberally it may vary the facts of the world, imagination can never transcend *itself* as a transcendental consciousness. It is beholden to the evidence of the first person singular. The reduction of my conscious experience to its most universal essence cannot, it seems, secure access to any self in general. My most universal essence always remains *my* most universal essence – for there is no access to the trans-individual through the transcendental. In other words, the phenomenological imagination can save us from the anonymity of facts; but it does not appear capable of saving us from the exclusivity of our own transcendental subjectivity.[61] Paul Ricoeur states Husserl's dilemma succinctly:

Phenomenology is a victory over brute fact by the method of imaginative variation ... Thus even the Ego must be 'imagined' in order to separate it from brute fact. This breaking away from my own contingency is essential to the birth of the *Ego meditans* ... The remarkable thing is that this passage to the *eidos-ego* brings into play only variations of my own ego and has no reference to the other in the second person. Thus I imagine myself as other without imagining an other. This is quite necessary since before constituting the other, my ego is the only ego ... in this way the eidetic ego definitely has no reference to the similarity between the first and second person and works its variations on the solipsistic plane.[62]

Solipsism is the most serious obstacle confronting Husserl's theory of imagination. It is all the more surprising, then, to discover him in the fifth Cartesian Meditation seeking to solve the problem *by means of imagination*. Husserl's argument is based on the following programme of imaginative variation: I am here (*hic*), the other is there (*illic*); but there (*illic*) is where I could be if I were to move. From over there (*illic*) I would see the same things but under a different perspective. Hence, through imagination I can co-ordinate the other perspectives to *my* place and to *my* perspective.[63] But because the life of the other is not given to me in an 'original production' (*Leistungen*), but merely in a fictive 'reproduction' in the mode of the '*as if* I were there', the life of the other can never become for me the equivalent of the one life of which I have originary experience, that is, my own. Husserl cannot escape the self-enclosing mesh which his own theory of imagination has cast. And his closest disciple in this area, Jean-Paul Sartre, was – as we shall see – to be equally troubled by this dilemma.

(f)
The importance Husserl attributes to imagining stems largely from its power of free variation which leads to the intuition of both noetic and noematic essences. But there is a third and more fundamental *eidos* which the phenomenological imagination can disclose: what Husserl describes as the 'ultimate telos (goal) for all our eidetic investigations, objective and subjective ... the *eidos* of a philosophy as the all embracing science'.[64]

This teleological *eidos* motivates all of human culture. It is, Husserl suggests, what first leads us out from the solitude of consciousness towards the otherness of a world. It is what regulates and presides over all other essences, noetic and noematic alike. It is, in short, the 'Eidetic Apriori' of all truth.[65]

Because of this conviction, Husserl is inclined to review the history of philosophy as a recently married man might review an adolescent diary: he speaks of it, retrospectively, as an 'asymptotic' striving for an ideal rationality, a complex of contradictory systems which, unbeknownst to itself, veils a 'concealed unity of intentional interiority' (*Verborgene Einheit intentionaler Innerlichkeit*). Husserl concludes accordingly that phenomenology is the 'sweet nostalgia' of all modern thought from Descartes to Kant.[66]

It is imagination, in the final analysis, which projects the ideal possibility of phenomenology as a rigorous universal science – an ideal sought after by all great thinkers in the history of philosophy. And it does so by freely varying the possibilities of the ultimate telos situating each past philosophy as a particular step on the way and suggesting the best-possible means whereby this telos might be realized in the future. In imaginative variation the history of thought emerges as a struggle towards the telos of absolute reason. Philosophy is shown accordingly to be a vocation of Western humanity which resulted at one particular period in the geometric objectivism of Galileo and Spinoza, at another in the more advanced transcendental subjectivism of Descartes, Hume and Kant, and in this century, still closer to the final *eidos*, in his own phenomenology.[67] But philosophy does not end with phenomenology. It begins again as if for the first time. Indeed, it is precisely through the phenomenological method of imaginative variation that even this final *eidos* is seen to imply the 'and so forth' of endless possibilities.[68]

In his later thought, Husserl became convinced that the teleological *eidos* guides not only the philosophical world but also the pre-philosophical life-world (*Lebenswelt*). In the *Crisis* and some of his archival manuscripts, he attempted to explain this correlation of philosophy and life by locating their common source in a universal programme of intentionality which expresses itself in a series of intersubjective operations (*Leistungen*). Husserl claims that the constitution of life-worlds evinces, despite its *prima facie* relativity, certain invariant 'habits' (*Gewohnheiten*) and 'typicalities' (*Wesensgesetzlichetypiken*). The imagination discovers these in free variation. By prescinding from any single *Lebenswelt*, it projects a whole variety of possible *Lebenswelten* and thus discloses the universal *eidos* of any single *Lebenswelt* whatsoever.[69] And so by tracing the worlds we live in back to their common intentional source (*Sinngenesis*) the imagination can divine the *eidos* of human society and project ways in which it might be historically brought about. In *The Origin of Geometry*, first published as an appendix to the *Crisis*, Husserl enunciates this possibility:

> In imagination we have the capacity of complete freedom to trans-
> form our human historical existence and what is there exposed as
> its 'life-world'. And precisely in this activity of free variation, and
> in running through the conceivable possibilities for the life-world,
> there arises with apodictic self-evidence, an essential general set
> of elements going through all the variants; and of this we can
> convince ourselves with truly apodictic certainty. This freedom and
> the direction of our gaze upon the apodictic invariant, results in the
> latter again and again, and can be fixed in univocal language as the
> essence constantly implied in the flowing, vital horizon.[70]

To the extent, then, that Husserl recognized this prospective power of imagination, he may be said to have founded an ontology of the *Lebenswelt*. Treating the present world as but one of many possible life-worlds, imagination contrives to discover the logos of its being and the telos of its becoming. Moreover, it is precisely this aim of imagination that constitutes, for Husserl, 'the ultimate and highest problem of phenomenology'.In his article for the *Encyclopaedia Britannica* he states this unequivocally as follows:

> Phenomenology recognizes its particular function within a possible
> life for man ... It recognizes the absolute norms which are to be
> picked out from this life of man, and also its primordial teleologi-
> cal–tendential structure in a striving towards the universal ideal of
> absolute perfection which lies to infinity, a striving which becomes
> free through the imaginative process of disclosure.[71]

Here, again, we confront the paradox of freedom and necessity which so deeply informs Husserl's treatment of the imagination. If imagination is that which *frees* us by suspending our servility to the facts of the 'natural' world and by returning us to the world of possibility, it is also that power of 'ideation' which discloses the laws of 'eidetic *necessity*'.[72] Free variation leads to necessary invariation. At this point a phenomenology of imagination points towards a phenomenology of transcendence. But, even though Husserl was well aware of this, he was reluctant to allow of anything which might transgress the limits of an 'absolute and presuppositionless' phenomenology.[73]

Husserl's unwillingness to carry phenomenology into the realm of fundamental ontology or theology (except for occasional mention of the ultimate telos of consciousness as a super-real entity) meant that his treatment of imagination could not escape the following impasse: if imaginative consciousness is wholly free it runs the risk of relativism; and if it is wholly necessary it runs the opposite risk of determinism.

Towards a teleology of possibility

The closest Husserl comes to addressing the question of the tran-scendence of imaginative meaning is, it seems, in his account of 'pure possibility'. Some indication of the relationship between imagination and possibility was implicit in all of Husserl's writings, but it was not until the *Cartesian Meditations* (1929) that he explicitly formulated its importance. In the second Meditation, Husserl describes phenomenol-ogy as an *a priori* science which concerns itself with the 'realms of pure possibility, pure imaginableness'.[74] 'Instead of judging about actu-alities,' he says, 'phenomenology uses imagination to judge about its *a priori* possibilities and thus at the same time prescribes rules *a priori*.'[75] This identification of *imaginableness* and *possibility* is made more explicit in the fourth Meditation when Husserl speaks of imagination as intuiting the essence of perception by reducing it to a world of *as-if*:

> We shift the actual perception into the realm of non-actualities, the realm of the as-if, which supplies us with 'pure' possibilities, pure of everything that restricts to this or that fact whatever. We keep these aforesaid possibilities ... just as a completely free 'imaginableness' of phantasy. Thus removed from all factualness, we reach the pure eidos of perception whose ideal extension is made up of all ideally possible perceptions, for every *fact* can be thought of merely as exemplifying a *possibility*.[76]

In his later works, Husserl tended to speak increasingly of transcend-ent horizons of possibility which stretch out beyond the given reality and mobilize consciousness as 'an intending-beyond-itself'.[77]

But there is an obvious ambiguity here as to whether this reaching out beyond the immediate presentness of our experience is a mere

31

projection of the *self*, or an encounter with something *other than the self*.[78] If imagination is merely conscious of possibilities fashioned within its own consciousness, we can no longer speak of the object of imagination as a transcendence. And, if this be the case, we find ourselves once again prey to the illusion of immanence. It would seem clear, however, that the originality of Husserl's theory of imagination lies in his interpretation of images as pure possibilities revealed *to* consciousness rather than fabricated *within* it.[79] Husserl thus finds himself back with the old question: If possibility is 'pure' – that is, emancipated from all ties with reality – then how does its freedom avoid degenerating into arbitrariness? If, on the other hand, possibility is 'real', it is no longer arbitrary, but surely at the expense of being pre-determined by an already given world?

This dilemma induced Husserl to search for some sort of transcendent telos which could satisfy the requirements of both freedom and necessity. Only in terms of such a telos, he believed, could possibility be said to remain *pure* and, at the same time, *motivated* by some goal towards which it strives. Such a *teleological possibility* would be that which unites all other possibilities into 'a universal constitutive synthesis'. Husserl defines it as an infinite regulative idea of which every 'presupposable system of possible objects of possible consciousness would be the *anticipative idea*'.[80]

The movement from actuality to possibility epitomizes, for Husserl, the intrinsic dynamism of human consciousness. On the level of philosophy, as we saw, this takes the form of a movement from the *natural* to the *eidetic* perspective.[81] This 'unnatural' movement must, however, be motivated *somehow*. And since it cannot be motivated by the natural world of facts – it being a surpassing of all that is factual – it can only be motivated by some telos which resides in the world of possibility itself.[82] This telos, Husserl informs us, constitutes an 'essential necessity' manifesting itself in the way in which any flow of freely varied possibles coheres into a certain ideal structure.[83] As such, the telos is not just a projection of human consciousness but something which human consciousness *discovers*:

What can be varied, one into another in the arbitrariness of imagination, becomes in itself a necessary structure, an eidos; and therewith *necessary laws* which determine what must necessarily belong to an object in order that it can be an object of this kind ... We need not *ourselves* bring about the overlapping coincidence, since, with the

32

successive running-through and the retaining-in-grasp of what is run through, it takes place *of itself*.[84]

This teleological necessity is not, therefore, a construction of the ego. It is, Husserl tells us, 'prior to all concepts we, as egos, may have of it'.[85] The actual ego is not the source of this possibility any more than the actual world is. On the contrary, both these actualities of ego and world find their source in possibility. As actualities, they remain but partial instances of their total horizons of possibilities. Thus, for example, my ego's ultimate possibility is the completion of my horizontal projections – the ultimate fulfilment of my past, present and future. Such, Husserl seems to suggest, is the telos which motivates all beings towards the condition of essences. And this confirms imagination as the indispensable power of intentionality which allows us to move beyond our actual world to the world of possibles where we reside as the possibility of total being. In brief, imagination is precisely that which can redeem us from our bonds of partiality by prefiguring the telos of totality.[86]

Because we can imagine we know that reality is not something given but an infinite metamorphosis. The absolute is not 'real', or at any rate not yet. The absolute is possible and, as such, can be intuited only through the imagination.[87] Husserl's notion of the telos as possibility calls for a free decision on the part of each consciousness to break through to the transcendence of the telos (be it the telos of a thing, an ego, philosophy or history itself); and to disclose (*entfalten*) it as a task for all. Imagination lies at the basis of such decision.

In the light of the above analysis of teleology, we are surely in a better position to review Husserl's overriding dilemma: how are the eidetic laws of possibility, which operate on the basis of an 'essential necessity', to be reconciled with the demands of imagination as a free intentionality? This apparent aporia prompted Husserl to make an important distinction between *motivation* and *causality*.[88] Whereas causality operates as an imposition of necessity on things; motivation, on the contrary, operates as an invitation to disclose the teleological laws of meaning. The latter alone allows for freedom and choice. And, although Husserl himself rarely couches this difference in such existentialist terms, his uncompromising rejection of all forms of determinism in the *Crisis* corroborates this view. Certainly, this was the interpretation which such close disciples as Levinas, Landgrebe, Heidegger and Sartre drew from his writings on the subject. Moreover, this revealing quotation from one of Husserl's unpublished manuscripts would seem further to substantiate the point:

> So we understand the absolute teleology which is the inseparable unity of all finite beings as a meaning-giving process which relates to each absolute subjectivity as the infinite way along which it moves itself towards its uniquely true being ... This operates in the clear consciousness of authentic humanity in the form of a *chosen* ideal.[89]

But, even if we accept that teleological 'motivation' is compatible with the demands of freedom, we are still left with the question of whether it is our absolute subjectivity which gives meaning to the telos in the first place, or vice versa. In the *Cartesian Meditations* Husserl declared that since 'transcendental subjectivity is itself the universe of all possible sense, i.e. every imaginable being whether immanent or transcendent, then an outside is precisely – nonsense'.[90] In the *Ideas*, on the other hand, Husserl appears to contradict this view. 'The absolute of transcendental subjectivity is in truth no ultimate,' he concedes, 'it is rather something which in a certain profound and wholly unique sense ... has its primeval source in what is ultimately and truly absolute.'[91] 'All being', Husserl tells us elsewhere again, 'is on the way' (*unter wegen*) to the realization of 'an ideal and absolute possibility'.[92] It is precisely this ideal telos which guides consciousness in its constitution of the world and calls each human subject to the creation of 'an absolutely perfect transcendental, total community'.[93] Such a teleological community would, furthermore, mark a gradual transition from subjective consciousness to an intersubjective communion with others based on the imaginative power of empathy (*Einfühlung*). Here Husserl's teleology takes an ethical, and at moments even theological, turn.

In one or two manuscript entries Husserl actually refers to this telos as 'God'. It is difficult to determine whether Husserl means by this the deity of Western monotheism or metaphysics.[94] But his insistence on the radical *otherness* of the divine telos – he uses such terms as *Uberwarheit, Uberwirklichkeit* and *Uber-an-sichlichkeit* to define it – suggests that he did not believe it was reducible to a projection of human subjectivity.[95] On occasion, Husserl even refers to the telos' power of motivation as 'grace'.[96] The transcendent status of this teleological possibility in no way jeopardizes Husserl's conviction that the freedom of human imagination is at all times preserved. Indeed, in his last writings he is careful to speak of humans being motivationally 'directed' rather than causally 'determined' by the telos – a significant distinction which indicates that the most sovereign possibility of our transcendental consciousness is such that we are entirely at liberty to realize it or not.

'In faith we may experience the teleology which directs us,'[97] Husserl informs us (faith meaning here the imaginative consciousness of the telos as our sovereign possibility). Because we are free to intend this possibility imaginatively, we are also free not to intend it. If there is evil in the world, it follows that we are entirely responsible for it. For evil only arises when humans refuse to intend 'the possibility of an absolutely perfect transcendental community'.[98] Because we are conscious of the possibility which may (for it is only a possibility) make all things necessary, we are totally free to intend or counter-intend this telos. In short, Imagination is what makes us absolutely free and, by extension, absolutely responsible.[99]

In many ways Marx's comment that Hegel's phenomenology reached the ideal but *in the mind only* could also be applied to Husserl's phenomenology. With the exception of some of the later manuscripts, Husserl's concern is almost invariably with a telos of Reason rather than of History. Furthermore, this telos proves to be a profoundly contradictory one. This is so, not only in the senses outlined above, but more particularly in the sense in which Husserl claims that the telos of phenomenology is at once (*a*) a presuppositionless and self-evident absolute, and (*b*) a goal which can never be reached 'absolutely' because of the 'asymptotic' nature of human intentionality.[100] In the first instance, philosophical reason is understood as the possibility of its *own* absolute foundation. In the second, philosophical reason is seen as an infinite striving towards some possibility *other* than itself.[101]

Husserl's formulation of possibility as *both* a self-grounding telos *and* a never-ending horizon of imaginative freedom is ambivalent, to say the least. The first part of this formulation was developed in an ontological direction by Heidegger in his *Letter on Humanism* (1947) – a text where he speaks of 'possibility' as a potency (*Vermögen*) by means of which Being 'appropriates' (*ereignet*) what is other than itself to what is the same as itself.[102] The second part of Husserl's formulation was taken up by Sartre in *Being and Nothingness* (1943) in his notion of possibility as a free projection of the human imagination. Husserl himself never succeeded, I believe, in reconciling the opposing exigencies of 'possibility'. His overall theory of imagination as the intention and intuition of possibility was altogether too confused and too inconsistent to resolve its own contradictions. Nevertheless, as Sartre justly acknowledged: 'Husserl blazed the trail and no study of images after him could afford to ignore the wealth of insights he provided.'[103]

Conclusion

Summarized in its most basic terms, Husserl's quandary is this: If imagination creates essential possibilities out of itself, how can it escape the charge of subjective idealism? And, if it does not so create them, who or what brings them about?

The closest Husserl comes to offering a hint of a solution is when he suggests that imaginative variation, as opposed to induction, does not *construct* a universal essence out of particular facts but discovers this essence to be the *a priori condition* of these facts.[104] This discovery is what Husserl calls 'constitution'. There is much confusion surrounding the phenomenological theory of constitution. The existentialist inter- pretation, based largely on the unpublished manuscripts at Louvain, maintains that Husserl meant constitution as a 'clarification' (*Klärung*) of the potentialities implicit in being.[105] This is what Merleau-Ponty calls the 'miraculous paradox of consciousness' which brings to light *afterwards* what was already there *before*.[106] It is in this sense also that Brand interprets Husserl's statement that the imagination does not deny the world altogether, but 'only prevents me from affirming that the assumed reality of the pre-given world has the value of an absolute foundation, so that I may examine the laws by which this world is constituted in the first place'.[107] Others – including Kockelmans, Spiegelberg and Suzanne Bachelard – lay the emphasis on the more idealist notion of constitution as a pure creation unrelated to the experience of being.[108]

The antinomies of imagination as a disclosure of essences notwith- standing, the fact remains that phenomenology could not exist without imagination. One of Husserl's disciples, Felix Kaufman, sums up its significance in the following portentous terms:

Phenomenology must be intuitive – and that means *imaginative* in the sense of eidetic intuition, or it will lose its identity as a philosophical movement ... Phenomenology ventures out into a new possibility of existence, an adventure of imagination – which, I submit, is the very destiny of man if he has imagination enough to grasp it.[109]

In conclusion we may say that Husserl's greatest contribution to our philosophical understanding of imagining was to have inaugurated a phenomenological redescription of the image as an intentional activity rather than a static representation. It is of course undeniable that his treatment was fragmentary in execution and often inconclusive in argument: one remains especially perplexed as to how, for example, the Husserlian account can succeed in relating the *essential* to the *existential*, the *transcendental* to the *historical*, or the *subjective* to the *intersubjective*. These criticisms aside, however, Husserl did serve the indispensable function of outlining the principal implications of an intentional theory of imagination. First, he showed that the image is an intuition (that is, presentification) of consciousness, closer to perception than to either the concept or the sign. Second, and perhaps most significantly, he revealed the distinct and *sui generis* natures of imagination and perception: the former as an 'as if' (or irreal intuition of the intended), the latter as a real one. But Husserl's claim that imagination and perception occupy two separate ontological regions was not only a resolution of traditional anomalies but also the creation of an entirely new one. The problem now was no longer how to distinguish the image and the percept – intentionality had provided the key here. It was how to justify the view that the imaginary can have any mode of *being* at all; or, more correctly, to discover what kind of being the image possesses if it is not the being of natural reality.

We saw how Husserl went close to providing an answer with his notion of the imaginary as possibility. But his discussion of this subject was vitiated by the opacity and incompleteness of his treatment, and it never succeeded in furnishing more than hints and guesses at a solution. Husserl himself was quite aware of this shortcoming. Indeed, he repeatedly insisted that his work was an appeal to future disciples of phenomenology and not in any sense a *fait accompli*. The appeal was not to fall on deaf ears. Subsequent reworkings of the phenomenology of imagining by thinkers as diverse as Sartre, Bachelard, Merleau-Ponty, Ricoeur and Lyotard are proof, as we shall see in the studies which follow, of Husserl's lasting if highly chequered legacy.

How, we may ask finally, has Husserl's phenomenology contributed to our threefold inquiry of imagining – epistemological, ontological and ethical? In answer to the *epistemological* question, Husserl has demonstrated how imaginative variation opens on to the eidetic realm of possibility where the intuition of 'essential truths' may take place. In answer to the *ontological* question, he has suggested how the bracketing of empirical facts can lead back to the transcendental experience of 'things themselves' (the phenomenological attitude). And, in answer to the *ethical* question, though not directly addressed, Husserl discloses the capacity of empathic imagination to move from subjectivity to intersubjectivity; and he intimates, furthermore, that this transition from self to other may uncover an ultimate teleological motivation.

Notes

1 J.-P. Sartre, *Imagination*, trans. F. Williams (Ann Arbor, Mich.: University of Michigan Press, 1962), pp. 134–5.
2 ibid., p. 81.
3 ibid., p. 83.
4 ibid., p. 117.
5 ibid., p. 146.
6 ibid., pp. 127–30.
7 Husserl, *Ideas: General Introduction to Pure Phenomenology*, trans. W. Gibson (New York: Collier, 1962), sect. 9.
8 ibid., pp. 171–94; also Sartre, *Imagination*, pp. xx–xxiii.
9 Husserl, *Ideas*, sect. 23.
10 ibid., sect. 42.
11 Husserl, *The Idea of Phenomenology*, trans. W. Alston (The Hague: Nijhoff, 1973), pp. 56–7: 'The consciousness in which the given object is brought to fulfilment is not like an empty box in which these data are simply lying; it is the "seeing" consciousness which, apart from attention, consists of mental acts which are formed in such and such ways.'
12 Husserl, *Ideas*, sect. 84.
13 Sartre, *Imagination*, p. 115.
14 Husserl, *Ideas*, sect. 23.
15 ibid., sect. 42.
16 E. Husserl, *Experience and Judgment*, trans. J. Churchill and K. Americks (Evanston Ill.: Northwestern University Press, 1970), p. 83.
17 Husserl, *Ideas*, sect. 23.
18 ibid., p. 416; Husserl, *Experience and Judgment*, pp. 258 ff.; E. Husserl, *Cartesian Meditations*, trans. D. Cairns (The Hague: Nijhoff, 1960), pp. 18, 127–9.
19 Husserl, *Ideas*, p. 123.

20   M. Farber, The *Foundation of Phenomenology* (Albany, NY: State University of New York Press, 1943), pp. 355–6, 385.

21   ibid., p. 411; also pp. 458, 462, 396. A certain hierarchy of intentional modes of consciousness begins to emerge, based on their degree of fulfilment. The lowest level is formed by the signitive acts which have no 'fulness' (intuition) at all. Both perception and imagination have fullness but, no matter how great the fullness of imagination, it is never as full as perception, for it does not give the object itself, not even in part. Consequently, Husserl talks of the 'genuine' fulfilment of perception in contradistinction to the merely 'figurative' fulfilment of imagination.

Though Husserl does at times concede that imagination is as valid as perception for the purpose of intuiting essences (for example, the essence 'red', the essence 'triangle'), the predominant view expressed in the *Logical Investigations* (1900–1) is that perception has ultimate superiority. Indeed, on one occasion he even refers to images as 'mere supplementaries' of a 'pure perception', the aim of the latter being to exclude gradually everything symbolic or pictorial so as to reach an adequate intuition of the object as it really is in its own original self-manifestation.

Husserl displays a similar preference for perception in his treatment of the subject in his next major work *The Phenomenology of Internal Time Consciousness* (1905; English trans. J. Churchill, The Hague: Nijhoff, 1964). Here Husserl rejects Brentano's theory that the origin of the apprehension of time lies exclusively in the sphere of imagination. He argues that Brentano failed to differentiate between time as perceived and time as imagined, because he failed originally to differentiate between the act of apprehending time and the object apprehended in time. On the basis of this difference Husserl distinguishes between 'primary memory' (based on an original perception) and a 'secondary memory' (based on imagination). The former he defines as being founded on a 'retention' of originally given percepts which are still lively enough to be 'presented'. The latter he defines as being founded on a 'reproduction' of percepts which are so far past that they can only be 'presented' mediately, that is, through the medium of an image. Since the image is prone to modification, however, there is no way of determining whether it refers to something self-given or not.

22   Husserl, *Ideas*, p. 287.

23   ibid., p. 281–5.

24   ibid., p. 80.

25   ibid., p. 416.

26   For conflicting definitions of 'irreality', see Husserl, *Ideas*, p. 432; *Experience and Judgment*, p. 268; *Cartesian Meditations*, p. 78; *Formal and Transcendental logic*, trans. D. Cairns (The Hague: Nijhoff, 1969), pp. 168–9. Another notable shortcoming in Husserl's treatment of imagination is his failure to distinguish between the *hyle* of internal and external images. Although he demonstrates how an external image and a corresponding perception can constitute different intentions and yet share the same *hyle*, he does not demonstrate how an internal (or mental)

image can have the same *hyle* as a percept. An example of an external image would be an intention based on Dürer's picture of the knight, death and the devil; an example of an internal image would be our image of these three without any such external picture to illustrate them.

Although in some passages in the *Logical Investigations* and the *Phenomenology of Internal Time Consciousness* he tended towards the view that the basic matter (*hyle*) of both an image and a percept is the same, in *Ideas* he declares such a view untenable. By stressing the importance of the 'reduction' in this work, Husserl rendered it impossible to distinguish a percept and an image by means of their respective positing or non-positing of the object intended. The reduction of the objects of both imagination and perception to the status of an 'irreality' eliminates any possibility of distinguishing between them by reference to their objective reality or unreality. In other words, if the tree perceived is just as 'irreal' as the tree imagined, how are we to know that the one is perceived and the other imagined? Husserl now recognizes that a difference in the noesis (intending act) of the transcendent object itself is not enough. There must also be a difference in the noematic *hyle* of the image and the percept:

> It may be in each case a matter of a blossoming tree and that tree may appear in each case in such a manner that a faithful description of *that which appears* as such would have to use scrupulously the very same terms. Yet the *noematic correlates are not for all that aany less different on essential grounds when we are treating of perception and imagination . . . Now the apparition is characterized as 'reality in flesh and blood', now as 'fiction' etc. These are characters which we find* as inseparable features of the perceived, imagined etc . . . as necessarily belonging to these in correlation with the respective types of noetic experience. (*Ideas*, p. 245)

This concession is by no means as unequivocal as it appears. What does Husserl mean when he says that we 'find' a difference between a perceptual noema and an imagined noema? Does this mean that the 'irreal' *hyle* can themselves motivate different types of intention? Or does it mean that the *hyle* are conditioned as different by the different noetic intentions? But if the latter be the case we are still left with the original question: What determines the intention as either percept or image in the first place? Once again, the circle. Husserl does offer a hint of a solution when he says that the *hyle* of an image calls for a 'spontaneous' intention, whereas the *hyle* of a percept does not. (This, as we shall see, was to become a major consideration of Sartre's theory of imagination). It was not, however, until the *Cartesian Meditations* (1929) that Husserl developed this insight into a comprehensive differentiation between a 'passive synthesis' of perception (operating according to a necessary association) and an 'active synthesis of imagination' (operating according to a free spontaneity) (pp. 80–1).

27 Husserl, *Ideas*, pp. 200–1.

28 ibid.
29 Martin Heidegger, 'On the essence of truth', in *Existence and Being* (London: Vision Press, 1949), p. 322.
30 Husserl, *Ideas*, p. 57.
31 ibid., pp. 198, 57.
32 ibid., p. 58. See Donald Kuspit, 'Fiction and phenomenology', *Philosophy and Phenomenological Research*, vol. 29 (1968), p. 19.
33 Husserl, *Phenomenology of Inner Time Consciousness*.
34 Husserl, *Ideas*, p. 200.
35 ibid., p. 309.
36 ibid., p. 306.
37 ibid., p. 312.
38 Husserl, *Formal and Transcendental Logic*, p. 245.
39 Husserl, *Ideas*, p. 313.
40 Husserl, *Formal and Transcendental Logic*, p. 245.
41 See Paul Ricoeur, *Husserl: An Analysis of His Phenomenology* (Evanston, Ill.: Northwestern University Press, 1967), pp. 91, 108, 128–9; see also M. Farber, *The Foundation of Phenomenology* (Albany, NY: State University of New York Press, 1943), pp. 385, 411–12; 441–2; Husserl, *Ideas*, pp. 312 and 123: 'Between perception on the one hand and, on the other, the presentation of a symbol in the form of an image, there is an unbridgeable and essential difference.'
42 Marvin Farber explicates this relationship between imagination, possibility and reduction succinctly as follows:

    It is thus seen that phantasy and the consciousness of possibility are essentially related to one another. Phantasy 'gives' possibilities originally. Reflection in phantasy yields possibilities of consciousness originallyy, and these are indubitable. The phenomenological reduction can thus be made in the infinite domain of phantasy. This extends the region of absolute giveness over the whole field of possible consciousness, as a sphere of 'transcendentally purified' possibilities. (Farber, *Foundation*, p. 528)

43 *Noesis* is the knowing and *noema* is that which is known.
44 See A. Gurwitsch, *Studies in Phenomenology and Psychology* (Evanston, Ill.: Northwestern University Press, 1966), p. 318.
45 We find here the important distinction between eide that can be instanced only in imagination, like centaurs, and those that can be instanced in actual experience. These latter, we must remember however, are only presented as eide through imagination. Husserl defines phenomenology as a science of the essence of things. By essences he means certain ideal contents which cannot be grasped within the natural attitude. They can emerge only through the 'possible' world of imaginative consciousness. Here any given thing may be abstracted from its actual instantiation in the world and freely varied through an infinite series of possibilities until such a point (which Husserl never specifies adequately) that an invariant structure emerges. This invariant

structure is what Husserl calls the essence or *eidos*. It has the advantage of being totally immune to the vagaries and contingencies of things as they exist factually; and as such it provides the imaginer with an intuition of the things as they exist ideally. W. Biemel (ed.), *Phänomenologische Psychologie, Husserliana*, vol. 9 (The Hague: Nijhoff, 1962), p. 14.

46 Husserl, *Ideas*, p. 200.

47 ibid., p. 71.

48 ibid., p. 71.

49 ibid., p. 72. The eidetic universal of imagination differs from the empirical universal of experience in so far as it is concerned with the *a priori* structure of an object. Imagination allows us to contrive fictional examples of an object which we could never encounter in the world: 'We stand then in a pure fantasy world, a world of absolutely pure possibilities' (ibid., p. 74). Because of this *ad libitum* nature of variation, the particular instance with which we began the process forfeits its priority. For we realize that we might well have begun with another instance of the *a priori* essence of the object and come across our original instance as just another of the infinite possibilities (*Experience and Judgment*, sect. 92).

50 Several phenomenological psychologists have illustrated this danger – Geld, Goldstein and Merleau-Ponty: see Gurwitsch, *Studies in Phenomenology* p. 394; also F. Kaufman, 'On imagination', *Philosophy and Phenomenological Research*, vol. C11 (1946): 'It is imagination through which man lives in devising new possibilities of life and world, transcending each given state and dissatisfied even with the satisfactions that mark a relapse into the inertia of patterned animal habits. Man's life acquires new meaning by virtue of the new meaning he can bring to and elicit from the world ... This is as in an artistic process where the painter emphasizes the features relevant to the constitution of the beauty he wants to reveal. Indeed, this awareness of possibility, this transposition of the potential into actual presence, which is characteristic of human existence, is in itself the work of the imaginative genius of man' (p. 379). See also in this connection Donald Kuspit, 'The dialectic of taste', *Journal of the British Society of Phenomenology*, vol. 4, no. 2 (1973), pp. 126–36. Husserl understood imagination to be precisely that organ which allows us to suspend our belief in the real world and to return to the origin of this real world in the 'irreal world' of intentional consciousness. This exploration of the intentional nexus where consciousness and world combine to form a single 'phenomenon' is the prerequisite of freedom. It is the concern of every human and the special concern of the artist. As J.-P. Sartre says in *What Is Literature?* (New York: Methuen, 1950), p. 63: 'The work of art is an imaginary presentation of the world in so far as it demands human freedom.'

51 Husserl, *Ideas*, p. 200. See also his *Experience and Judgment*, p. 173: 'In the actual world, nothing remains open; it is what it is. The world of imagination "is", and "is" such and such, by the grace of the imagination which has imagined it; a complex of fictions never comes to an end that does not leave open the possibility of a free development in the

sense of a new determination'; and also Farber, *Foundation*, p. 441: 'Since the production of phantasy-images is subject to our will to a much greater extent than that of perception and positings in general, we are accustomed to relate possibility to phantasy-imagining.'

52 Husserl, *Ideas*, p. 189; see also his *Logical Investigations*, Vol. 1, pp. 252 ff.

53 Husserl, *Ideas*, p. 200.

54 Kuspit, 'Fiction and phenomenology', p. 25.

55 ibid., p. 27.

56 Husserl, *Ideas*, pp. 200–1. And Husserl continues: 'These are indeed fruits of the imagination but in respect of the originality of the new formation, of the abundance of detailed features and the systematic continuity of the motive forces involved, they greatly excel the performances of our fancy, and moreover, given the understanding's grasp, pass through the suggestive power of the media of artistic presentation with quite special ease into perfectly clear fancies.'

57 Husserl, *Experience and Judgment*, p. 330.

58 Husserl, *Logical Investigations*, sect. 31–3; see also Gurwitsch, *Studies in Phenomenology*, p. 192.

59 Husserl, *Logical Investigations*, pp. vi, 31–3.

60 Husserl, *Cartesian Meditations*, pp. 128–9.

61 For lucid critical commentaries on this vexed relationship between imagination and solipsism in Husserl's phenomenology, see Ricoeur, *Husserl*, pp. 92–108; and L. Landgrebe, 'Husserl's department from Cartesianism', in R. Elveton (ed.), *The Phenomenology of Husserl* (Chicago, Ill.: Quadrangle, 1970), pp. 208–33 and 280–8.

62 Ricoeur, *Husserl*, p. 108; and Husserl, *Cartesian Meditations*, pp. 116–30.

63 ibid., pp. 128–9.

64 ibid., p. 36.

65 ibid., pp. 154–6.

66 E. Husserl, *The Crisis of European Sciences and Transcendental Phenomenology*, trans. D. Carr (Evanston, Ill.: Northwestern University Press, 1970), pp. 165–80. See also Gurwitsch, *Studies in Phenomenology*, p. 423–4.

67 Husserl, *The Crisis*, pp. 173–8. This principle of a teleological eidos holds good for the historical development of the imagination itself, from the realist tendencies of the Greek and medievalist philosophies, to the subjectivist leanings of Kant and Hume, which, though leaving much to be desired in themselves, pointed the way to the phenomenological concept of imagination as an intentional and constitutive power. Thus, the phenomenological imagination, as an agent of free discovery, proceeds to discover the curriculum vitae of its own historical becoming. Imagination becomes both the organ and the object of phenomenological research.

68 Husserl, *Ideas*, pp. 414–18; also Kuspit, 'Fiction and phenomenology', pp. 123–5, and Kaufman, 'On imagination', p. 372.

69 cf. Gurwitsch, *Studies in Phenomenology*, p. 420 ff.; J. Kockelmans, *The Philosophy of Edmund Husserl* (New York: Anchor, 1957) pp. 450–73; R.

Zaner, *Phenomenology and Existentialism* (New York: Capricorn, 1973), pp. 293–6.

70   *The Origin of Geometry*, appendix to *Crisis*, p. 372.

71   Husserl, *Ideas*, pp. 82–3; see also on the relation between imagination and telos: André de Muralt, *The Idea of Phenomenology*, trans. G. Breckon (Evanston, Ill.: Northwestern University Press, 1974), pp. 53–6; Gurwitsch, *Studies in Phenomenology*, p. 422–6; L. Dupré, 'Husserl's thought on God', *Philosophy and Phenomenological Research*, vol. 29 (1969), p. 201. This talk of possible life-worlds is reminiscent of Leibniz. Despite many striking similarities between the two philosophers (see Husserl, *Cartesian Meditations*, pp. 139–41), the parallel in this instance is a superficial one. Husserl is concerned with a free variation of possibilities effected by us not, as Leibniz held, by God. There is, to be sure, a teleological Possibility which calls us to our task in the first place, but Husserl seems to suggest it is entirely up to us to accept or reject this vocation (that is, to accept or reject 'the best of all possible worlds'). See Dupré, 'Husserl's thought on God', pp. 201 ff.

72   Husserl, *Ideas*, p. 415.

73   Dupré, 'Husserl's thought on God', p. 208.

74   Husserl, *Cartesian Meditations*, p. 28.

75   ibid., p. 28.

76   ibid., pp. 70–1.

77   ibid., p. 46; also pp. 122–36.

78   If we view possibility as something beyond consciousness, then imagination becomes a dialogue between the self and the other-than-self (ibid., pp. 137–8, 148–9). The latter is the only view consistent with Husserl's original definition of the image as intentional; that is, as a consciousness of something other than consciousness itself.

79   Representation in this sense may be broadened to signify not only revival from the past *per se*, but also a revival from the past in the shape of a projection into the future. Either way, however, the possibility represented in consciousness is one generated from its own depths: an Odysseus returning to his Ithaca – a circle.

80   Husserl, *Cartesian Meditations*, p. 54; also pp. 154–6. Martin Heidegger provides an interesting gloss on the notion of imagination as an anticipation of 'essences' in *The Basic Problem of Phenomenology*, trans. A. Hofstadter, (London and Bloomington: Indiana University Press, 1988), pp. 106–7: 'It is the anticipated look of the thing, sighted beforehand, that the Greeks mean ontologically by eidos, idea ... The anticipated look, the proto-typical image, shows the thing as what it is before the production and how it is supposed to look as a product. The anticipated look has not yet been externalized as something formed, actual, but is the image of imag-ination, of fantasy, phantasia, as the Greeks say – that which forming first brings freely to sight, that which is sighted.' Is this not what Husserl means by 'Constitution'?

81   *Husserliana*, vol. 8 (The Hague: Nijhoff, 1956–9), p. 121.

82   ibid., pp. 92–8.

83 Husserl, *Cartesian Meditations*, p. 137. See also Elveton (ed.), *The Phenom-enology of Husserl*, pp. 270–6; W. Wieland, 'The problem of teleology' in *Articles on Aristotle* (London: Duckworth, 1975), pp. 141–61.
84 Husserl, *Experience and Judgment*, pp. 341–3. See also on this notion of 'horizons': Elveton (ed.), *The Phenomenology of Husserl*, pp. 280–8, 14.
85 Husserl, *Cartesian Meditations*, p. 71. See also ibid., p. 60–1, where Husserl argues that essences are not 'truths for us' but 'truths in themselves'.
86 ibid., pp. 60–1.
87 Muralt, *Idea of Phenomenology*, pp. 54–62.
88 Husserl, *Cartesian Meditations*, p. 75. See also Husserl's Louvain *Manu-scripts*, hitherto referred to as *M.S.*, pp. 98–9, and Elveton (ed.), *The Phenomenology of Husserl*, pp. 25 ff., 292 ff.
89 *M.S.* VIII, 1, p. 7. See here also H. L. Van Breda, 'Husserl et le problème de Dieu', in *Proceedings of the Tenth International Congress of Philosophy* (Amsterdam, 1949), pp. 1210–12. Also Xavier Tillette, 'Husserl et la notion de la Nature', in *Revue de métaphysique et de morale*, vol. 70, pt 3 (1965), pp. 257–69.
90 Husserl, *Cartesian Meditations*, p. 85.
91 Husserl, *Ideas*, p. 236.; *M. S.*, E. III, 4, p. 66.
92 *M.S.*, E. III, 4, p. 26.
93 *M.S.*, E. III, 4, p. 61.
94 Husserl's most characteristic designation of God is as the supreme *Eidos* which 'gives all the constituting activities unity, meaningful coherence and teleology'. It is 'no mundane being' he says, 'but a final Absolute'. See here S. Strasser 'Das Göttes problem in der Spätphilosophie Edmund Husserl', in *Philosophisches Jahrbuch* (1967), pp. 131 ff.; also L. Dupré's claim that Husserl's Deity is an immanent pantheistic Telos rather than a transcendent and personal God ('Husserl's thought on God'). He infers, and with some justice, that Husserl's appeal to a Deity, like that of Kant and Descartes before him, is to a sort of philosophical *deus ex machina* which would resolve enigmas and ambiguities otherwise unresolvable. See also Elveton on Husserl and the Absolute, *The Phenomenology of Husserl*, pp. 43, 182 ff.
95 *M.S.*, E. III, 4, p. 62.
96 ibid., E. III, 1, p. 5.
97 ibid., E. III, 10.
98 ibid., E. III, 4, p. 61.
99 ibid., E. III, 4, p. 47: 'Man lives by faith and that is precisely why he lives in a world that has meaning for him and which he constantly confirms to the extent that he does justice to it. Correlatively, his existence in the world has meaning from him; he cannot give him-self up or give up the world ... precisely because he constantly negates the evil in himself and outside of himself as that which he recognizes to be co-responsible.' Husserl doesn't succeed in solving the problems of imagination and possibility by his appeal to a divine teleology, highly reminiscent of Aristotle and Kant (see Dupré, 'Husserl's thought on God', p. 214). He served a great purpose however, in

locating the link between imagination and God in the world of possibility.

100 Husserl, *Cartesian Meditations*, p. 151. This contradiction between the absolute and asymptotic charcter of teleology is evident in his conclusion to the *Cartesian Meditations*:

> Our meditations, we may venture to say, have in the main fulfilled their purpose, namely: to show the 'concrete possibility' of the Cartesian idea of a philosophy as an all-embracing science grounded on an absolute *foundation* ... though of course in the form of an *endless* programme. (p. 152)

101 Landgrebe provides a detailed and scholarly analysis of this precise problem in his article 'Husserl's departure from Cartesianism', pp. 259–302. Note particularly his discussion, pp. 298–301. Elveton also offers a critical account of the paradoxical nature of Husserl's pronouncements on 'teleological possibility'. He concludes as follows: 'Is this teleology itself entirely compatible with the possibility of a fully achieved science of transcendental origins, or are human reason and self-understanding by their very nature always "on the way" to such a result? Precisely how can these two motifs complement each other?' (*The Phenomenology of Husserl*, p. 36).

102 See particularly Heidegger's *Letter on Humanism* in Zaner's *Phenomenology and Existentialism*, pp. 149–50: 'Thinking ceases when it withdraws from its element. The element is that by means of which thinking can be thinking. It is the element which is potent, which is potency ... It brings thought into its essence.' Heidegger is availing of a certain play of words here. The verb *vermögen* means 'to be able'; the noun *Vermögen* means 'Potency' in the sense of 'power' or 'possession'. Later in the letter, Heidegger states clearly what he means by possibility: 'Being as the element [of thought] is the quite power of the loving potency, i.e. of the possible. Our words 'possible' and 'possibility' however, are, under the domination of logic and metaphysics taken only in contrast to 'actuality', i.e. they are conceived with reference to a determined viz., the metaphysical – interpretation of Being as *actus* and *potentia*, the distinction of which is identified with that of *existentia* and *essentia*. When I speak of the 'quite power of the possible' I do not mean the possible of a merely represented *possibilitas*, nor the *potentia* as *essentia* of an *actus* of the *existentia*, but of Being itself, which in its loving potency commands thought and thus also the essence of man, which means in turn, his relationship to Being.'

103 Sartre, *Imagination*, p. 143.

104 Husserl, *Cartesian Meditations*, pp. 101, 148.

105 ibid., pp. 84; and R. Boehm, 'Husserl's concept of the absolute', in Elveton (ed.), *The Phenomenology of Husserl*, pp. 177–204.

106 J. Merleau-Ponty, *The Phenomenology of Perception*, trans. C. Smith, (New York: Humanities Press, 1962), p. 30.

107 Husserl, *M.S.*, IX, 15, pp. 27–8.

108   Kockelmans, *Philosophy of Edmund Husserl*, pp. 237–67, 137–42.
109   Kaufman, 'On imagination', pp. 372–3.

Suggestions for further reading

As there is no single work by Edmund Husserl on imagination one must rely on selected passages from a variety of early and late texts, in particular *Logical Investigations*, Vol. 2, bk 6, trans. J. Findlay (New York: Humanities Press, 1970); *Ideas*, trans. W. Gibson (New York: Collier, 1962); *Cartesian Meditations* trans. D. Cairns (The Hague: Nijhoff, 1960); *Formal and Transcendental Logic*, trans. D. Cairns (The Hague: Nijhoff, 1969). The best secondary sources on Husserl's treatment of images, imagination and fiction are Jean-Paul Sartre's conclusion to *Imagination*, trans. F. Williams (Ann Arbor, Mich.: University of Michigan, 1962), and two accessible and engaging articles by Donald Kuspit, 'Fiction and phenomenology', *Philosophy and Phenomenological Research*, vol. 29, (1968), and Felix Kaufman 'On imagination', *Philosophy and Phenomenologicial Research*, vol. C11 (1946). The most comprehensive secondary source is M. Saraiva's scholarly if somewhat technical book, *L'Imagination selon Husserl* (The Hague: Nijhoff, 1970); but this is not yet available in English translation.

2

The existential imagination

(Sartre)

Jean-Paul Sartre, one of the founders of French existentialism, took up the phenomenology of imagining where Husserl left off. He opened the brackets of phenomenological intuition, affirming that any description of tthe *essence* of imagining must necessarily include analysis of its *existential* circumstances and consequences. Sartre was determined to combine the results of Husserl's eidetic researches with the existentialist cooncerns of thinkers such as Kierkegaard and Heidegger, whose writings had already profoundly influenced him in the thirties. The question Sartre put to imagination was not simply what it meant as an activity of consciousness but how such an activity informed our everyday being-in-the-world.

Although Husserl never dedicated any single work to the imagination, Sartre devoted his first two major philosophical studies to this subject. The first of these, *L'Imagination* (later translated as *Imagination*), appeared in 1936. It was designed primarily as a critique, from the perspective of phenomenology, of the main philosophical and psychological theories of imagination from Descartes to behaviourism, culminating with a critical exposition of Husserl's theory of the image. Sartre's conclusion charts the course for his own second work on the imagination:

> Husserl blazed the trail, and no study of the image can afford to ignore the wealth of insights he provided. We know that we must start afresh attempting above all to attain an intuitive vision of the intentional structure of the image ... It might be that on the way we would have to leave the realm of eidetic psychology and resort to

experimentation and inductive procedures. But eidetic description is the required starting point. The way is open for a phenomenological psychology.[1]

This passage states the inspiration and strategy of Sartre's principal work on the imagination, *L'Imaginaire: psychologie phénoménologique de l'imagination* (1940) – translated as *The Psychology of Imagination*.[2] And it is in the controversial 'Postscript' to this book that Sartre outlines, as we shall see, the most innovative existential implications of imagining.

Four characteristics of the imaginative consciousness

Sartre's inaugural move in *The Psychology of Imagination* is to amplify the Husserlian thesis that the image is an act of consciousness. To avoid any misunderstanding, Sartre distinguishes between the properly phenomenological use of the term 'consciousness' (*Bewusstsein*) to designate an active process of intentionality and the more habitual designation of the term (for example, in empirical psychology) as a given mental state. Sartre elaborates here on his earlier argument in *Imagination* that the essential nature of imagining cannot be grasped until we overcome the traditional 'illusions of immanence' – that is, that the image is (*a*) a mere representation having the same nature as the material reality it represents; and (*b*) a mere psychic content subject to the same laws as all other psychic contents. By providing concrete and convincing demonstrations of how images are unique intentions of consciousness, Sartre resolves to consolidate Husserl's challenge to the traditional understanding of images as second-hand sensations.

Sartre thus sets out to develop Husserl's contention that imagining is to be distinguished from perceiving not by reference to the objects it intends, but by reference to the act of intending. The mental image is not just a thing existing alongside other things; it is a unique *orientation* of consciousness towards things. 'The two worlds, real and imaginary,' as Sartre puts it, 'are composed of the same objects: only the approach to these objects varies.' What defines the imaginary world, and also the world of the real, is an attitude of mind. The image and the percept are not therefore different *objects* of consciousness; they are different ways of being *conscious* of objects:

The image is the relation of consciousness to the object; in other words, it means a certain manner in which the object makes its appearance to consciousness, or if one prefers, a certain manner in which consciousness presents an object to itself.[3]

For this reason Sartre displays a preference for such phrases as the 'consciousness of something as an image' or 'the imaginative consciousness of something' rather than the traditional designation 'mental image'. To have an image of someone is not to have a consciousness of the *image* of someone, but to have the imaginative consciousness of that person. 'The imaginative consciousness I have of Peter is not', Sartre points out, 'a consciousness of the image of Peter: Peter is directly reached, my attention is not directed on the image but on an object.'[4] Sartre explains in painstaking detail what Husserl had, for the most part, only contended: that a phenomenology of imagination would establish that an image is not an object in consciousness but an act of consciousness which intends an object beyond consciousness.

Sartre also goes further than Husserl in his conviction that images are often 'positional' rather than 'neutral'. In fact, for Sartre, neutralization is but one of four modes in which imagination posits its objects. These modes are (1) as non-existing, (2) as existing but elsewhere, (3) as existing but absent, (4) as neither existing nor non-existing.[5] An example of the first would be the image of an object which we know doeeees not exist – say, the image of Peter's head with the body of a centaur. An example of the second would be the image of an existing someone or something in a particular place other than here – say, the image of the absent Peter at the North Pole. An example of the third would be the image of an existing someone or something in no particular place other than here – say, the image of the absent Peter as simply absent but nowhere. And an example of the fourth would be a 'dis-positional' image, that is, an image the object of which has been neutralized with regard to the positing of its existence, for example, an agnostic's image of the dead Peter in heaven.

Sartre spends much space in *The Psychology of Imagination* extrapolating Husserl's basic insight that perception and imagination differ by virtue of their intentional character. Perception, he points out, may intend the object (in this instance Peter) as distant or near, hazy or clear, but it always posits him as *real*. By contrast, imagination may posit Peter as non-existent, absent, elsewhere, and so on; but it always posits him as *unreal*. When I see and imagine my friend Peter, it is the same object who is intended in both instances and the same I who intends him. Consequently, it can only be the intentional rapport *between* the intended object and the intending subject which constitutes the variant term. In perception my intention presents Peter as he really is: as he is 'seen' by me. In imagination, by contrast, my intention presents Peter in an 'unreal' way: not as he is but as he is imagined to be. Both reach the same Peter; but the former reaches him in the direct manner of encounter, the latter in the indirect manner of invention.

The matter is not, however, quite as simple as this neat antithesis between reality and unreality suggests. If it is true that the image presents the object in an *unreal* way, it is equally true that what it wishes to present is more often than not the *real* object. Curiously, the very point of my inventing an image of Peter may be that of trying to grasp the ungraspable Peter himself, that is, of trying to 'possess' the real Peter as he is in himself. Imagination is, Sartre notes accordingly, 'an incantation destined to produce the object of one's thought, the thing one desires, in a manner that one can take possession of it'.[6] Otherwise put: the way in which we take possession of an object of imagination is by 'presenting' it in an unreal way, as if it were real.[7]

Imagination is a *sui generis* mode of intentionality which frequently seeks to deny what it specifically is (unreal) in favour of what it would like to be (real). But, while the image is different from the percept in its mode of intention (unreal rather than real), it is often similar in *purpose* (the intuitive possession of the object). Thus, from the outset Sartre intimates the essentially 'absurd' project of imagination – to affirm what it must always negate, to possess what must always remain intangible, to realize an object by unrealizing it.[8]

The second characteristic of the image isolated by Sartre is the phenomenon of *quasi-observation*. Because the imagining of Peter is only a presentation of Peter *as if* he were really present, the object does not yield the full-blooded richness of perceptual observation, but only a 'quasi' observation. The image cannot teach us anything. As a pure invention of our consciousness, it contains nothing that we did not put into it; and, therefore, nothing that we do not already know.[9]

Sartre contrasts the apprehension of an object (for example, a cube) which an image affords with that afforded by a percept and a concept. By means of a detailed phenomenological description he reveals that:

(1) the percept is a progressive complex of different real presentations: to perceive a cube is to present it 'gradually' and 'exactly' from all its sides;

(2) the concept is a single and simultaneous knowledge of the conceived: to conceive a whole cube is to know all of its determinations (length, breadth, height, weight etc.) 'simultaneously' and 'exactly';

(3) the image, though 'simultaneous' like the concept and 'presentative' like the percept, differs from both in that it fails to provide an 'exact' apprehension of the object intended.

Moreover, while concepts for the most part posit the existence of abstract and universal natures, and while percepts posit the existence of concrete and sensible natures, images ignore all considerations of real existence, and posit the unreal existence of anything at all – be it abstract, universal, concrete, sensible or otherwise.[10]

Sartre is particularly eager to draw our attention to the distinction between the fullness of perception and the 'essential poverty' of quasi-observation. He accounts for this phenomenon as follows:

In a word, the object of the perception overflows consciousness constantly; the object of the image is never more than the consciousness one haaas; it is limited by that consciousness; nothing can be learned from an image that is not already there.[11]

In perception, Sartre says, one can increase one's knowledge of a given object through one's observation. I can, for instance, count the columns of a temple as I walk around it. Also in perception I can observe and learn more about the relationship of this temple with other objects which surround it – for example, trees, sky, street; or about the relationship of parts within the object – for example, columns and altar and roof. In imagination, by contrast, the temple is given in the single act of intending it. The image is entirely determined by the knowledge I use to create it. It can therefore reveal nothing new. So that when I imagine a temple I find that it floats immediately into my consciousness, total and unresisting. But, by the same token, as soon as I try to observe this imagined temple, seeking a more detailed knowledge of its architecture, measurement and ornamentation, I discover that such observation cannot inform me of anything more than I already had to know in order to intend the image in the first place. I discover, in other words, that it is only a *quasi*-observation, not an actual one.[12]

If in perception everything presents itself as being what it is, in imagination everything presents itself as being what it is not. The image follows its own *sui generis* laws of time, space and generalization, and defies the logic of ordinary apprehension.[13] To be sure, I do grasp a temple. But it is an *absent* temple; and it only appears to me to be *present* by in some way 'magically possessing' what it intends. The phenomenon of quasi-observation is, in short, a paradox.[14]

Sartre's phenomenological descriptions lead accordingly to the conclusion that imagination and perception can never overlap in so far as they constitute two heterogeneous modes of observation. Even though the image differs from the concept by virtue of its ability to 'presentify' its object intuitively, it falls far short of its perceptual goal. While prompting us to appropriate the thing intended by virtue of its quasi-presentation, the image fails to meet the essential richness of real perception.[15]

Moreover, because imagination is a mode of consciousness, it follows that it must be in some way cognizant of its own pseudo-status, asserts Sartre. More simply, in order to present its object as quasi-real, imagination must be conscious of first positing it as unreal.[16] This crucial phenomenon of double-think was to play a central part in Sartre's later discussion of dreaming, fascination and hallucination as modes of imaginative consciousness. And it was also to provide the basis for his famous existential notion of 'bad faith' in *Being and Nothingness*.

The third essential characteristic of the image identified in Sartre's description is that of *nothingness*. Since every act of imagination is constituted either by positing its object as absent, non-existing, existing elsewhere, or as not existentially posited at all, it follows that the object is invariably presented as 'nothing'. To say I have an image of Peter is, Sartre claims, equivalent to saying not only 'I do not see Peter', but also 'I see nothing at all'.[17] It might be more correct to say that, while *intentionality* and *quasi-observation* are characteristics of the imagining act, *nothingness* is a characteristic of the imaginary world itself. But Sartre is not always consistent in distinguishing between these two aspects of the image.

Sartre goes further than Husserl, moreover, in establishing a radical existential dichotomy between the worlds of the real and the unreal. Whereas Husserl tended to view the absolute antithesis of imagination and perception as but one of several forms their relationship could take, Sartre posited this as the *only* existential form compatible with a thorough phenomenological description.[18]

For Sartre the worlds of perception and imagination are mutually exclusive. To posit the imaginary is *ipso facto* to negate the real. But it is because imagination is essentially 'lacking' in the mundane richness of perception, precisely because it nihilates the real world which determines perception, that it is free. By positing the world as nothingness rather than reality, imagination reveals itself as *freedom*. This last point is pivotal to Sartre's entire existentialist philosophy.

Sartre goes on to argue that the nothingness of the imaginary takes three main forms: (1) spatial unreality; (2) temporal unreality; and (3) the unreality of intra-world relationships.

In the imaginary world spatial relationships are entirely *sui generis*. They do not emerge as normal series of organized external relationships. The distance and size of an imaginary object do not depend on its relationships with other objects as the distance and size of a real object do. Moreover, if the imagined object is itself given with an imaginary background, this latter exists only in relation to it. The imagined room in which the imagined Peter appears is a mere appendage to Peter. It exists and has meaning only in so far as he occupies it. If Peter leaves the room, then the room will have to leave with him. The relationship between the imagined Peter and the room is not one of contiguity and exteriority, as it is in the real world. It is one of 'internal interdependence'.[19]

The temporal dimension of the imaginary world is equally unreal. The duration of an imaginary event is not commensurate with the duration of the imaginative act which intends it. And so, if in reverie, I imagine myself running for ten hours through a forest, the reverie itself may only last for several seconds. Sartre suggests that the objects of imaginative consciousness have a certain timeless quality. Alternatively, the imagined object may be a synthesis of past, present and future times, for example, if I imagine my brother, he may appear as an amalgamation of child, boy and man. Imagined time may be faster or slower than real time. A fiction can recount a hundred years of history in a minute – or extend a split second of experience into hours. Fictional time can be reversed and repeated at will, unlike real time. The time of an imagined object is integral to it, and cannot exist apart from it.[20]

Third, the imaginary world evinces the unreality of intra-world relationships. Sartre maintains that phenomenological description reveals the image to be totally lacking in the quality of individuation which prevails in reality. Hence the image of someone can often appear as a collage of different perspectives, and can easily dissolve into the image of someone entirely other. Furthermore, an imagined object may be endowed with contradictory qualities: a face may appear upside down or back to front or with six eyes. This imaginative phenomenon was, incidentally, ingeniously exploited by many of the surrealist and expressionist painters, especially Picasso, Chagall and Braque. Whereas the different parts of a perceived object are related to each other in a predictable and coherent way, in the imaginary world no such relationships occur. If I alter any part of an imagined object, the whole object will either change completely or not change at all. Thus Sartre attempts to account for the jerky and discontinuous nature of imagining where each single image stands isolated from every other, acting upon nothing and being acted upon by nothing other than itself. Because of this shifting and unreal status, the image can never do more than simulate presence. It is haunted by an essential *lack of existence*.

The fourth and last characteristic described by Sartre is that of *spontaneity*. Sartre's position here is largely an extrapolation of Husserl's original theory of the image as an 'active genesis'. The image is spontaneous in that it posits *nothing* and so is always immediately present to, and identical with, itself. The imaginative intention reveals itself as it realizes itself.[21]

A perceptual consciousness appears to itself as being passive, but an imaginative consciousness presents itself to itself as a spontaneity which produces and holds on to the object as an image.[22] In other words, if perceptual consciousness is passive before the object which determines its perception, imaginative consciousness cannot be determined by its object because the object of imagination is nothingness. The image's 'existence' owes nothing to the object of consciousness: the image is created in the act of imagining.[23] At this stage in his argument Sartre seems to confuse the object as it appears in the image (a nothingness) and the object as aimed at through the image (a transcendent entity). But this should not prevent us from admitting a general validity to his distinction between the *passivity* of perception and the *spontaneity* of imagination. Sartre is surely phenomenologically correct in describing the spontaneous character of imagining as 'a magical act by which one seeks to possess *all at once* an object, which for perception presents itself only gradually, by degrees, and never as a whole'.[24]

From this account the image emerges as a productive activity sustaining itself by a spontaneous flow of consciousness. Insisting on the *sui generis* nature of this spontaneous flow, Sartre hopes to strengthen Husserl's refutation of the classical view that the image resides in consciousness as a derivation of perception or thought. And, even though Sartre will go on in the second part of this work to argue that the image has both a cognitive and an analogical component, his purpose at this stage is to make quite clear that *image, percept* and *concept* remain 'essentially' distinct intentions of consciousness. For Sartre, it would be as absurd to say that these intentions overlap as it would be to say that a body is simultaneously solid, liquid and gaseous.

The phenomenon of impersonation

Sartre does admit of variations in the *degree* of imaginative spontaneity. He proclaims the necessity of distinguishing between the purely mental image which (because it relies on nothing outside of itself) possesses the highest degree of spontaneity and non-mental images which are less spontaneous in that they are related to an external analogue; for example, a painting or photograph.[25] In the case of a portrait, the canvas and colours act as an analogue for the person depicted. Sartre thus classifies the spontaneity of images according to the way they relate to such physical analogues: in painting, the spontaneous act of imagination is very dependent on external analogues, whereas in dreaming or fantasizing the analogue becomes more and more an integral part of consciousness itself.

Sartre defines the relationship which the imagination engenders between the portrait-analogue of King Charles and the absent King Charles himself as a 'magical' one. Though absent in an absolute sense, the person depicted in a portrait becomes present in a relative sense through the magical enlivening of the analogue. Once imaginatively intended, King Charles seems mysteriously to incarnate himself in the lines, colours and shapes which originally constituted a mere object of perception.[26]

Sartre traces this phenomenon of magical incarnation back to the primitive belief that portraits or possessions of a buried ancestor-king preserve him as present (alive) even when absent (dead); or to the use of effigies, relics and shibboleths in magico-religious rites.[27] And, although Sartre spends no more than a few pages in relating this imaginative phenomenon to such symbolic practices, it is already intimated that his most significant contribution to a phenomenology of imagination will be on the level of existential anthropology rather than psychology *per se*.

This phenomenon of symbolic presentation is also operative in mime or impersonation. Here Sartre offers a lucid and convincing description of the imaginative process whereby Franconay, a famous French mimic, uses her own small body with the aid of a straw hat and a fat protruding lip to 'presentify' the absent Maurice Chevalier. From the point of view of perception, this straw hat and fat lip are nothing more than Franconay's hat and lip. From the point of view of imagination, however, they become signs which, when imaginatively apprehended by the audience, magically incarnate the person they signify – Maurice Chevalier.[28]

Sartre describes this relationship of the object impersonated, Chevalier, and the analogue of impersonation, Franconay, as one of *possession*.[29] The impersonator presents the impersonated by allowing herself to be 'possessed' by his most essential features. In order to do this, she – not unlike the portrait painter or photographer – tries to capture the most general and typical traits of the person in the form of some analogue: the aim of analogical 'typicality' being to solicit us, the beholders, to project the image of the person on to the actor's persona.[30]

Here we find the seeds of Sartre's central notion of projection, perhaps the single most important theme of his existential ontology. Simply stated, the creative imagination of the artist – impersonator, painter or photographer – requires the re-creative imagination of the beholder if its intended image is to be intentionally imagined. Without the imaginative project of the beholder the artwork remains a static nexus of gestures, hints and traces: a material substrate bereft of life.

Sartre's descriptive analysis also takes note of instances where consciousness creates images without any signs inherent in the analogue itself. He cites as examples the way we read images into stains, clouds, arabesques, flames, tea leaves or coffee grains. Here the role of projection is more clearly in evidence, for the analogue itself is totally passive, indeterminate and without directive. Sartre has surprisingly little to say on the significance of this transition from reciprocal acts of imagination (such as mime), where the analogue has as much to reveal as the consciousness has to project, to unilateral acts of imagination (such as reading tea leaves), where the analogue has nothing to reveal and consciousness everything to project.[31] His failure to make such distinctions is symptomatic of an increasing tendency to view imagination as solipsistic – a tendency which, as we shall see, ultimately leads to the existential dualism between the for-itself and in-itself of *Being and Nothingness*.

The paradox of the imaginary life

Sartre's investigations open up a whole new world of existential 'unreality' – what he calls the *imaginary life*. This life is the source of both our existential freedom and our enslavement: an existential paradox intimately related to the phenomenological paradox, noted above, that 'the image knows a certain fullness together with a certain nothingness'.[32]

We saw how for Sartre the operations of imagination are 'magical' ones in so far as they conjure up the objects of our desire, and enable us to take instant possession of them. There is always, as Sartre puts it, something 'imperious and infantile' in such a process, a refusal to take distance or difficulty into account. But this refusal to be bound by normal constraints contains its own nemesis: although everything obeys the emperor of imagination – appearing and disappearing at its beck and call – it only obeys in so far as it constitutes an empire of nothingness. The real and the imaginary are always separated by the Chinese wall of *le néant*. 'The world of the imaginary is completely isolated,' writes Sartre. 'I can only enter it by unrealizing myself in it.'[33]

Desire plays a pivotal role in our imaginary life. One may have a desire which is, at first, basically diffuse, devoid of precise intentionality. In organizing itself into an imaginative creation the desire acquires a certain specificity, intensity and coherence.[34] But the image, Sartre repeatedly points out, is not something which pre-dates the desire and affixes itself to it from the outside. This would be to treat imagination as a sort of labour exchange for images. The image, as phenomenologically described, is an unreality which can never be the *cause* of intentions. It is no more nor no less than an intentional creation of our own desire. Unlike Pygmalion, it cannot bring its creation into reality. It can lend it life, but only its own life – and only momentarily. The pride of the image-maker, as Sartre illustrates with his habitual literary flair, hangs on a thread of self-deceit. He is a creator enthralled by his own creations:

> The faint breath of life we breathe into images comes from us, from our spontaneity. If we turn away from them they are destroyed . . . Kept alive artificially, about to vanish at any moment, they cannot satisfy desires. But it is not entirely useless to construct an unreal object for it is a way of deceiving the senses momentarily in order to aggravate them, somewhat like the effect of sea water on thirst . . . it is but a mirage, and in the imaginative act desire is nourished from itself. More exactly, the object as an image is a definite want; it takes shape as a cavity.[35]

Moreover, the fact that our images are fleeting, protean and ambiguous serves to aggravate our sense of uneasiness.[36] Because the image is essentially unreal, it cannot furnish the same density and individual locality afforded by the realities of perception – hence our experience of the imaginary object as never being fully itself, as always remaining an elusive presence which functions as a perpetual abstention from being, an 'anti-world'.[37]

Because desire projects itself into an image of the desired object, which it then invokes as if it were really present, Sartre argues that an image has *in itself* no emotive power. It is not the image that is persuasive, erotic or disgusting. It is we who persuade, excite and disgust *ourselves* by the very act in which we construct the image. Sometimes the affective function of our intention overleaps itself and induces in us certain violent behavioural reactions such as nausea or vomiting; and we often misinterpret these as responses to an independently existing 'thing'. But for Sartre such nausea could not be the effect of any repugnant quality *in* the image. An image is an unreality which has no qualities unless given by us. The quality of repugnance is, therefore, but a consequence of the free development of the imaginative emotion as it exceeds its own affective role and returns to plague the inventor. This repugnance before the 'unreal' image must of course differ radically from the repugnance experienced before a 'real' perception, for the imaginative consciousness is determining *itself*. The emotive behaviour of the imagination feasts on its own reflection. And so Sartre tenders the rather perplexing suggestion that if we are repelled by an image we are, in fact, repelled by nothing other than ourselves.[38]

The imagination thus emerges as a labyrinth of mirrors, and the imaginer himself as both Theseus and the Minotaur. The implications are ominous. And Sartre's claim that when a lover imagines his beloved it is his desire for her that causes her 'unreal' face to appear to him and not her 'unreal' face that excites him with desire in the first place lends a tragic narcissism to the whole Sartrean interpretation. As soon as the beloved is absent for some length of time, my desire becomes something engendered not by her as an existing presence, but by me in order to fill in her absence. As long as she could be *perceived*, my feeling could always be surprised by a new richness, a new depth in her presence hitherto undiscovered. But as a mere image she can never be more than a correlative of my feelings for her. Consequently, once translated into the alien currency of fiction, she displays a basic poverty. She becomes, as Sartre puts it, 'scholastic'. The image of the beloved is like a corpse desperately trying to give itself the kiss of life. Each time the imaginative intention tries (and ultimately fails) to reincarnate the absent beloved as a 'real presence', the image loses more and more of its particularity.

At this point Sartre offers the intriguing hypothesis that love letters are awaited with such impatience not so much for the news they contain as for their concrete and particular existence, their ability to revivify an affective analogue which is dwindling from within. Increasingly distanced from the real presence of the beloved – which alone could infuse the analogue with a new lease of life – desire resorts to the ploys of imagination. And, given Sartre's reading, it ultimately degenerates into a sort of 'impoverished' love, a love for love's sake, a love that is in love with nothing other than itself.

This implies that an imaginary affection cannot be genuinely *felt*; since the object no longer positively affects me. It is an icon issuing from a void within the imaginer. The imagination allows for no 'passion' in its real and etymological sense (Latin *patio-iri*, to suffer or allow things to happen to one). There is no longer any contact, receptivity or dialogue. There is only the imagination writing love letters to itself, answering its desire with its own desire. Sartre illustrates this point further with the following vivid anecdote:

One could speak of a dance before the unreal, in the manner that a corps de ballet dances around a statue. The dancers open their arms, offer their hands, smile, offer themselves completely, approach and take flight, but the statue is not affected by it: there is no real relationship between it and the corps de ballet. Likewise, our conduct before the object cannot really touch it, qualify it any more than it can touch us in return; because it is in the heaven of the unreal beyond all reach.[39]

In this heaven of the unreal, desire becomes the dupe of its own duplicity, the victim of a barren and abstract object: what Sartre calls, in a memorable phrase, 'the empty absolute'. Our fascination for such unreality derives, of course, from the fact that the beloved-as-imagined will always prove more amenable to the whims of the lover than the beloved-as-real. But the price that must be paid for such unresisting complaisance is the price of solipsism. Unlike the real object with its inexhaustible wealth of resources, the unreal object can never be more than my desire for it.

Sartre goes on to argue, rather provocatively, that in the instance of 'infatuation' this is exactly what the lover seeks. His analysis here of the self-enslaving role of imagination is quite masterly and accentuates the suspicion that his real interest lies more in the existential meaning than in the eidetic method of human imagining. Pining away for an intangible person, the infatuated lover of Sartre's description knows deep down that any 'real' contact with this person would temper the excess and cool the fever of his passion. By restoring him to a certain reasonableness and self-possession such contact would, of course, considerably heighten his chances of winning over the loved one. But it is just such a tempering which the infatuated person most fears. He reckous his 'real' advantage as nothing compared with the loss he thinks he will suffer by the diminution of his present 'imaginary' passion. The touch of reality must be avoided at all costs; for by offering an avenue to the desired end it threatens to free us from the excitement of our 'imaginary' torments. At this point in Sartre's analysis we are reminded of the vexed lovers of their own love which people the pages of literature: Malvolio, Don Juan, Julien Sorel and Emma Bovary – characters who imagine a romantic world uncontaminated by reality but rediscover all the boredom of the real in the imaginary.

Pathologies of imagining

The pathological implications of such behaviour are evident, and Sartre does not hesitate to identify them. He cites the example of a neurotic who believes himself to be suffering from cancer but in fact is the victim of his own anguish. Unlike the *real* victim of cancer, the neurasthenic will dispense all his energy in trying to suffer more rather than less, in trying to convince himself of a disease which he *knows* despite himself (and cannot but know since he created it himself) to be an unreality:

> He cries out in order to bring on anguish, he gesticulates in order to bring it into his body. But in vain: nothing will fill in that annoying impression of emptiness which constitutes the reason and basic nature of his outburst.[40]

Sartre also cites the example of the coward who enacts brave deeds in fantasy but shirks, if the opportunity arises, any contact with practical reality.[41] After all, images *qua* images can have no consequences other than the ones I give them: the blood will only flow from the fictional bullet-wound if I will it to do so. This radical difference between real and imaginary behaviour accounts for what Sartre calls the 'continuous hiatus between the preparation and the action itself'.[42] And one might recall here the example of Hugo in Sartre's play *Les Mains sales* who is obsessed by the 'imagined' consequences of his act to the point that he procrastinates *ad infinitum* and is unable to reach any decision to act at all. Bereft of all recourse to reality, Hugo cries out against his own impotence: 'I live on a stage.'[43]

Sartre also discusses the role played by imagination in other pathological phenomena such as obsession, fascination, hallucination and schizophrenia. Contrary to the Romantic cult of 'divine madness', Sartre insists that the glorification of insanity and excess was, and still is, a fallacious one. If the schizophrenic imagines so many amorous scenes, he writes, 'it is not only because his real love has been disappointed, but above all, because he is no longer capable of loving'.[44]

While the object of perception sets up what Husserl called a 'claim to reality' (*Seinsanspruch*), the object of the image, by contrast, is always a non-thetic consciousness of itself as a creation of nothingness.[45] The question must then be asked how the patient can believe in the image which he is conscious of having created in the first place. Elaborating on his existentialist maxim that all humans are responsible for their own behaviour, Sartre ingeniously interprets this as a form of double-think, rooted in a fundamental disintegration of consciousness. Divided against himself, the patient claims that the hallucination or obsession *imposes* itself on the mind, as if the image were some extraneous thing set over against consciousness. This illusion, Sartre insists, can only arise out of a violent existential opposition between self and non-self:

> Consciousness is here a sort of victim of itself, clinched in a vicious circle, and every effort made to get rid of the obsessing idea is precisely the most effective way to bring it about ... the self is no longer an harmonious integration of enterprises in the external world. There are some spasms of the self, a spontaneity that liberates itself; it occurs as a resistance of the self to itself.[46]

Thus, when a patient speaks of evil thoughts which are 'given' to him, he is merely bearing witness to his own self-alienation. Sartre goes on to explain that such ideas of external 'influence' arise out of the victim's simultaneous belief that he is and is not responsible for producing these images. Accordingly, the belief in demonic possession is a fallacy which stems from a misunderstanding of the phenomenon of *counter-spontaneity*: an intentionality which both asserts *and* negates itself at the same time. Lacking an integrated centre of intentionality, man's consciousness disintegrates; and its images are erroneously interpreted as being *other* than the very consciousness which produced them. Sartre warns us here, however, not to confuse this phenomenon of disintegrated consciousness with the notion of the *unconscious*. Human existence is consciousness through and through. The pathology of imagination results not by consciousness being possessed by 'demonic' or 'unconscious' images set over against it, but by consciousness being set over against itself. 'Possession' can only be possession of consciousness by itself.

Following this line of reasoning, *dreams* should also be seen (though Sartre prefers to ignore this implication) in a pathological perspective, since here, too, we find consciousness captivated by its own creations. In the dream, as in ordinary images, everything that happens does so not because the objects are themselves present to my intuition, but because I imagine them to be so. Consciousness becomes intrigued by the visual possibilities of a whole series of affective impressions and ceases to see itself as an imaginative projection. The dreamer is one who walks through the world of his own creation, utterly seduced by the characters he imagines for himself:

> My [dream] consciousness is that of a world into which I have pro-jected all my knowledge, all my interest, all my memories and even

the necessity of being-in-the-world which imposes itself upon the human being. I have projected all that, but I did so in the imaginary mode of the image which I now construct. What has happened if not that consciousness was completely taken in? It entered completely into the game and it itself was determined to produce syntheses in all their richness, but only in an imaginary way.[47]

This phenomenon of total enclosure in the imaginary is what Sartre calls 'fascination'. And the dream is its most explicit manifestation since consciousness is here compelled to follow its own fascination without constraints. But, if Sartre speaks of compulsion, he makes sure to distinguish sharply between 'determinism', which suggests an influence from *without*, and 'fatalism', which refers to the self's submission to its *own* influence. Fatalism, not determinism, is the existential counterpart of freedom. The dreamer is 'unfree' precisely because he has lost his sense of being-in-a-world, an awareness which would have permitted him to withdraw from his oneiric imaginings and redirect his consciousness towards another modality of consciousness (perception or reflection, for example). Sartre is thus compelled to admit that, although non-thetically conscious of itself even while dreaming, the self can no longer free itself. It has traded in its freedom for fatalism.

'This is the reason', says Sartre, 'why the world of the dream like that of the reader occurs as completely magical; we are haunted by the adventures of the persons in our dreams as we are haunted by the heroes of a novel. It is not that the non-thetic consciousness of imagining ceases to grasp itself as a spontaneity but it grasps itself by means of a spell-bound spontaneity.' However, what gives the dream its 'unique nuance of fatality' is that 'the events occur as not being able not to happen, in correlation with a consciousness which cannot help imagining them'.[48]

There is a crucial difference, of course, between the aesthetic attitude of the *reader* and the oneiric attitude of the *dreamer*. The former retains the freedom to revert to the real world at any moment, to perceive the book as a mere tangle of black lines on white pages, or to stop and reflect upon the moral character of the hero or heroine. Always implied in aesthetic identification is the possibility of aesthetic distance. One sympathizes with the fortunes of fictive heroes rather than being *fascinated* by them in any 'fatalistic' way. Consequently, while aesthetic illusion is like dream-illusion in that both demand a suspension of disbelief, it differs in that its suspension is a *willing* one.

Sartre's tendency to play down such distinctions in *The Psychology of Imagination* is all the more surprising in view of the central role which he ascribes to individual will and responsibility in *Being and Nothingness*.

To break from the enchantment of the dream cannot, for Sartre, be a matter of voluntary decision. One may, indeed, be able to say to oneself 'I am only dreaming'. One may struggle to break out of one's own dream. But everything we say and do is transubstantiated, despite ourselves, back into the imaginary – like foam reconverted into water. Sartre ends up contending that we may only be awoken from the dream by either (1) an external stimulus (such as a door banging) too strong to be assimilated as material for an imaginative analogue; or (2) an emotion of fear or horror so real in its evocation that it breaks the fetters of nightmare and motivates a reflection; or (3) a natural caesura in the dream story itself (I am executed, I fall off a cliff, I kill the monster) which causes consciousness to hesitate momentarily, and thus occasions the transition to another mode of intentionality – wakefulness.

According to Sartre's analysis, to dream is to live a fiction in such a way as not to be able *not* to live it. He is thus led to the rather alarming conclusion (though he never acknowledges it) that *dreaming* is just as pathological a manifestation of imagination as *schizophrenia* or *neurasthenia*. In so far as it is condemned by its own creation, dreaming evinces both the power and the danger of imagination:

> Just as King Midas transformed everything he touched into gold, so consciousness is itself determined to transform into the imaginary everything it gets hold of: hence the fatal nature of the dream ... it is the odyssey of consciousness dedicated by itself, and in spite of itself, to build only an unreal world.[49]

By failing to distinguish sufficiently the degree of pathology in such different modes of the imaginary life as infatuation, dreaming or schizophrenia, Sartre tended to confound the notions of sanity and insanity, sickness and health. On this reading of the situation, one of two conclusions are likely: either all those who imagine (dream, love an absent person, and so on) are sick or all the mentally sick are gifted imaginers. As it transpired, Sartre was ultimately to opt for the former conclusion. And in *Being and Nothingness* this would express itself in the view that all human beings – because they project an impossible ideal (the synthesis of the in-itself-for-itself) – are useless passions in an absurd world.

Sartre's phenomenological account of imagination thus reaches the conclusion that the nothingness of the imaginary life is the source of both our pathology and our liberty.

Towards an ontology of imagination

In a substantial postscript to *The Psychology of Imagination* Sartre explores the critical implications of his hypothesis that imagining is a negation of reality. He departs at this point from the realm of psychological description and embarks on an investigation of the existential significance of the imaginary life. This existential inquiry concerns itself with two primary questions: (1) the *ontological* question of what a human being must be in order to imagine; and (2) the *aesthetic* question of what art must be if it is a creation of imagination.

In the postscript Sartre reveals the underlying ontological motivation of his two works on imagination. And this revelation involves a novel evaluation of the 'unrealizing' (*néantisant*) powers of imagining. In addition to its pathological tendencies to captivate and enthrall consciousness, the imaginary life now emerges as the primary condition of all human consciousness as a temporal being-in-the-world. Reviewing the findings of both *Imagination* and *The Psychology of Imagination*, Sartre poses the ontological question in the following terms: (*a*) 'Is the imaginary function a contingent and metaphysical specification of the essence of consciousness or should it rather be described as a constitutive function of that essence?'; and (*b*) 'Are the necessary conditions for realizing an imaginative consciousness the same or different from the conditions of possibility of consciousness in general?'[50]

Starting with the first formulation of the question, Sartre sets out to determine what a consciousness must be in order for it to imagine. To this end he prosecutes the view that the *sine qua non* for a consciousness to be able to imagine is the power to posit a hypothesis of unreality. Having provided throughout his analysis ample evidence of the four main ways in which such a hypothesis may be made – as absent, non-existent, existing elsewhere or neutralized – he now explores the significance of the fundamental factor common to them all: negation (*néantisation*). But since the negating act of imagination always remains a consciousness *of* something the crucial question still to be asked is: What is imagination a conscious-ness of?

In attempting to answer this question Sartre makes an important existential distinction between 'being-in-the-world' and 'being-in-the-midst-of-the-world'. Viewed as a 'being-in-the-midst-of-the-world', one is a simple spatio-temporal object which can be manipulated and measured like other objects in the world. As a 'being-in-the-world', however, one is a specifically human consciousness which is always consciousness of an object, and by the same token consciousness of *not* being this object. The 'of' distinguishes consciousness from objects at the same time as it relates it to them. Because it is inten-tional, consciousness possesses a power of withdrawal such that it can negate the objects of which it is conscious. The terminology here is Heideggerian, and Sartre does not hide his debt. At several points during the postscript, he explicitly acknowledges the influence of Heidegger's account of *Transcendenz* in *Being and Time* (1927) on his own theory of the image as a 'surpassing' of thingness towards nothingness. Nor is it insignificant that some ten years before the publication of *The Psychology of Imagination* Heidegger had argued in *Kant and the Problem of Metaphysics* (1929) that the transcendental imagination is the temporalizing-projecting source of human existence, and thus the prototype of *Dasein*.[51]

Imaginative consciousness involves a *double* negation. When we imagine, we first posit a world in which our imagined object is absent, in order that we may then imagine a world in which our imagined object is present.[52] To imagine something therefore is (1) to constitute the 'world' as a synthetic totality – by means of a nihilating withdrawal from it; and (2) then to negate this 'worldly' existence by positing something that is *not* of this 'world' (an absence, a nothingness, a pseudo-world).[53]

The image acts in this wise as a negation of the already negated world – rather like the negative of a photographic plate where the world emerges precisely through its own inversion. Without the negating power of imagination, the real 'world' no less than the imaginary 'world' could not be constituted as 'world' at all. Regrettably, Sartre's thinking here is far too concise, and not very coherent for those unfamiliar with Heidegger's notion of *Dasein* as a surpassing-negating of the world. But this discussion represents Sartre's first explicit approach to existential ontology, even though it was not until three years later in *Being and Nothingness* that he clearly and consistently worked out his ontological theory of negation. At this point, his analysis still exhibits much confusion and an inordinate dependence on Heideggerian terminology.

Sartre concludes the postscript by answering both formulations of the ontological question in the affirmative. First, if we accept the phenomenological concept of imagination, we must admit, he says, that the conditions for an imaginary consciousness *are* the same as those for consciousness in general. Second, in so far as we admit that the negating power of imagination is constitutive of the very essence of consciousness (as opposed to being a mere specification of it), it is impossible to conceive of a consciousness which would *not* be imaginative. For if a consciousness could not imagine, it would be 'engulfed in the existent and unable to grasp anything but the existent'.[54]

Sartre thus endorses Husserl's view that it is imagination which allows us to escape from the constraints of immediate reality and to regard it with a critical eye, that is, to transcend the *actual* and project ourselves into the *possible*. Deprived of this surpassing power, consciousness would be submerged in the manifold of the given. In other words, if the *excess* of imagination results in a pathology of self-immersion, then the *lack* of it results in the equally undesirable extreme of self-surrender to the chaos of existence. Imagination is both our health and our disease.[55]

While Sartre's psychological analysis of imagination tended to stress the connection between nothingness and enslavement, his ontological analysis reverses the coin and explores the fundamental link between nothingness and freedom. The emphasis here is on the existential fact that in order to imagine something consciousness must be free from all reality. It is the unrealizing power of consciousness which endows it with freedom *vis-à-vis* the real. 'The unreal is produced outside of the world by a consciousness which stays in the world, and it is because he is transcendentally free that man can imagine.'[56]

Sartre does not hold, however, that every act of freedom must be an act of imagination in the *full* sense, that is, an act of *double* negation. But it must be at least an act of imagination in the implicit sense, an act of *single* negation. This implicit act of imagining is equally requisite in the constitution of our everyday real 'world' – or what Sartre often calls our 'situation'. 'The realizing consciousness', as he puts it, 'always includes a retreat towards a particular imaginative consciousness which is like the reverse of the situation and in relation to which the situation is defined.'[57] Otherwise stated, it is the *possibility* of the unreal – or the other-than-real – which provides us with the freedom to found the real; it is the hint of an absent world which pulls our present one into shape. The reason for this complex pairing of the *real* and the *unreal*, which in Sartre's later ontology will emerge as a dualism of *being* and *nothingness*, is best expounded by the author himself:

> The imaginary appears on the foundation of the world, but recip-rocally all apprehension of the real as world implies a hidden surpassing towards the imaginary. All imaginative consciousness uses the world as the negated foundation of the imaginary and reciprocally all consciousness of the world calls and motivates an imaginative consciousness as grasped from the particular meaning of the situation ... So imagination, far from appearing as an actual characteristic of consciousness, turns out to be an essential and transcendental condition of consciousness.[58]

Towards an existential aesthetic

In the second part of the postscript Sartre discusses the implications of his ontology of imagination for an existential aesthetic. His premiss is that the being of a work of art is a non-being; and his procedure is to demonstrate how this is so in such various arts as painting, music and literature.

If I apprehend a picture of Charles VIII, I may choose to view it as a reality or as an image. As a reality, I merely *perceive* different materials – canvas, oil, paint, frame, light – which may be destroyed with the strike of a match. As an image, however, Charles VIII cannot be destroyed – any more than David Copperfield could be destroyed by tearing up a particular edition of a Dickens novel, or the Seventh Symphony of Beethoven by planting a bomb in the orchestra-pit where it is being performed. The aesthetic image which moves us and which we venture to praise or blame is an *unreality* (though one might regret here that Sartre did not opt for the Husserlian term 'fiction' in his discussion of art, as the term 'image' carries too many visual connotations. It is difficult, for example, not to feel awkward when referring to a piece of music as an 'image').

The image of Charles VIII is the consummation of an act of con-sciousness which aims to present the absent king through a material analogue. Aesthetic qualities do not exist *in* the painting itself but rather in the way in which our intention is fulfilled by the image. A picture is dead until it is imagined. Galleries with nobody in them are cemeteries. Berkeley's *esse est percipi* becomes Sartre's *esse est imaginari*. Every time a spectator assumes an imaginative stance he casts a particular spell over the person or thing intended which renders it present in its absence. Sartre argues from this to the rather startling conclusion that the 'beautiful' does not refer to actual things but to an aesthetic property of no-thingness. What is beautiful, he says,

> is something which cannot be experienced as a perception and which by its very nature is out of this world ... The fact of the matter is that the painter did not *realise* his mental image at all: he has simply constructed a material analogue of such a kind that everyone can grasp the image provided he looks at the analogue. But the image thus provided with an external analogue remains an image.[59]

Since it is impossible that the imaginary be made real, it is absurd to speak of beauty as an objective entity. Beauty does not exist in beautiful objects, but in a certain mode of intending objects beautifully. Sartre's existential phenomenology thus injects new life into the jaded maxim that beauty is in the eye of the beholder. It reveals that aesthetic appreciation is a particular way of intending an unreal object; that it is not directed to the empirical canvas, but passes through it towards the re-creation of an image. But this is only partially true. Sartre seems to ignore the fact that many art forms, particularly non-figurative sculpture and painting, rely on their material *texture* (rough, smooth, jagged, shiny, slippery) for their effect.

Sartre's insight is arguably most fitted to the art of acting, as might be expected from a playwright. The actor, he points out, does not actually become Hamlet but serves as an analogue of gestures by means of which the audience may resurrect the absent prince. To abet this resurrection the good actor will voluntarily assist in the transformation of himself into an unreal Hamlet. He will subordinate his given self to the imaginary self of the emerging Hamlet. It is not 'the character who becomes real in the actor, but the actor who becomes unreal in his character'.[60]

This analysis also holds good for the art of music. If we consider the matter carefully, we discover that the Seventh Symphony can be reduced neither to its performance nor to its historical creation by

Beethoven. It *exists*, to be sure; but not on the actual score-sheets, nor in the notes issuing from the actual orchestra. It exists elsewhere, out of reach, beyond the real. The symphony, of course, needs the real in order to exist. It needs an actual performance to serve as analogue to its imaginative re-creation. But the analogue only functions in so far as it is negated as a reality and becomes an unreality. Sartre is not claiming that art exists in some Platonic heaven or other-world. To claim that a Beethoven symphony or the Prince of Denmark exists elsewhere does not mean that they exist some *where* else. It simply means that they are other than every *thing* that exists here. We do not actually behold Prince Hamlet or the Seventh Symphony; we *imaginatively* behold them. And it is precisely this shift from perceptual to imaginative consciousness that determines the *sui generis* nature of art.

Sartre offers the interesting suggestion here that it is this mutual exclusiveness of intentionalities which accounts for the peculiar dis-comfiture one experiences when leaving a theatre or concert-hall. The unease is engendered not by the passing from one *place* to another – from hall to street – but by passing from one *attitude* to its opposite – from imagination to perception. 'Aesthetic contempla-tion is an induced dream and the passing into the real is an actual waking up.'[61]

Sartre submits that this fact exposes the myopia of those who persist in confounding the aesthetic with the moral. Art can never be moral, in his view, for morality is only concerned with reality while art is, in its essence, an existential reversal of reality. His analysis here sheds some new light on the 'disinterested' character of aesthetic experience so often spoken about by Kant, Schiller and Schopenhauer (though later repudiated by Sartre himself in *What Is Literature?*, 1947). For the author of *The Psychology of Imagination*, beauty is always unreal and so can never be used by an 'interested' attitude:

It is untouchable, it is beyond our reach; hence arises a sort of sad disinterest in it. It is in this sense that we may say that great beauty in a woman kills the desire for her. In fact we cannot at the same time place ourselves on the plane of the aesthetic where this unreal 'herself' which we admire appears and on the realistic plane of physical possession. To desire her we must forget she is beautiful, because desire is a plunge into the heart of existence, into what is most contingent and most absurd.[62]

The existential crisis of value

The inaccessibility of beauty has worrying implications for the role of 'value' in our everyday existence. If beauty, as an aesthetic construct of imagination, is unrealizable in our contingent lived experience, then what of 'value' which Sartre equally identifies as an imaginary project? The problem is this: freedom is the supreme value of our existence. It is that goal towards which all our existence *tends* (*se dirige*). But it is also that which is *presupposed* by our existence – as the power to negate what is and project what might be. And this power, as we have seen, derives from imagination. We thus discover ourselves back in the solipsistic circle where imagining is both the origin *and* end of our existence.

Sartre's most succinct formulation of this relationship between the existential value of freedom and imagination comes in his conclusion to *The Psychology of Imagination*:

> We may conclude that imagination is not an empirical and super-added power of consciousness; it is the whole of consciousness as it realizes its freedom. Every concrete, real situation of consciousness in the world is big with imagination in so far as it always presents itself as a withdrawing from the real.[63]

Although there is some confusion in Sartre's mind as to whether man is free because he imagines or imagines because he is free, the important point is that consciousness is freedom in so far as it is always transcending the real towards the imaginary. 'There could be no developing consciousness without an imaginative consciousness', Sartre says, since 'that which is denied must be imagined'.[64] Thus understood, the imaginary serves as a sort of provisional telos towards which consciousness strives in its perpetual negation of the given.

The nearest Sartre comes to an acknowledgement of this telos is in his allusions to the 'meaning' or 'value' of imagination.[65] Stating that all imaginative consciousness uses the world as the negated foundation of the imaginary, Sartre adds that 'reciprocally, all consciousness of the world calls and motivates an imaginative consciousness as grasped from the particular *meaning* of the situation'.[66] This notion of meaning (*sens*) or value (*valeur*), appearing in the conclusion of *The Psychology of Imagination* for the first time, is to play a central role in Sartre's whole existential theory of possibility-projection in *Being and Nothingness*.

Even though Sartre never adverts to the link himself, it is undoubtedly in this discussion of imaginative freedom and value that one discovers the most fundamental line of continuity between the two works.

While all our acts are freely motivated in some way Sartre seems to suggest that we only truly become free when we lucidly and reflectively assume this freedom. We do this, he says, by discovering that the power to imagine is our 'essential and transcendental condition of consciousness'.[67] Only by such a discovery can we grasp the 'meaning' of the situation which is the telos mobilizing our surpassing of the real in the first place:

> When the imaginary is not posited as a fact, the surpassing and the nullifying of the existent are swallowed up in the existent; the surpassing and the freedom *are there* but are not revealed; the person is crushed in the world, run through by the real, he is closest to the thing. However, as soon as he apprehends in one way or another the whole as a situation, he retreats from it towards that in relation to which he is a lack.[68]

Sartre seems to be suggesting here that as soon as we discover ourselves as *lack* we discover that we are lack only in relation to a goal which we are not. It is precisely this teleological image of fullness which serves as the concrete motivation of the imaginative structure of consciousness. Our imagining therefore is not generally an *arbitrary* expression of freedom. It is not an empty void but a nothingness teleologically directed towards some ideal which, Sartre concedes, 'represents at each moment the implicit meaning of the real'.[69]

This view is also intimated in Sartre's treatment of the work of art. He argues that the Seventh Symphony of Beethoven is a *nothingness* in the sense that it cannot be reduced to the real sounds which a real orchestra plays from a real score-sheet. These merely comprise the analogue of the symphony; but the symphony itself is not subject to the laws of empirical reality. It is a no-thing which can only be imagined. It seems quite obvious that Sartre employs the term 'nothingness' here to denote neither arbitrariness nor emptiness, but some ulterior meaning beyond both reality *and* consciousness. This nothingness could not, of course, exist without consciousness and reality, that is, without the imaginative negation of the latter by the former. But such negation is merely the prerequisite. It accounts for the non-existence of the world, not for the existence of the imaginary. And yet the imaginary itself seems to

73

require some form of *positive* existence also, some particular telos which it prefigures or incarnates.[70]

Only such a teleological reading can resolve the contradiction between the imagination's claim to both freedom *and* fascination. If, according to Sartre, the imagination can become fascinated by the images which it intends, and if it is true that imagination is a *sui generis* mode of consciousness which relates to nothing other than itself, then how is one free to break this fascination? In other words, even if it were possible to be fascinated by pure nothingness – a highly dubious supposition in itself – how could it then be possible ever to negate this nothingness since negation must always be negation of *something*. Taking the example of our being fascinated by an impersonator, it seems impossible to explain our freedom to switch our mode of intention so that we may 'perceive' the real person behind the imaginary one (Franconay behind Chevalier), as long as one holds that imagination can have recourse to nothing outside of itself. But experience tells us that we are in fact free to switch our intention in this way. When watching Cordelia or Hamlet die on stage we can always take solace in the reminder that such suffering is 'only pretend' and that as *real* actors they are not suffering at all. Indeed, the whole principle of tragic catharsis by pity and fear presupposes this ability to move freely between imaginative identification (pity) and actual distance (fear). Brecht was to make great use of this factor in his famous alienation effect (*Verfremdungseffekt*). Or, on a more everyday level, we might point to how an adolescent fascinated by the image of a television star breaks the spell as soon as he realizes that she is not a goddess at all, but merely an ordinary human being.

However, Sartre's dualist theory of the image cannot, I believe, adequately account for this phenomenon of *transition*. By failing to explain how the image exists in a manner different from both consciousness and reality, he excluded any possibility of explaining how one can mediate between them. In short, only if the image is beyond not only the reality which it negates but also the imaginative consciousness which intends it can one account for the fact that one is free and fascinated at the same time – that is, aware that the image is not real while behaving *as if* it were. In order to be consistent with his initial description of the image as empty consciousness, Sartre appears to have no choice but to revise his existential definition of imagination as an agent of freedom. If the image is a nothingness with no existence other than the consciousness which intends it, then one is simply not free not to be fascinated.[71] Such revisions were not made.

I have spoken of the 'existence' of nothingness several times. Indeed, it seems impossible to avoid such paradoxical expressions once we take Sartre's claims for the image seriously. If beauty, for instance, is an epithet which can only be attributed to nothingness, then clearly nothingness is not the mere lack of reality – as Sartre originally described it – but some sort of ontological *telos* towards which each consciousness surpasses the actual.

Some hint of a solution is to be found in the Husserlian notion of the image as a disclosure of the possible. As intentional possibility, the image is sufficiently present to function as a *telos* which mobilizes the imaginer's transcending of reality. Sartre himself seems very close, on occasion, to conceding the positive existence of such a teleological horizon of possibles in the light of which imaginative acts seek to unrealize the real. As when he admits that imagination must retreat towards 'something'.[72] But he is reluctant to grant this 'something' any positive ontological status. I think this refusal must be ultimately understood in terms of Sartre's fetish of freedom.

Sartre peremptorily excludes any consideration which might obstruct the *chemins de la liberté*. In *The Psychology of Imagination* and later again in *Being and Nothingness*, he will only allow of a two-tiered model of existence: the first called freedom (or *être-pour-soi*), the second called non-freedom (or être-en-soi). Freedom represents the power of imaginative consciousness to unrealize the given world, and is thus synonymous with nothingness. Non-freedom represents the given world unrealized by consciousness. Sartre could not admit of any third tier to this model for the basic reason that he could not tolerate the suspicion of human liberty being sponsored by any agency other than itself. Either freedom or necessity. There is no in-between. But this uncompromising fidelity to the unconditionality of freedom sometimes nudges Sartre towards the old trap of dualism – the pincer-jaws of being and nothing.[73] The ghost of Descartes hovers imperceptibly between the lines of Sartre's early texts.

In a world where everything is either *pour-soi* or *en-soi*, anything redolent of synthesis is rejected as absurd. Although Sartre frequently characterizes the imagination as that which enables us to apprehend things as pointing to a meaning beyond themselves, he ignores the teleological implications of this view. But the fact remains that the *meaning* of things can only be imagined, not perceived. Indeed, it is highly significant that Sartre's own philosophical procedure, especially in *Being and Nothingness*, is based on just this implied use of imagination. Objects are phenomenologically described and intuited by Sartre, not simply for their own sake, but in so far as they embody a significance beyond themselves. For instance, Sartre's famous description of a waiter's project to unite his *pour-soi* (freedom) and his *en-soi* (being in-itself) presupposes the use of imagination to intuit this 'meaning' in all of his gestures – for as *perceived* they are no more than gestures. Similarly, Sartre suggests that our likes and dislikes are symbolic of a whole way of being-in-the-world. If we are drawn to skiing or repelled by viscous substances it is symbolic of our desire to transcend the habitual intractability of matter. Sartre develops a whole inventory of such existential patterns of behaviour – structured by symbolic 'value' – in a concluding section of *Being and Nothingness*, entitled 'Existential psychoanalysis'.[74]

Such 'value' is best understood as the imaginary 'possibility' of things. If Sartre is correct in *Being and Nothingness* when he rejects the traditional notion of possibility as something existing *in* things, he is mistaken in regarding it as a mere projection of consciousness. Imaginary 'possibility' must be ontological in a *positive* sense – different from both the being of reality and the non-being of consciousness. It must be positively ontological in order to *be* that of which the imaginative intention is conscious; it must be different from reality in that reality is precisely that which is negated in its name; and it must be different from consciousness in that consciousness is always conscious *of* the image as something different from itself.

If the traditional error was, according to Sartre, to regard possibility as determined by the same being as actuality (*ens in potentia* being a determination of *ens* or a logical *possibilitas* existing in the mind of a Supreme Being), then his own error is to reduce possibility to the mere invention of an empty choosing will. Sartre would not admit of possibility as a third ontological category between the extremes of consciousness and reality, for its dialectical implications seemed to jeopardize the unconditional sovereignty of freedom. Accordingly, in *Being and Nothingness* he dismisses the possibility of a dialectical synthesis between the *en-soi* and the *pour-soi* as 'absurd', while at the same time identifying this as the Supreme Value towards which all things are teleologically directed. Freedom ousts dialectic, but only at the price of absurdity. It is a pyrrhic victory.

The existential question of value, which arises in *The Psychology of Imagination* for the first time, is one of the most central concerns of

Sartre's subsequent ontology. While going under the name of 'beauty' in *The Psychology of Imagination* (1940) it is rechristened the *'pour-soi-en-soi'* synthesis in *Being and Nothingness* (1943). And as we move from his ontology to his literary writing we find Sartre referring to value straightforwardly as 'Being' – contrasting it with the absurd contingency of man's 'existence' (see the concluding passages of *Nausea*). This nomenclature is witnessed most clearly in his novels and plays, though it is also operative throughout his considerable corpus of aesthetic criticism. Finally, in his later political philosophy, and especially his existentialist-Marxist *Critique of Dialectical Reason* (1960), Sartre designates value as a 'Concrete Universal' resulting from historical praxis.[75] But, whether value is denominated as 'Beauty', 'Being', the 'For-itself-in-itself' or the 'Concrete Universal', it always refers to that ideal synthesis which eye has not seen nor ear heard, but only imagination imagined. And it is precisely because it is *imagined* – and *only* imagined – that it invariably constitutes for Sartre an 'empty absolute'.

Conclusion

Perhaps the most obvious objection to Sartre is his tendency to treat imagination in a pathological light. This is explicit in his treatment of the 'abnormal' expressions of imagination – hallucination, schizophrenia, neurasthenia; but is also present, if diplomatically understated, in his treatment of such 'normal' forms of imagination as dreaming, infatuation, fascination or aesthetic appreciation. We find here the germs of Sartre's famous existentialist doctrine that man is an absurd, useless and nauseated creature. Since Sartre's analysis in *The Psychology of Imagination* seems to imply that every attempt to negate reality is in some sense a symptom of pathologial self-deception, the unreality of the imagination cannot be construed as anything other than an existential infirmity.[76] Furthermore, since Sartre insists that the very constitution of our world is ultimately based on such an unrealizing power, he has no option but to conclude that all humans are pathological by nature – crippled by their own nothingness. Imagination emerges in the final analysis as an illness which aesthetic man, everyman, cannot afford to do without.[77]

Another major objection to Sartre's concept of imagination concerns his dualism between the real world of moral practice and the unreal world of art. 'The real is never beautiful,' Sartre asserts in *The Psychology of Imagination*, 'beauty is a *value* which can only apply to the imaginary and whose essential structure involves the nullification (*néantisation*) of the world'. That is why, he concludes, 'it is foolish to confuse ethics and aesthetics'.[78] By thus defining their relation as incorrigibly antithetical, Sartre is in effect denying that art can ever be practical or that praxis can ever be artistic. Not only is this view incompatible with many of his later aesthetic theories – in particular his argument for a 'committed literature' in *What is Literature?* – it is also based on a reductive conception of the nature of art.[79] For, even if one credits Sartre's view that the aesthetic and the real can never function in the same mode of intentionality *at the same time*, it does not thereby follow that we are obliged to deny *any* relationship between them. Precisely as alternative, and alternating, orientations of consciousness, art and ethics may fruitfully interact. Sartre could not concede this simple truth because he was committed to a dualist account of existence, based on an uncompromising antagonism between the real and the imaginary.[80] What Sartre's existential philosophy of imagination failed to address adequately is the fact that if reality without fiction is blind, fiction without reality is powerless.

Notes

1 J.-P. Sartre, *The Psychology of Imagination* n.t. (New York: Citadel Press, 1948), trans. from the French, *L'Imaginaire: psychologie phénoménologique de l'imagination* (Paris: Gallimard, 1940), p. 143.

2 It is unfortunate that the English translation of this book was entitled *The Psychology of Imagination*. This allows for a misunderstanding of the function of the word *phénoménologique* in the original title, where it serves to dispel any impression of an empirical approach to the subject which the word *psychologie* would be likely to connote. As one critic justly remarked, 'though the book makes use of psychological investigations, it is clearly a work of philosophy throughout': A. Manser, *Sartre: A Philosophic Study* (London: Athlone Press, 1966), p. 20. And at this point in his career, philosophy for Sartre was synonymous with phenomenology. See three main essays prior to *Imagination* (1940): 'La transcendance de l'ego', in *Recherches philosophiques* (1937); 'Une idée fondamentale de la phénoménologie de Husserl, l'intentionnalité', in *Nouvelle Revue française* (1939); *Esquisse d'une théorie des emotions* (Paris: Hermann, 1939).

3 Sartre, *Psychology of Imagination*, p. 8.

4 ibid., p. 8.

5 ibid., p. 16.

6   ibid., p. 177.
7   ibid., pp. 23–5. Therefore, even though imagining and perceiving are two mutually exclusive intentions, 'whenever we think imaginatively of some individual objects it will be these objects themselves that will appear to our consciousness ... as they are, that is, as spatial entities with determinations of form and colour etc.' (p. 160).
8   See similar point: I. A. Bunting, 'Sartre on imagination', *Philosophical Studies*, vol. 19 (1970).
9   *Psychology of Imagination*, p. 13. He defines it concisely as follows: 'We are in effect, in an attitude of an observation, but it is observation which tells us nothing. If I imagine the page of a book, I am in the attitude of a reader; *I look at* the printed lines, but I do not *read*. And, ultimately I don't even look at them, for I already *know* what is written.'
10 ibid., p. 10; see also on this point E. Casey, *Imagining: A Phenomenological Analysis* (London and Bloomington: Indiana University Press, 1977), pp. 12–17. Sartre's analysis here is, unfortunately, more suggestive than systematic. Certainly a more adequate contrast between the concept and the image is required. This shortcoming is perhaps due to the fact that Sartre dedicated considerable space to the discussion of the precise role which knowledge plays in imagination in the second half of the book. We shall reserve our criticisms therefore until we reach this discussion.
11 *Psychology of Imagination*, p. 12.
12 Sartre maintains that this 'quasi' characteristic is evidenced in the notable absence of all the laws of time, space and identity in images. We shall be returning to this point.
13 This shall be discussed in detail in the next section.
14 ibid., p. 129. See also: 'I can do nothing with this object which I believe able to describe, decipher, enumerate. The visible object is there, but I cannot see it – it is tangible but I cannot touch it – audible but I cannot hear it' (ibid., p. 126).
15 ibid., p. 17. 'But even a quasi–presentation of reality presupposes some sort of observational stance. For it is only, Sartre declares, when we 'assume the attitude of observers in the realm of sensible intuition that the words "absent", "far from me" etc. can have a meaning'.
16 ibid., pp. 17–18: 'Alive, appealing and strong as an image is, it presents its object as not being. This does not prevent us from reacting to the image as if its object were before us ... as if it were a perception. But the false and ambiguous condition we reach thereby only serves to bring out in greater relief what we have just said: that we seek in vain to create in ourselves the belief that the object really exists by means of our conduct towards it: we can pretend for a second but we cannot destroy the immediate awareness of its nothingness.' See also here Bunting, 'Sartre on imagination', p. 238; R. Goldthorpe, 'Sartre's theory of imagination', *Journal of the British Society of Phenomenology*, vol. 4, no. 2 (1973), pp. 116–17.
17 Sartre, *Psychology of Imagination*, pp. 17, 179 ff.
18 ibid.: 'The unreal object appears as out of reach in relation to reality. Consciousness can only negate reality by stepping back or withdrawing

from reality grasped as a totality ... The condition necessary for a consciousness to be able to imagine is dual: one must be able to posit the world in its synthetic totality; and at the same time posit the imagined object as out of touch with this synthetic whole, that is, at the same time to posit the world as nothing with respect to the image.' I have slightly modified the original translation here. The original passage is to be found on p. 233 of the French edition.

19 ibid., p. 167.
20 ibid., pp. 15–16.
21 ibid., p. 14.
22 ibid., p. 19.
23 ibid., pp. 116–17.
24 Quoted in J. P. Feel, *Emotion in the Thought of Sartre* (New York: Columbia University Press, 1956), p. 42.
25 Sartre, *Psychology of Imagination*, pp. 22 ff. See also E. Kaelin, *An Existentialist Aesthetic* (Madison, Wis.: University of Wisconsin Press, 1962), pp. 40–3. This distinction prefigures Sartre's distinction between subjective motivation (*motif*) and objective motivation (*mobile*) in *Being and Nothingness*, trans. H. Barnes (New York: Citadel Press, 1956).

Having phenomenologically described the four essential characteristics of imagination, Sartre next proceeds to a description of its 'essential' function. He distinguishes here between images as immediate intentions and images as mediated intentions. Immediate images are quite simply synonymous with psychic images. Mediated images, by contrast, are those mediated by some form of material analogue external to the psyche – portraits, caricatures, signs, imitations, photographs, etc. Mediated images combine to form what Sartre calls 'the image family'.

My immediate image of Peter differs from my mediated image of Peter, not by virtue of its intention – both intend an absent Peter as present – but by virtue of the material analogue which carries the intention. In the case of the latter – say, a portrait of Peter – the material which carries the intention exists externally and may also be 'perceived' as a mass of lines and colours on a canvas. In the case of the purely immediate image, on the other hand, the material which carries the intention exists internally as a form of psychic disturbance, and can under no circumstances be perceived (*Psychology of Imagination*, p. 25).

The intention of every member of the image family is the same: to make an absent object present. It is only in regard to the material analogue for this intention that they evince a difference of degree (ibid., pp. 26, 40–74). We saw in our last chapter how Husserl's notion of *hyle* was often inconsistent, fragmentary and at times even contradictory. In his detailed discussion of the role of the hyletic or material analogue in the various members of the image family, Sartre endeavours to redress some of his mentor's shortcomings.

Sartre holds that the purpose of the image is to make an absent object present, even though that object cannot be made an object of perception. Since imagination is intentional in its essence, every imaginative act of consciousness must be consciousness *of* some analogue which acts as a sort of equivalent of the absent object (p. 23). When I try to imagine my friend Peter I want, Sartre says, 'to make him present to me'. And as I cannot bring him before me directly as a perception 'I have recourse to a certain material which acts as an analogue, as an equivalent, of the perception' (p. 23). To imagine Peter by conjuring up a mental image of him, or by looking at a photograph or caricature, are 'three situations with the same form, but in which the material differs' (p. 24). Consequently Sartre claims that no phenomenology of imagination is complete until the various analogues of the 'image family' are adequately described.

Sartre seems at times to confuse the absent object *of* which the image is the intention, and the present analogue *of* which the image is also the intention. Sartre would no doubt respond to this objection by stating that the image of a centaur is merely consciousness of the analogue (lines on a page) as a means towards a consciousness of the transcendent object (the centaur itself). This is all very well so long as the analogue is also transcendent of consciousness, as it is, for instance, in the case of lines on a page which exists outside the mind. But when the image is immanent in consciousness, as in the case of all mental images, then it would seem that the image cannot be consciousness *of* the analogue at all. For the analogue is now no longer other than consciousness but consciousness itself. Indeed, it seems at times that Sartre's theory of the mental image comes perilously close to the traditional illusion that images are copies immanent *in* consciousness.

26 ibid., p. 32. This phenomenon of imaginative reincarnation occurs also in the instance of the photograph-analogue. If I am imaginatively conscious of a photograph of Peter, then I am animating this celluloid analogue in order to *present* this absent person. The shades, figures and curves of the celluloid itself merely guide and carry our imaginative intentionality to its fulfilment. See ibid., pp. 120, 160–70, 180–7; also see Sartre, *Situations IV* (Paris: Gallimard, 1952), pp. 371–2.

27 E. Gombrich (*The Story of Art*, New York: Phaidon, 1950, pp. 31–40) and J. Berger (*Ways of Seeing*, Harmondsworth: Penguin, 1972, pp. 94–108) have both developed this Sartrean insight into a thorough analysis of the whole historical phenomenon of portrait-painting.

28 Sartre, *Psychology of Imagination*, p. 40. Although Sartre uses signs here as 'expressive' components of the material analogue (Franconay) which may imaginatively intend the 'essential' feature of the absent Chevalier, elsewhere he makes a strict distinction between the sign and the image. The material of the sign, he argues (p. 28), is totally indifferent to the object it signifies (that is, the steel pointer with 'Paris' written on it bears no resemblance to Paris) and is related to it solely by means of convention. The material of the image by contrast closely resembles the absent object which it presents (that is, the portrait of King Charles does resemble King Charles). In brief, while the sign points, the image presents. Sartre argues accordingly that there is a certain *internal relationship* (p. 42) between an object and the image of that object, what he calls a relationship of 'presence' or 'possession', whereby via the material analogue the object itself appears to consciousness in a surrogate form. The sign by

contrast is *externally related* to the object which it signifies and remains visually empty; it in no way pretends either to present or to possess the transcendent object (p. 120). And elsewhere again Sartre makes yet another distinction: 'In every image, even in the one which does not posit that its object exists, there is a *positional determination*. In the sign as such this determination is lacking. When an object serves as a sign it causes us to envision something at the very outset, but we affirm nothing about this something, we limit ourselves to envisioning it' (p. 31). These distinctions between the image and the sign are most informative, and one can only regret that Sartre also used 'sign' in an entirely different, that is, imaginative, sense as in the Chevalier example above.

29 ibid., p. 40.
30 ibid., p. 73. This goes some way also to accounting for the 'typicality' or 'generality' which, as we saw in our discussion of quasi-observation, is so integral to the image. It also sheds some interesting light on Da Vinci's theory of *Sfumato* which held that blurred outlines and nebulous features always led to a better portrait in so far as they enlisted the reciprocal imaginative activity of the beholder in order to create from them a vivid and coherent image. See Gombrich, *Story of Art*, p. 228.
31 An example of reciprocal imagination would be the appreciation of a portrait; an example of unilateral imagination would be reading the future from coffee beans.

Sometimes, Sartre remarks, consciousness acts imaginatively without the aid of any external analogue whatsoever. Examples of this would be dreams or purely psychic reveries. Here the material analogue is internal to consciousness itself. It is, moreover, so contingent upon the imagining intention that it actually appears and disappears with it. Sartre's most original contribution here lies in his treatment of the hypnagogic image.

The hypnagogic image is defined as a certain mode of intention which is 'fascinated' by itself. As such it lacks any form of detachment which could enable it to resist the charms of its own effective projections; and so it succumbs to a form of 'fatalism'. Sartre describes with customary phenomenological vividness how in a state of languor consciousness can create hypnagogic images out of the luminosity of an internal field of phosphenes, and then proceed to respond to its 'lifelikeness' (*Psychology of Imagination*, p. 62–4). This enslavement results from the fact that imaginative consciousness is no longer fully aware that the power of the image is its own power and not some external fate (ibid., p. 67).

In so far as hypnagogic images are created from an *internal* psychic movement of phosphenes, they lack that sense of critical distance which characterizes normal imaginative projection. This latter quality of distance would apply to all forms of artistic imagining or even to our construing shapes in coffee beans. In these instances a certain detachment is preserved *vis-à-vis* the 'magic' of the images. There is always a certain 'willing' in the suspension of disbelief. But once the material analogue is internalized and becomes psychic the charms of one's own creation cannot be resisted without difficulty. Imagination has no longer any 'reference point' outside itself; and so it tends to conjure up all sorts of images and invest them with an independent existential status.

What Sartre fails to determine adequately, however, is what distinguishes hypnagogic or delerious images from the normal mental image, given the fact that neither have recourse to any reference outside themselves. Sartre also fails sufficiently to appreciate that this state of imaginative enslavement, which he calls 'fascination', is as applicable to images with external analogues as it is to those with internal ones. We need only look to the mindless hysteria produced by such contemporary phenomena as propaganda, advertising and 'pop' hysteria to be reminded of this (ibid., p. 21). Indeed, it is probably correct to say that 'fascination' is far more pernicious in such public and collective projections than it is in the internal and private projections of hypnagogic imagery.

The absence of external analogues is by no means sufficient to account for the phenomenon of 'fascination'. Contrary to Sartre's suggestions, the greatest 'fascination' is often invoked by images not created by the private consciousness at all, but by some public power totally external to it. This is, of course, particularly true of mass-media experience; a factor which should have been obvious to Sartre even as early as 1940, when radio, cinema and the mass broadcasting of political rallies were already features of the day. But this oversight in Sartre's analysis does not seriously impair the originality and suggestiveness of his insight into the whole phenomenon of imaginative 'projection' and 'fascination'.

Sartre shows that all imagined analogues (of the image family), whether internal or external, psychic or physical, free or fascinated, constitute a movement of magical projection. This Sartre calls 'the symbolic movement' (ibid., p. 74). All symbolic imagining presupposes both an intention of consciousness and a material analogue of some sort. The first factor has been described at great length and poses no problem. The second factor poses no problem either, in so far as it refers to an external analogue: for example, a photo or portrait, which can be perceived and 'described' after or before it is imagined. In so far as it refers to an internal or mental image, however, Sartre concedes that it is impossible for the method of phenomenological reflection to 'describe' it. The moment imaginative consciousness passes away, the internal analogue which carries the image passes away also. But the analogue of every act of imagining must, for the phenomenologist, be something which can be perceived as transcendent *of* consciousness, rather than a mere element *in* it (ibid., p. 75–6). The issue becomes problematic.

32 ibid., p. 120. Enumerating several pertinent experiments, Sartre illustrates his earlier statement that the space and time of the image world are totally unique and totally 'unreal' (pp. 180–1). He convincingly demonstrates that we can neither count the instants of an imagined act nor compare the real time taken to imagine an act with the time internal to that act itself. The same essential difference, he shows, applies to imagined 'space' as testified by our failure to count the columns of an imagined parthenon.

33 ibid., p. 188.

34 'It cannot be denied that my hunger, my sexual desire, my disgust undergo an important modification in passing through the imaginative state' (ibid., p. 198).

35 ibid., p. 179.

36 ibid., pp. 137, 196.

37 ibid., p. 206: 'The evasion to which they [images] invite us is not only of the sort which is an escape from actuality, from our preoccupations, our boredom, but an escape from all worldly constraints; they seem to present themselves as a negation of the condition of being in the world, as an anti-world.'

38 ibid., p. 205.

39 ibid., p. 205.

40 ibid., p. 205.

41 ibid., pp. 211–12.

42 ibid., p. 209.

43 J.-P. Sartre, *Les Mains sales*, Act 4, sc. 2.

44 Sartre, *Psychology of Imagination* p. 212.

45 ibid., p. 214.

46 ibid., pp. 222–3.

47 ibid., p. 243.

48 ibid., pp. 231–50.

49 ibid., p. 255.

50 ibid., pp. 259–60.

51 See my discussion of Heidegger and the transcendental imagination in the *Introduction* and in the study of 'The hermeneutical imagination' below (in particular the opening section); and in *The Wake of Imagination* (London: Unwin Hyman, 1989), pp. 189–95.

52 See Hazel Barnes's elucidation of this complex process in her introduction to Sartre's *Being and Nothingness* (New York: Citadel Press, 1956).

53 But the imagination is not an arbitrary power of negation. On the contrary, it negates the world from a very definite point of view, that is, the one which permits the positing of the real absence of the object unreally present as an image. Sartre takes up again and develops Husserl's original example of the centaur:

> For the centaur to emerge as unreal, the world must be grasped as a world where-the-centaur-is-not, and this can only happen if consciousness is led by different motivations to grasp the world as being exactly the sort in which the centaur has no place ... It is the being-in-the-world, grasped as a concrete and individual reality of consciousness, which is the motivation for the construction of any unreal object whatever and the nature of that unreal object is circumscribed by that motivation. (*Psychology of Imagination*, pp. 268–9)

The real 'world' emerges as a synthetic totality by means of a primary negation; the imaginary 'world' emerges as the inversion of this totality, by means of a secondary negation of this real 'world' – to which it is always tied by the umbilical cord of its 'point of view'. The unreal 'world' as a twofold negation must therefore always be constructed on the basis of the real 'world' which it denies (p. 270). From this observation, Sartre deduces three features of the act of imagining: (1) *Constitution* – it constitutes the 'world' which prior to consciousness merely existed as an undifferentiated and unsynthesized manifold; (2) *Negation* – it negates this 'world' on a second plane and from a particular point of view; (3) *Isolation* – it isolates the object intended by this second negation as something beyond the real 'world', that is, as something unreal and out of reach (p. 263).

54 ibid., p. 271.
55 ibid., p. 271. 'The gliding of the world into the bosom of nothingness and the emergence of human reality in this very nothingness, can happen only through the position of something which is nothingness in relation to the world, and in relation to which the world is nothing. By this we evidently define the structure of imagination ... We therefore conclude that imagination is not an empirical and super-added power of consciousness, it is the whole of consciousness, as it realizes its freedom.'
56 ibid., p. 271.
57 ibid., p. 272.
58 ibid., p. 273.
59 ibid., p. 255.
60 ibid., p. 278.
61 ibid., p. 281.
62 ibid., p. 282. See also Kaelin, *Existentialist Aesthetic*, p. 126: 'In fact, when Sartre's phenomenological ontology replaces Plato's transcendental idealism poets became liberated from the latter's moral condemnation on the very same metaphysical considerations which brought about the proposed censorship. If the artist is dealing only with an analogue of the aesthetic object, which is unreal, there is no longer any ground for the charge of fomenting the passions of criminals. The attitude of aesthetic contemplation precludes the activity which is thought detrimental to well-being.'
63 Sartre, *Psychology of Imagination*, p. 270.
64 ibid., p. 272.
65 ibid., p. 273.
66 ibid., p. 273.
67 ibid., p. 273.
68 ibid., p. 273.
69 ibid., p. 272.
70 See Gaston Bachelard's critique of the contradictions in Sartre's theory of imaginative projection in Chapter 3 below.
71 Sartre's official theory rejects this reading. *Psychology of Imagination*, p. 127: 'An image has no persuasive powers but we persuade ourselves'; and again, p. 28: 'However touching or strong an image may be, it gives its object as not being (*comme n'étant pas*).' G. Todes more than any other critic comes close to something like this teleological interpretation of the imaginary in his article 'A comparative phenomenology of perception and imagination', in *Journal of Existentialism*, vol. 7, no. 25 (1966), p. 15.

Rather than talking of the 'imaginary object', Todes talks of the 'imaginary idea': 'The imaginative idea is not, strictly speaking, produced *in* our imagination. It is produced *by* our imagination but only as the imaginative instrument for producing images in our imagination as representing the imaginative idea with which we produced them; but the imaginative idea is not itself entertained in our imagination. We imagine some image . . . but we imagine *that* some imaginative idea obtains.' Todes's treatment of the image as possibility is as suggestive as it is vague: 'Only an image indirectly produced by means of an imaginative idea appears capable of further occupying us in a progressive unfolding of its significance. Such an image "illustrates" its controlling idea in such a way as to reflect the idea itself, by somehow making all its possible aspects implicitly apparent in the one imagined aspect which *appears* to stand for them all. In this way, a single image controlled by an imaginative idea reveals the possibility of many other imaginary representations of this same idea. Our sense that we can actualise these possibilities is our sense that we can progressively unfold the significance fully implicit in the given image' (ibid., p. 12.)

72   Sartre, *Psychology of Imagination*, p. 272. The implication here is that, since consciousness must be always consciousness of something, the moment it negates the reality it was perceptually conscious of it must simultaneously posit *something* else which it is imaginatively conscious of.

73   Alphonse de Waelhens argues that Sartre never succeeded in reconciling his dualist and phenomenological approaches, and that accordingly phenomenology was greatly prejudiced: 'A philosophy of ambiguity', introduction to J. Merleau-Ponty's *Structure of Behaviour* (Boston, Mass.: Beacon, 1963), trans. A. Fischer from original *La Structure du comportement* (Paris: Presses Universitaires de France, 1949), pp. v–xv. Merleau-Ponty himself and Bachelard express a similar view: see chapters below. But it is E. Kaelin in his 'Phenomenology in Sartre's theory of Images', *Existentialist Aesthetic*, p. 46, who offers the neatest formulation of this critique:

> For Sartre, consciousness is pure spontaneity. In what sense therefore, can an object affect a consciousness in perception? Sartre claims that it does not. But if this is so, what is the relation between consciousness and object in an act of perception? The statement which constitutes the phenomenological axiom 'every consciousness is conscious of something' solves the issue by fiat and the question is begged. We still face the issue of discriminating between percept and image. To call the one an object and the other an intention is perfectly valid, if only one can describe the nature of the relation between object and intention in an act of purely perceptive awareness. Since Sartre chooses to bind himself between two disparate explanatory categories, the 'pour-soi' and the 'en-soi', spontaneity and determined essence, he has failed to solve the problem of perception, as others have failed. The question of the interaction of the two orders of existence has clearly been begged.

74 See here Mary Warnock's discussion of Sartre's 'method of concrete imagination' in her 'Imagination in Sartre', in *British Journal of Aesthetics*, vol. 10, (1970), pp. 333–6. For Sartre's 'existential psychoanalysis', see *Being and Nothingness*, pp. 557–75.

75 J.-P. Sartre, *The Critique of Dialectical Reason* (London: NLB, 1976).

76 Sartre, *Psychology of Imagination*, pp. 213–30.

77 René Lafarge, *Jean-Paul Sartre: His Philosophy* (Dublin: Gill & Macmillan, 1970), p. 46.

78 Sartre, *Psychology of Imagination*, pp. 254 and 281. Several critics, notably T. Flynn, 'The role of the image in Sartre's aesthetic', *Journal of Aesthetics and Art Criticism*, vol. 23 (1974), p. 438; Iris Murdoch, *Sartre* (London: Fontana, 1953), pp. 68, 100–3; and A. Desan, *The Tragic Finale* (New York: Harper, 1960), p. 11 ff., have argued that Sartre's penchant for sharp and irreconcilable dichotomies derives ultimately from a lingering Cartesian dualism.

79 Flynn, 'Role of the image', p. 437.

80 See Desan, *Tragic Finale* pp. xix, 190 ff., M. Saraiva, *L'Imagination selon Husserl* (The Hague: Nijhoff, 1970), p. 152.

Suggestions for further reading

The two obvious primary sources are *Imagination* trans. F. Williams (Ann Arbor, Mich.: University of Michigan Press, 1962) and *The Psychology of Imagination* (New York: Citadel Press, 1948). The former is a somewhat technical survey of modern theories of the image from Descartes and Leibniz to Hume and Husserl. For a properly philosophical analysis of imagination, one has to await Sartre's final chapter on Husserl. *The Psychology of Imagination* is an original and highly detailed exercise in phenomenological psychology. The most interesting insights into Sartre's existential ontology are contained in the fourth part of the book entitled 'The imaginary life' – dealing with the 'Unreal and behaviour', the 'Pathology of imagination' and 'The dream' – and the postscript where Sartre explicitly invokes Heidegger's existential account of being-in-the-world to outline his theories of imagination's role in freedom, transcendence and art. The most useful secondary sources on Sartre's philosophy of imagination are I. A. Bunting, 'Sartre on imagination', *Philosophical Studies*, vol. 19 (1970); R. Goldthorp, 'Sartre's theory of imagination', *Journal of the British Society of Phenomenology*, vol. 4, no. 2 (1973); E. Kaelin, *An Existentialist Aesthetic* (Madison, Wis.: University of Wisconsin Press, 1962); and Mary Warnock, 'Imagination in Sartre', *British Journal of Aesthetics*, vol. 10 (1970).

3

The poetical imagination (Bachelard)

With over ninety influential publications to his name, Gaston Bachelard is justly celebrated for his contribution to the phenomenology of poetic imagining. Originally a philosopher of science, he turned more and more in his later writings in the fifties and early sixties to a series of studies on the origin of the creative imagination. Bachelard saw the need for such studies arising as much from the crisis of modern science as from that of modern poetics. In *Le Nouvel Esprit scientifique* published in 1934, he was already speaking of the 'poetic endeavours of mathematicians'; while in *Le Matérialisme rationnel* (1953) he tendered the bold claim that 'scientific language is in a state of permanent semantic revolution'. And so, as his reflections on the epistemological sources and breaks of the sciences developed – culminating in a radical critique of the limits of deductive Euclidean reason – Bachelard began to turn his attention more directly to the workings of the poetic imagination itself. The following became his central questions: Where do we locate the poetic act of creation? In the human initiative of making? In the matter and form of the thing made? Or in the minds of the recipients themselves – for example, the reading community? Bachelard's answers to these questions prompted him towards a poetics of imagining deeply influenced by Husserl's phenomenology but extending well beyond its limits and exerting a decisive influence on the *nouvelle critique* of the sixties.

Against the structuralists and the positivists, Bachelard argued for a return to the human subject. But Bachelard's humanism differed from that of his phenomenological colleagues in this significant respect: he sought to release the phenomenology of imagining from what he considered its Cartesian or idealist remnants (as witnessed in the early Husserl and Sartre). His was a 'subversive humanism' which conceived of the human being as a de-centred subject nourished by a poetic power which transcended its control. Bachelard called for another humanism which – in Mary McAllester's phrase – 'reinvents man, against idealism, beyond conventional notions of subject and object'.[1]

The Archimedean point of Bachelard's poetics is what he terms, in *The Poetics of Space* (1957), the 'ecstasy of the novelty of the image'. This experience of novelty is no longer attributed to a transcendental subject, nor indeed to an existential one: the *novum* of the imaginary surpasses the consciousness which intends it. If eidetic phenomenology credited the power of the human subject to intuit timeless essences, and existential phenomenology hailed human imagination as the autonomous centre of all meaning, Bachelard was more modest in his claims. His poetic phenomenology describes imagination as a perpetual interaction between the human subject which imagines and the image itself. Imagination is thus recognized to be conscious of something other than itself which motivates, induces and transforms it.[2]

What is this *something other*? Here Bachelard gives a further inflection to the phenomenological concept of possibility adumbrated by Husserl and Sartre: the world of possibility, at once invented and discovered by imagining, is the source of *both* scientific and poetic creation. 'In recalling those fine mathematical symbols where the possible and the real are allies', he asks, 'might one not invoke the images of Mallarmé?'[3] And Bachelard goes on to claim that 'the possible is homogenous with being itself'. What the imaginative sources of science and poetry share in common is a creative ability to break with the everyday 'facts' of *Homo faber* and transmute each one of us into a *Homo aleator* – someone able to explore those imaginary possibles which emerge into existence at the intersection between self and world.[4] Scientific and poetic creation both derive from a deeper *poiesis* wherein imagination and reality make and remake each other.

Subjectivity and trans-subjectivity

In *L'Eau et les rêves: essai sur l'imagination de la matière* (1938), Bachelard writes: 'In its birth and emergence the image is, in us, the subject of the verb to imagine ... The whole world comes to imagine itself in human reverie.'[5] In this pithy pronouncement we find a neat illustration of the difference between Sartre's and Bachelard's phenomenologies of imagination. While both agree that the image is an act of intentional consciousness, they differ radically in their interpretation of this. Sartre sees it as a circle of self-involvement; Bachelard as the spiral of man's dialogue with the world.

For Bachelard creativity is not negation of being, but 'a flare-up of being in the imagination'. It is precisely in the creative act that the world comes to know itself in the images of man. This strange fact can only be comprehended, Bachelard insists, in terms of phenomenology – 'In order to clarify the problem of the poetic image, philosophically, we shall have to have recourse to a phenomenology of the imagination'.[6] And he goes on to explain that by this he understands a 'study of the phenomenon of the image when it emerges into the consciousness as a direct product of the mind, soul and being of man'.[7] Bachelard is, of course, fully alert to the difficulties involved in a phenomenology of imagining which admits that each new image is a creation. And yet he is adamant in resisting Sartre's solipsistic conclusions. He writes:

This crisis on the simple level of a new image, contains the entire paradox of a phenomenology of the imagination, which is: how can an image, at times very unusual, appear to be a concentration of the entire psyche? How – with no preparation – can this singular, short-lived event constituted by the appearance of an unusual poetic image, react on other minds and in other hearts, despite all the barriers of common sense, all the disciplined schools of thought, content in their immobility?[8]

Bachelard's whole phenomenology of imagination is concerned with providing an answer to this question, that is, with providing a justification for a *dialogical* interpretation of the image.

Taking up again the Husserlian quest for a 'science' of imagination, Bachelard also acknowledged phenomenology as the best alternative to the reductionism of associationist psychology. It alone, he agreed, could provide access to the neglected intentional structures of creative consciousness: 'Only phenomenology – that is to say, consideration of the *onset of the image* in an individual consciousness – can help us to restore the subjectivity of images and to measure their fullness, their strength and their trans-subjectivity.'[9] Time and again in his prefaces, Bachelard confirms that such a method of unprejudiced description most adequately grasps the image as a *sui generis* act of consciousness, rather than a thing in consciousness.[10]

Bachelard was no less critical of the orthodox psychoanalytic method which he felt to be as reductive as traditional psychology in its approach to the image. Freud himself defined the image as a sublimated coating for repressed and neurotic impulses.[11] The psychoanalytic method was thus officially conceived as a means for unmasking this veneer, treating the image as a symptom to be diagnosed and deciphered, rather than as something to be admired and appreciated for its own sake.[12] Otherwise put, psychoanalysis tried to explain the flower by the fertilizer. It suspected images of subterfuge – of hiding some original meaning behind a mask.

For Bachelard, however, images are much more than occasions of frustration or sublimation. They are free expressions – created not from pressure but from play, not from necessity but from inventiveness. For this reason Bachelard endorses Sartre's repudiation of the 'determined' imagination of psychoanalysis in favour of the 'symbolic' imagination of phenomenology. Phenomenologically viewed, the imagination is not the repository of childhood traumas, but the cradle of a renewed world. 'On principle', as Bachelard says, 'phenomenology liquidates what is past and confronts what is new.'[13] But unlike Sartre's analysis, which often considered imagination in a pathological light, Bachelard's phenomenology defined it as the ultimate 'happiness of expression'. He rejected what he regarded as Sartre's solipsism and hailed the image ,as the self's stepping stone to the other-than-self.[14] Consequently, the imaginative being-there (*être-là*) of the individual is conceived by Bachelard as a *well-being* rather than a *non-being*. What for Sartre was the epitome of human infirmity is now acclaimed as the epitome of health.[15]

In so far as it condemns the 'representational' theories of the traditional psychology of the imagination, Bachelard's analysis corroborates the phenomenological conviction that the image is an act which transcends reality and frees us from the constraints of both past and present.[16] The image is to be understood as a *genesis* not an *effect*; and this is possible only in a poetics where the suspension of causal preconceptions allows for an assessment of the unprecedented nature of its being. Against classical psychology, Bachelard claims that 'a phenomenology of imagination can have no truck with a reduction of the image to a merely predicational form of expression; it must *live* the images directly, for when an image is new, the world is also new'.[17] Above all, Bachelard deploys phenomenology because of its unique capacity to penetrate to the significance of the image as *origination*. 'I chose phenomenology', he says, 'because of its ability to highlight the image's virtue of origin, to grasp their very being as originality.'[18]

This phenomenological emphasis on the *originality* of images leads in turn to the discovery of their *trans-subjectivity*. Unlike Sartre, who saw the intentional uniqueness of each image as implying self-enclosure, Bachelard marvelled at the mystery that the image can be both *unique* to the originating consciousness and yet *common* to different subjects. For Sartre, the image was construed as a world of monologue between the mind and itself. It could be *occasioned* by an analogue in the external world, but as an image it remained the prerogative of private subjectivity. And it was because it could not reach beyond its own nothingness that it was defined by Sartre as an 'essential poverty'. For Bachelard the image was revealed as a world of dialogue *between* intentional subjects: .

> It appears to us that the essential transsubjectivity of the image cannot be accounted for in terms of objectifying methods. Only phenomenology – that it is to say, the consideration of the origin of the image in consciousness – can enable us to understand the subjective source of images and at the same time, their transsubjective significance.[19]

For both Sartre and Bachelard, the phenomenological analysis of imagination involves ontological conclusions – a disclosure of the essence of our being-in-the-world.[20] But, whereas the former describes man's imaginative existence as fundamentally 'ipsorelative', the latter paints an entirely different picture of the imaginer as 'aliorelative', that is, intentionally directed towards the *other* rather than the self. Similarly, while Sartre often appears to regard imagination as one particular mode of intentionality which leads to the discovery of the fundamentally negating power of consciousness, Bachelard reverses the emphasis and regards negation as but one of the many powers of imagination. Though he agrees with Sartre's definition of imagination as a *sui generis* power distinct from perception and conception,[21] he views this distinction as the basis for a fruitful interplay. Thus Bachelard can hold that 'what man imagines dictates what he *perceives*'; and that 'it is necessary to imagine too much in order that we may *think*, and so *realize*, enough'.[22] Bachelard insists accordingly that the imagination's negating of reality is not a passage into nothingness but the prerequisite of a redemption of the real. 'To create an image is', he says, 'to renovate our power of seeing the world which for so long has been smothered in lazy familiarity.'[23] In other words, the imaginary for Bachelard is not so much a world of *un-reality* as of *sur-reality*. It does not deny reality *per se*, but only the ossified and habitualized crust of reality. It does not annihilate the real world; it mobilizes its potencies of transformation.

'The imagination is not', Bachelard states, 'a faculty which fabricates images of reality; it is a power which forms images which surpass reality in order to change reality. It is the power of a sur-humanity.'[24]

Rêve and rêverie

Bachelard makes an important distinction at this point between imagination as *rêve* and as *rêverie*. *Rêve* is synonymous with the pure negation of reality (à la Sartre) and is equated by Bachelard with common dreams of escapism or sleep. On the other hand, *rêverie* designates imagination as a constant re-creation of reality.[25] The imagination as reverie is the guardian of the emergence of being. It is the purest expression of human freedom[26] – residing at that interstice where being takes leave of itself and launches into becoming. Playing on the Greek etymology of the term, 'phantasy', Bachelard affirms that it is precisely because the imagination (*phantasia*) is concerned with being in its origination and emergence (*phainesthai*) that it calls for a phenomenology (*phainomenon*). Indeed, the artist is renowned for his imagination because he attends more acutely than most to the logos of being's emergence in the world. The aesthetic imagination responds and corresponds to the Word of existence. And in this context Bachelard fully approves Van der Berg's maxim that 'poets and painters are born phenomenologists'.[27] But imagination is fundamentally tied to phenomenology not just because it caters for the *appearing* of being, but because it exemplifies more intensely than any other human activity the principal insight of phenomenology – namely that man is an intentional being who 'ceaselessly lives above his being'.[28]

The Bachelardian notion of the imagination as sur-real, rather than unreal, does not lapse, as might first be expected, into the traditional error of confounding the imaginary and the real. As sur-real, it remains both *sur*-real and sur-*real*; that is, it succeeds in preserving the claims of both iconoclasm (as a critical surpassing of the real) and incarnation (a commitment to the real). For Bachelard there is a continuous path between the imaginative and the real even as there is a discontinuous divide. In *La Poétique de l'espace* he elaborates on this paradox as follows:

> By the swiftness of its actions, the imagination separates us from the past as well as from reality; it faces the future. To the *function of reality*, wise in experience of the past, should be added a function of irreality, which is equally positive. Any weakness in the function of irreality, will hamper the productive psyche. If we cannot imagine, we cannot foresee . . . the function of the real and the function of the irreal must be made to cooperate.[29]

We summarize the main differences between Bachelard and Sartre here by saying that, while the latter saw the image as a surpassing of the real towards nothingness, the former saw it as a surpassing of the real towards a renewed reality. Consequently, Bachelard can discard the Sartrean thesis that the image results from a degradation of consciousness, and hold instead that it is imagination which unites consciousness with the world and with itself. It is imagination, in other words, which leads the subject towards his ultimate telos as *l'homme reconcilié*.[30] Hence the poet's fascination with images which, in Coleridge's phrase, 'yoke together opposites'. The imagination strives towards a syncopation of contrary elements, as Bachelard demonstrates in his graphic analysis of the fascination shown byyy artists for images of 'roundness' (the synthesis of horizontal and vertical impulses), 'androgeny' (the synthesis of the *animus* and the *anima*) and 'cosmic harmony' (the synthesis of the *natura naturans* and the *natura naturata*).[31] Imagination is the great synthesizer of our universe: 'Imagination has the integrating powers of the tree. It is root and branch. It lives between earth and sky. Imagination lives in the earth and in the wind. The imaginative tree is imperceptibly the cosmological tree, the tree which summarizes a universe, which makes a universe.'[32] We saw how for Sartre the imagination became enchanted by its own creations and fell to the worship of an 'empty absolute'. For Bachelard the absolute intended by man is so ontologically rich that it can not ever be 'observed', only 'admired'.[33] Sartre had little time for Bachelard's optimism and explicitly denounced his notion of imaginative 'quality' in his conclusion to *L'Etre et le néant*. In *La Terre et les rêveries de la volonté* (1948), Bachelard wrote the following reply:

The imagination of qualities moves beyond given reality. We experience sensual joys but we make of them songs ... Quality is, for us, the occasion of such great valorization that the passional value of the quality supplants our consciousness of the quality. The manner in which we love a substance and acclaim its quality, reveals certain resonances in our being. The imagined quality reveals us to ourselves as qualifying subjects. And what proves that the field of imagination covers all and surpasses the field of merely perceived qualities is the fact that the resonance evoked in the subject manifests itself under the most dialectically opposed aspects: exuberance and concentration, the man of a thousand welcoming gestures and the man collected together in his sensible pleasure.[34]

This conception of imagination as poetical inspiration and expiration of being resists Sartre's notion of imagination as nihilation, a notion which – as we saw – ultimately condemns consciousness to solitary confinement. Sartre's view is *egological*: all attempts to move beyond the self and project oneself towards being rebound off the frontiers of the ego and slide back into consciousness. He could not accept Bachelard's belief that imagination 'valorizes' the world. For the very concept of valorization presupposes a positive content in the imaginer in order to ground the valorizing intention. The Sartrean imagination is defined by the lack of all positivity.[35] And, what is more, the 'real' – its counterpart – is treated as a pure positivity of being in-itself equally incapable of grounding value.

Bachelard, by contrast, conceives of the imagination not as privation but as audition – an acoustics of the *other* than self.[36] His poetical model of imagination is two-dimensional: at once a giving and a taking, a projection and a discovery, a centrifugal exodus towards things and a centripetal return to the self. This notion of an 'interlacing rhythm' which spans the breach between subjectivity and being epitomizes the Bachelardian theory of poetics.

The material and the dynamic

Bachelard groups his poetic reflections on the various types of imagining under two main headings – the *material* and the *dynamic*.

The material imagination is concerned with the affiliation of images according to certain archetypal elements, in particular those of air, fire, water and earth. Bachelard believes these primary material elements to be connected in some way with internal make-up. The being of certain materials *corresponds* with the being of the human subject. Matter supplies the 'images which are necessary for the virtualities of the soul to be distinguished and developed'.[37] Through the objects' intentional otherness, a reciprocal energy is produced by consciousness' encounter with matter:

> Matter is our energetic mirror; it is a mirror which focuses our powers in illumining them with imaginative joys ... In other words, in the realm of the imagination the dualism of subject and object is presented at its truest equilibrium ... Matter contains beauty as an affective space hidden in the interior of things.[38]

Poetic correspondences between the self and the material elements are not so much a question of intellectual abstractions from matter as discoveries of the self in matter. Matter harbours an objective correlative for all our possibilities within itself. And so the material imagination can, Bachelard maintains, 'find in the very depth of materials all of the symbols of the inner life'.[39] At such privileged moments, imagination and matter are commensurate.

This commensurability does not mean sameness. Different poetic minds will see different things in the same material element. Water, for example, has one set of symbolic correspondences in Melville's *Moby Dick* and quite another in Yeats's 'The Stolen Child'. In the former it provokes feelings of awe, threat, terror. In the latter it represents lyrical escapism. And the same diversity of reverberation is to be found, as Bachelard realized, in the elements of fire, air and earth, each of which receives separate and comprehensive attention in his works. The pleasure common to all our poetic experiences of these elements is that of discovering ourselves in what is other than ourselves – or what Robert Frost called the 'pleasure of ulteriority'.

Bachelard's researches into the material imagination are by no means confined to the four elements. Other archetypal motifs cited by Bachelard as capable of engendering associations of 'ulteriority' are the womb, the shell, the labyrinth, the snake, the forest and the house. These archetypal symbols, as he explains, are not isolated images but axes around which a host of images may conspire to evoke typical human experiences.[40]

They do not 'determine' us like ancestral memories (Jung) or personal histories of libidinal desire (Freud). They are concerned with
origins in a very different sense – in the sense of making us originators
of our own future and allowing us to intuit matter teleologically
as a task to be discovered rather than a thing to be negated. As
Bachelard states:

It is not a question here of the survival of primitive phantasms.
The figure of origin is rather transformed into a symbol for the
constructive reunion of contraries, into a truly 'reconciling symbol'.
This archetype in its functional signification does not point backwards
but forwards towards an end which is not yet attained.[41]

Thus we see that in his understanding of symbolism Bachelard was
once again in profound disagreement with Sartre. Where Sartre saw
the symbol as invention of the self – irredeemably confined to the
significance which the self gave it – for Bachelard it constitutes an
archetypal conjoining of self-contents with other-than-self contents. The
imagination's allegiance is not only to an origin in one's own subjective
consciousness, but also to an origin in the *other* which motivates the
self's perpetual movement towards its end. Here Bachelard approximates more to the Husserlian notion of the teleological imagination
than to the Sartrean.

Bachelard's theory of imaginative archetypes attempts to obviate both
the egological psychology of Sartre and the reductive psychoanalysis of
Freud. His aim is to inaugurate what he calls a 'counter-psychoanalysis'.
This would be motivated by a poetics of listening as opposed to the
standard analytic of unmasking which decomposes the image in order
to situate its sources in the neuroses of the imaginer's past. In a sense,
Sartre is guilty of this kind of unmasking in his interpretation of the
fascination for the imaginary in Genet, Baudelaire or Flaubert in terms
of some personal pathology of existence. Bachelard believed, for his
part, that images can have a life of their own and that in order fully to
appreciate the ontological dimension of images one must be prepared
on occasion to 'forget one's private past for the sake of the speaking
power of reverie'.[42] Here Bachelard's philosophy recalls Oscar Wilde's
aesthetic of the Mask and T. S. Eliot's theory of the impersonality of
the artist.

One must be careful of misunderstanding, however. Bachelard has
no wish to advocate a monistic principle of Being à la Parmenides. To

classify images according to archetypes is in no way to detract from the multiplicity of their being. The fact that one proclaims certain images to be 'isomorphic', as Bachelard often does, is not to suggest that they are synonymous or reducible the one to the other. It is simply to suggest that they share certain archetypal properties which transcend the law of individuation in its limiting and isolationist sense. But they do so not in order to deny the plurality of existence, but to enable a plurality of existents to partake in a community of experience – at once trans-subjective and trans-historical.[43] In this sense, Bachelard rescues imagination from the Sartrean circle of solipsism, without falling into the opposite extreme of monism.

Bachelard relates the archetypal filiation of images to an 'essential cosmicity'.[44] The material imagination, he claims, finds its echo in a cosmic rhythm which beats at the heart of matter. To 'imagine' the rhythm of any primary element is to create a liaison between this element as the systole and the diastole of one's own innermost self. This is why the different elements characterize different imaginative temperaments – Nietszche as a lover of air, Poe a lover of water, Lawrence of fire, and so on. In brief, by creating images from the materials which mirror his own being, the poetic imaginer enters into dialogue with his own self, rather than dividing him from himself as Sartre maintained.

The material imagination thereby constitutes an at-one-ment between self and self, and self and other, a repose. Its tempo is a languorous one, and it tends towards a condition of tranquillity.[45] But every primary image harbours within itself a certain diversity or contradictoriness; and this means that it foments movement and becoming even as it approaches immobility and rest. This concomitant principle of becoming leads us to the second principal dimension of poetical imagination – the *dynamic*.

The dynamic imagination is the formal counterpart to the material.[46] It articulates man's desire for the free-ranging, more spiritual modalities of being. To this end it strives continually to subject matter to motion. For example, in the order of dynamic imagination, all forms are furnished with perpetual movement. One cannot imagine a sphere without having it turn, an arrow without having it fly, a woman without having her smile.[47]

This second major form of the poetical imagination throws new light on the concept of archetype. As an agent of dynamism the originality of the Bachelardian notion is thrown into relief. The stress here on the transformative will of the human subject differs from both the Neoplatonist conception of the archetype as an Immutable Idea, and its more sophisticated Jungian one as an innate repository of the Collective Unconscious.[48] The archetype now emerges as the expression of an instinctual intentionality in humans which, while indeed being 'regulative' as the Neoplatonists suggested and 'collective' as Jung realized, remains essentially anterior to the predetermining principles of these two theories. As dynamic will, we are determined neither from below (by ancestral archetypes) nor from above (by transcendental ones). We are not determined *by* anything, but re-create ourselves in response to certain archetypal correspondences between consciousness and matter. So that if I imagine I am flying, for example, this is not necessarily as the Neoplatonists might suggest because God 'implanted' this image of 'ascent' in my mind; nor indeed, as Jung might suggest, because such an experience engraved itself *in illo tempore* into primitive consciousness. I imagine I am flying, according to Bachelard, because such an image is one among other expressions of a free *will to movement*.

Confronted with the materials of the world, the dynamic imagination charges our drive to form and cultivate. We are, as Bachelard once put it, 'like demiurges before the kneading-trough: we structure the becoming of matter'.[49] For this imagination, matter does not signify an intractable and viscous resistance to freedom. It is rather a call to our freedom, the very paste of possibility from which we must wrest new forms.

Language and logos

On several occasions, Bachelard identifies the dynamic *will to movement* with what he calls a *will to Logos* – the will to attune oneself to the speaking of Being itself. In this connection he distinguishes between 'metaphors' which are mere mental illustrations of perceptions and 'images proper' which are the utterances of an essential dynamism of being:

> The metaphor gives concrete body to impressions otherwise difficult to express. It bears a merely accidental relationship to the being of the imagination. The image ... on the contrary, takes all its being from imagination. The image, pure product of the absolute imagination, is a phenomenon of being, the specific phenomenon of speaking being (*être parlant*).[50]

This connection between poetical expression and imagination is a vital one for Bachelard and is deeply related to his conception of humans as intentional beings. Most of the time, we mask the intentional power of our language by using words in a strictly utilitarian or 'metaphorical' way. This power is revealed, however, the moment we use words 'imaginatively'. Bachelard illustrates this point in his discussion of the literary image – a discussion which occasionally reads like an indirect rebuttal of the Sartrean claim in *What Is Literature?* that the true writer is one who rejects the poetic approach to language in favour of an ideological aesthetic where words are used as 'loaded weapons'. 'The literary image', writes Bachelard, 'does not come to dress a naked image, nor to give word to a mute image. The imagination, in us, speaks ... every human activity wishes to speak. When this word becomes conscious of itself then human activity desires to write ... Literature is not therefore the offshoot of another activity. It is the fulfilment of human desire as it emerges in imagination.'[51]

Bachelard situates this will-to-logos at the root of the dynamic imagination.[52] It is a *projection* of our creative logos that is at the same time a *discovery* of the created logos of the world. This deep phenomenological rapport between imagination and language is first explored by Bachelard[53] (though Paul Ricoeur and other hermeneutic phenomenologists would develop it further). Certainly, there is no adequate discussion of it in either Husserl or Sartre. If anything, Sartre's theory of the heterogeneity of image and sign pointed to a denial of any such link. Bachelard's acoustic model of imagination resists Sartrean dualism by revealing the creative role of listening in our poetic relationship with a nature that *signifies* and *speaks*.

Images are born directly from the murmuring voice – to which one listens in speaking nature. Yes, as so many poets have said, nature speaks for those who listen to it. Everything speaks in the universe, but it is man, the great speaker, who says the first words.[54]

In general terms, of course, Bachelard's notion of the image as intentional dynamism concurs with Husserl's and Sartre's rejection of the traditional 'faint-copy' theory. In *La Terre et les rêveries de la volonté* (1948), Bachelard declares it his express intention to refute this doctrine clearly and to establish instead a thesis which affirms the primordial and irrepressible character of the creative imagination.[55] This vindication of the creative power of the imagination is accompanied, moreover, by the conviction that any human deprived of this power is 'just as neurotic as someone deprived of the function of the real'.[56] Far from being the traditional faculty for receiving and combining second-hand impressions, imagining as Bachelard conceives of it is an activity which de-forms the habitual status of being and in-forms it with the status of becoming. Hence Bachelard's famous definition of a human being as one who continually renews himself by means of the imagination: 'Man is a being *to be imagined*.'[57] But because we are so firmly immured in habit and convention our innate need for endless renovation is all the more acute. This need finds expression – when it does find expression – in the dynamic critical activity of imagination which Bachelard calls *iconoclasm*.[58] The iconoclastic function of imagination serves to demystify not only the immobilizing prestige of reality but also the 'fascinating' power of imagination itself. Bachelard thus avoids the Sartrean confusion concerning the role of imagination as both freedom and fascination, by making a distinction here between 'authentic' and 'inauthentic' imagination:

> To be authentic, all imagination must learn again how to dream ... and at the same time, how to break the fascination of images in order to keep the way clear for imagination's propulsion towards the absolute ... the authentic image renews not by a renunciation of imagination but by its fulfilment ... it does not represent something, it addresses someone.[59]

It was, arguably, Sartre's failure to appreciate fully this distinction between authentic and inauthentic imagination that led to his blanket characterization of the imagination as an impoverishment of being.

For Bachelard, then, the image does not only serve as the intuitional fulfilment of an intention – as with Husserl and Sartre. It designates a dynamic propulsion towards novelty which is quite as destructive of its own 'inauthentic' images as it is of 'inauthentic' reality. That is to say, it is both critique of reality and auto-critique at the same time. The dynamic imagination smashes all idols of stasis in favour of continual metamorphosis. And here Bachelard makes the original point that imagination can be a discriminating *valorizing* agency as well as an *aesthetic* one. This, proclaims Bachelard, 'is one of the great ontological principles of imagination: valorization decides being'.[60] In such manner, Bachelard seeks to resolve the yawning divide between an aesthetics of the imaginary and an ethics of the real announced by Sartre in his postscript to *The Psychology of Imagination*.

By recognizing imagination as an intentionality of self-transcendence rather than of self-fascination, Bachelard succeeded in exonerating it from the traditional charge of idolatry, dating back to the Hebraic prohibition of 'graven images'.[61] In Bachelard's view, our fascination for the 'empty absolutes' of our own imagination cannot but be short lived for the reason that the very imagination which idolizes its creations is at the same time driven by an opposing instinct for dynamic renewal. This recognition of a *double intentionality* in imagination – one material tending towards incarnation and repose, the other dynamic and tending towards disinvestment and unrest – was what constituted for Bachelard the unmistakably poetical nature of this power. Indeed, the complementary tensions between the rival propensities of imagination are exemplified in the way in which opposite character types are drawn to each other in the great works of Western literature. Just as Greek tragedy operated on the opposing archetypes of Apollo and Dionysius (as Nietzsche had it), modern fiction also offers many examples of the imaginative attraction exerted by one character on its opposite – for example, Jane Eyre and Rochester, Prince Mishkin and Nastasia Philipovna, Bloom and Molly, Narciss and Goldmund, Aschenbach and Esmerelda, Raskolnikov and Sonia, Sabina and Theresa.

If we were to deprive imagination of this poetic complementarity, its material instinct would gravitate towards a condition of inertia, its dynamic instinct towards a condition of frenzy. The poetical imagination balances these two tendencies of form and matter and makes of their difference a fecund interplay. As Bachelard himself puts it: '... the imagination of movement calls for the imagination of matter and vice versa.'[62] Thus, for example, the freedom *from* the world affected by the dynamic imagination is converted into the material imagination's freedom *for* the world. And precisely because of this poetic interplay, the world for which we are now freed is always *other* than the world from which we are freed. In the discovery of this other world the self discovers its 'other' self.[63] By generating this dialogue between my other-self and the other-world, the poetical imagination reveals new possibilities of being.

In sum, while the dynamic imagination discovers an objective grounding in matter, the material reveals itself by means of a certain rhythmical dynamism. As the instrument of such poetic play, the imagination finds itself in a world of which it is both the creature and the creator. 'When the imagination speaks', Bachelard muses, 'which speaks, I or the world?'[64] The archetypes of imagination, we now realize, can only emerge as the world's confirmation of an imaginative intention. They are responses to an address – fertile interlacings between the human subject and reality. Bachelard's repudiation of the Sartrean theory of imagination as *néantisation* could not be more explicit: 'Imagination does not know non-being ... the man of reverie lives by his reverie in a world homogenous with his being ... In reverie, there is no more not-I. In reverie, the *not* no longer functions: all is welcome.'[65]

Conclusion

Perhaps Bachelard's most significant contribution to the phenomenology of imagination was his disclosure of the poetical role of *language*. His increasing emphasis on the working of a *logos* of poetical interaction between the imaginative consciousness and the images themselves represented a decisive advance on both the eidetic phenomenology of Husserl and the existential phenomenology of Sartre. Bachelard's claims for the linguistic dimension of poetic imagining in the 'Rêveries de mots' section of *Poétique de la rêverie* and in his introduction to *La Poétique de l'espace* clearly mark this change of focus. The following passage from the latter text prefigures the linguistic turn of Ricoeur's hermeneutics of imagination: 'By its very novelty, the poetic image sets all linguistic activity in motion ... It becomes a new being of our language, it expresses us in making us what it expresses ... Here expression creates being ... In this manner, the poetic image, as a happening of the logos, is personally new to us.'[66] It is because the poetic expressions of imagination decentre (*défixe*) our human being that we can be redefined as *des êtres entr'ouverts*.[67] The being of the human subject, as a being who imagines, is not a fixed point but an endless spiral of movement. The origin of poetic imagining is neither a transcendental ego nor a negating *pour soi* – it is a becoming of language which demands perpetual rebirth.[68]

This motif of spiral motion challenges the limits of traditional humanism – which saw each human subject as an autonomous point of meaning – and calls forth one of Bachelard's favourite metaphors, that of *verticality*. Imagination's deepest leaning is towards a vertical transcendence which strives to 'return to a liberty of the possible'.[69] It is because the poetic image always operates under the vertical sign of ever newer possibilities of being that we rediscover ourselves as beings always ahead of ourselves (*des êtres en avant*).[70] This affirmation of a radical verticality of depth and height is the ultimate conclusion reached by Bachelard's reflections on the origin of poetic reverie:

> Is to meditate on an origin not to dream? And to dream of an origin not to surpass it? Where the deep image rises, it endures. It rediscovers a profundity or intimates an elevation. It rises or descends between sky and earth. It is polyphonic because it is polysemantic.[71]

It is at such moments of vertical correspondence that the voice of the poet responds to the 'voice of the world'.

Notes

1 Mary McAllester, 'Bachelard twenty years on: an assessment', *Revue de littérature comparée*, no. 2 (1984), p. 166.
2 See McAllester's informed discussion of this theme, ibid., pp. 173–177.
3 G. Bachelard, *Le Nouvel Esprit scientifique* (Paris: 1934), p. 60.
4 ibid., p. 119.
5 G. Bachelard, *L'Eau et les rêves: essai sur l'imagination de la matière* (Paris: Gallimard, 1938), p. 22. Hereafter cited as *Eau*.
6 G. Bachelard, *La Poétique de l'espace* (Paris: Presses Universitaires de France, 1957), trans. M. Jolas (Boston, Mass: Beacon Press, 1969) p. xiv. Hereafter cited as *PE*
7 ibid., p. xiv.
8 ibid., p. xv.
9 ibid., For the best commentaries on the phenomenological nature of Bachelard's theory of imagination, see G. Durand, *Les Structures anthro-lopologiques de l'imaginaire: introduction à l'archétypologie général* (Paris: Presses Universitaires de France, 1963), pp. 9–56; M. Mansuy, *Gaston Bachelard et les elements* (Paris: Corti, 1967); Hélène Tuzet, *Le Cosmos et l'imagination* (Paris: Corti, 1965); V. Thierrien, *La Révolution de Gaston Bachelard en critique littéraire* (Paris: Klincksieck, 1970); F. Dagognet, 'Gaston Bachelard, philosophie de l'imaginaire', *Revue internationale de philosophie*, vol. 51 (Belgium, 1960), pp. 34 ff., and E. Kaplan, 'Gaston Bachelard's philosophy of imagination', *Philosophy and Phenomenological Research* (1972), pp. 1–24.
10 Bachelard rejects the procedure of the traditional psychologist as follows: 'Pour lui l'image est double, elle signifie toujours autre chose qu'elle même' (*La Flamme d'une chandelle* (Paris: Presses Universitaires de France, 1961), p. 10; hereafter cited as *La Flamme*). 'Le mot image

est lourd de confusion dans les ouvrages de psychologie: on voit des images; on garde des images dans la mémoire. L'image est tout sauf un produit de l'imagination' (*PE*, p. 16).

11 S. Freud, *Civilization and Its Discontents*, trans. by J. Strachey (New York: Norton, 1962), p. 27.

12 See here also M. Préclaire, *Une Poétique de l'homme* (Montréal: Bellarmin, 1971).

13 *PE*, p. xxviii; cf. 'If it is concerned with the past it is so as "value" never simply as fact. The recalled past is not simply a past of perception. Already, since one remembers, the past is designated in reverie as a value of image. Imagination colours from the very beginning the pictures it likes to review. To return to archives of memory, one must go beyond facts to regain values ... Reveries are impressionist paintings of our past': G. Bachelard, *La Poétique de la rêverie* (Paris: Presses Universitaires de France, 1960), pp. 89–90; hereafter cited as *PR*.

14 *PE*, pp. xii, xiv, xxv; also Durand, *Structures*, pp. 19–21; C. Ramnoux, 'Avec Gaston Bachelard vers une phénoménologie de l'imagination', *Revue de métaphysique et de morale*, vol. 70, no. 1 (1965), pp. 30–2; and Kaplan, 'Bachelard's philosophy', p. 18: 'Bachelard's phenomenology of imagination views the image as the origin, not the product, of a new consciousness, restoring to language its autonomy'; 'The metaphor comes to give a concrete body to an impression difficult to express. But it is relative to an imagination, takes its whole being from imagination' (*PE*, p. 79). Bachelard's insistence on the psychological purity of absolute imagination is a reflection of his polemical position in favour of a phenomenology of imagination in his last two monographs on imagination: 'The poetic image illumines consciousness with such a light, that it is quite vain to seek unconscious antecedents for it'; 'The literary image should be the birth of a new meaning, rather than a resumé of old ones'. (*PR*, p. 3)

15 Mansuy, *Bachelard*, p. 136: 'C'est le sujet sain qui intéresse Bachelard plus que le malade. L'imagination matérielle est une imagination de la plénitude calme, une imagination de l'intimité et du repos qui se pelotonne sur elle même aucune passivité mais dans une intense possession de soi.' Indeed, Bachelard discusses various attempts to use imagination in psychotherapy, especially those of Robert Desoille: see *L'air et les songes* (Paris: Corti, 1943), pp. 129–45 (hereafter cited as *Air*); *La Terre et les rêveries de la volonté* (Paris: Corti, 1948), pp. 392–4 (hereafter cited as *Volonté*). *Eau*, pp. 10, 6; *La Terre et les rêveries du Repos* (Paris: Corti, 1948), p. 82 (hereafter cited as *Repos*). Today new advances have been made in this area by J. L. Singer, *Daydreaming: An Introduction to the Experimental Study of Inner Experience* (New York: Random House, 1966).

16 'L'imagination, dans ses vives actions, nous détache à la fois du passé et de la réalité. Elle ouvre sur l'avenir. A la fonction du réel, instruite par le passé, telle qu'elle est dégagée par la psychologie classique, il faut joindre une fonction de l'irréel' (*Eau*, p. 23); cf. *PE*, p. 16 (all references to this work unless otherwise indicated will be to the English translation, Boston, Mass.: Beacon Press, 1969); Dagognet, *Bachelard*, p. 33, and Kaplan, 'Bachelard's philosophy', p. 3.

17 *PE*, p. 58. See similar point expressed by Paul Ricoeur in *Finitude et culpabilité*, Aubier, 1960 Vol. 2, pp. 20 and 2: 'Nous cherchons maintenant une détermination phénoménologique des images ... entendons par là une étude du phénomène de l'image poétique quand l'image émerge dans la conscience comme un produit direct du coeur, de l'àme, de l'être, de l'homme saisi dans son actualité.'

18 *PR*, p. 2. Also *PE*, p. xv.

19 ibid., p. 3; cf. M. Dufrenne on Bachelard's theory of imagination as trans-subjective reciprocity in *La Poétique* (Paris: Presses Universitaires de France, 1963) p. 184 ff.

20 *Air*, p. 24: 'Nous n'hésitions pas à prendre prétexte des observations psychologiques pour développer nos propres thèses sur la métaphysique de l'imagination, métaphysique qui reste pourtant, notre but avoué.'

21 Bachelard was quite as adamant as Sartre in his insistence that the image differs from both the concept and the percept. On several occasions he explicitly expounded the view that imagination exceeds the homeostatic limits of conception: 'Les images ne sont pas des concepts. Elles ne s'isolent pas dans leur signification. Précisément elles tendent à dépasser leur signification. L'imagination est alors multifonctionelle' (*Repos*, p. 3). 'Les images ne se laissent pas classer comme les concepts. Même lorsqu'elles sont très nettes, elles ne se divisent pas en genres qui s'excluent' (ibid., p. 289). 'To specify exactly what a phenomenology of the image can be, to specify that the image comes *before* thought, we should have to say that poetry, rather than being a phenomenology of the mind, is a phenomenology of the soul. We should then have to collect documentation on the subject of the *dreaming consciousness*' (*PE*, p. xvi). Bachelard was even more determined that there be no confounding of the radical heterogeneity between perception and imagination. He tells us that if we look at a flame 'imaginatively', we transcend its concrete perception and behold a resonance which leads beyond itself to some 'other' dimension. We no longer view it as a thing in itself but as a hint of something more, as a dis-position of openness and becoming: 'Le flamme nous force à imaginer. Devant une flamme, dès qu'on rêve ce que l'on aperçoit n'est rien au regard de ce qu'on imagine' (*La Flamme*, p. 12). He states accordingly that to perceive and to imagine 'sont aussi antithétiques que présence et absense. Imaginer, c'est s'absenter, c'est s'enfoncer vers une vie nouvelle' (*Eau*, p. 10). The image is not a copy but the spontaneous inspiration of an 'au-delà' which breaks the procrustean conformity of the real. See Préclaire, *Poétique*, pp. 89–100.

22 G. Bachelard, *On Poetic Imagination and Reverie*, ed. Colette Gandin (New York: Bobbs Merrill, 1971), p. 23. Or again: 'On ne peut étudier que ce qu'on a d'abord rêvé: la science se forme plutôt sur une rêverie que sur une expérience' (quoted Préclaire, *Poétique*, p. 17); 'Nous verrons avec quelle facilité, avec quel naturel, le génie assemble la pensée à l'imagination; comment chez un génie l'imagination produit la pensée – loin que ce soit la pensée qui aille chercher des oripeaux dans un magasin d'images' (*Air*, p. 25).

23 ibid., p. 34.

24 *Eau*, p. 23.
25 E. Minkowski, 'Imagination?' *Revue Internationale Philosophique*, Brussels, vol. 51, 1960, p. 12–13. See also Dufrenne, *Poétique*, p. 183.
26 *PE*, p. xiii; Ramnoux, 'Avec Gaston Bachelard', p. 41; Dagognet, 'Gaston Bachelard', p. 37; Kaplan, 'Bachelard's philosophy', p. 17. The creative imagination is concerned with the deformation of perception in order to produce 'changing' images. (*Air*, p. 149). It is because imagination affords a freedom from a mental imitation of reality and sponsors a process of self-transcendence that Bachelard's phenomenology of imagination demonstrates a profound moral commitment, 'to reestablish imagination in its living role as the guide of human life' (*Air*, p. 209). Elsewhere he explicates this point: 'Le vie morale est donc, elle aussi, comme la vie de l'imagination, une vie cosmique; le monde entier veut la rénovation' (*Eau*, p. 202).
27 J. H. Van der Berg, *The Phenomenological Approach in Psychology* (Chicago, Ill.: C. Thomas, 1955), p. 67.
28 See this point: *Air*, pp. 14–17, 30, 97, 110–11, 290, 296, 300; *Volonté*, pp. 199–200, 371; *Repos*, pp. 295, 304. See also Kaplan on this point: 'Participating in an act of self-consciousness in imaginative creation, the dreamer of reveries is aware of himself as a creator (poetizing-I). This self-consciousness is the spiritual freedom of man in reverie' ('Bachelard's philosophy', p. 21).
29 *PE*, p. xxx.
30 *PE*, pp. 211 ff.
31 For the best examples of such images of synthesis see *PE*, pp. xx and 235 ff. Relevant commentaries: Kaplan 'Bachelard's philosophy', pp. 5–6; Dagognet, 'Gaston Bachelard' pp. 38–40.
32 *Repos*, pp. 299–300.
33 *PR*, p. 46.
34 *Volonté*, p. 80–1. For commentary on Bachelard's rejection of Sartre's dualism in favour of dialectic, see Minkowski, *op. cit.*, pp. 4–5, 27–30. See also Dufrenne on Bachelard's rejection of Sartre's solipsistic imagination in *La Poétique*, p. 185 'Mais le pour-soi n'est pas séparé et vide s'il est capable d'être inspiré du vrai. Les analyses de Bachelard vont en sens inverse: elle suggèrent plutôt que la Nature naturante sollicite l'humanité et oriente l'imagination'.
35 J.-P. Sartre, *Etre et le néant* p. 695.
36 cf. Ramnoux, 'Avec Gaston Bachelard vers une phénoménologie de l'imagination', *Revue de Métaphysique et de Morale*, vol. 70, no. 1, 1965, p. 42, and Dufrenne, *Esthétique et Philosophie*, Paris: Klincksieck, 1976.
37 *Volonté*, p. 357.
38 Ibid. pp. 23–4.
39 *Eau*, p. 202. See also ibid., pp. 46–7: 'Ainsi les parfums verts comme les prairies sont évidemment des parfums frais; ce sont des chairs fraîches et lustrées, des chairs pleines comme des chairs d'enfant. Toute la correspondance est soutenue par l'eau primitive, par une eau charnelle, par l'élément universelle.' For other instances of Bachelardian Correspondence see Ramnoux, 'Avec Gaston Bachelard' pp. 33–4, 40. Note

also the close similarity here to the Thomistic notion of correspondence: Marras, 'Scholastic roots of Brentano's conception of intentionality' (read at the International Congress 'Tommaso d'Aquino nel suo VII Centenario' in Rome on 18 April 1974), pp. 9 ff.

40 *Volonté*, p. 211. See also Kaplan, 'Bachelard's philosophy', p. 7: 'Imagined images are sublimations of notions revealed by the archetypal structure of the collective unconscious ... this sublimation is not one of formal determinism but of *process*, the fundamentally dynamic characteristic of imagination, e.g., sublimation as a transcendence of rigid psychological complexes.' Mansuy makes a similar point: 'Les inventions de l'imagination échappent au déterminisme. Si telles nuances de la rêverie changent avec les temps et les lieux, il n'en va pas de même des façons de rêver fondamentales qui, seules, intéressent Bachelard. Car l'un de ses buts est d'inventorier les songes que l'humanité fait depuis des millénaires et qui correspondent aux expériences essentielles, aux grandes émotions à le mannière d'être, bref, aux archétypes de l'homme' (*Bachelard*, p. 132).

41 Quoted in Préclaire, *Poétique*, pp. 81–2. Also *PE*, p. xx; *Eau*, p. 16: 'Aux matières originelles où s'instuit l'imagination matérielle sont attachées des ambivalences profondes et durables ... Et cette propriété psychologique est si constante qu'on peut en énoncer, comme une loi primordiale de l'imagination, la réciproque: une matière que l'imagination ne peut faire vivre doublement ne peut jouer le rôle psychologique de matière originelle. Une matière qui n'est pas l'occasion d'une ambivalence psychologique ne peut trouver son double qui permet des transpositions sans fin.' Bachelard maintains in fact that every material valorized by the imagination harbours a contradiction within itself, and this is why the poets can speak of the black secret of milk, the goodness of the serpent, the hardness of water or the seed that must die in order to live (see Mansuy, *Bachelard*, p. 168). Bachelard is convinced of the pervasiveness of this principle of constant interchange: 'Impossible d'échapper à cette dialectique: avoir conscience de brûler, c'est se refroidir; sentir une intensité, c'est la diminuer' (*La Psychanalyse du feu*, (Paris: Gallimard, 1938, p. 217).

42 *La Flamme*, p. 41. This creative and autonomous power of reverie is particularly apparent in poetry: 'Cette image que la lecture du poème nous offre, la voici qui devient vraiment nôtre. Elle prend racine en nous-mêmes. Nous l'avons reçue, mais nous naissons à l'impression que nous aurions pu la créer, que nous aurions dû la créer. Elle devient un être nouveau de notre langage, elle nous exprime en nous faisant ce qu'elle exprime; autrement dit, elle est à la fois, un devenir d'expression et un devenir de notre être. Ici, l'expression crée de l'être' (*Air*, p. 283). Compare this with the view of Binzwanger, another phenomenologist, in *La Science des rêves*: 'Le rêve comme toute expérience imaginaire est un indice authentique de transcendence; et dans cette transcendence le monde nous parle; il parle dans un langue de symboles. Un symbole est une image fournie par la Nature même. Dans l'image de l'enfance originelle, le monde parle de sa propre enfance: il dit quelque chose de soi qui, exprimé par le monde, est tout autant lever de soleil que naissance d'un enfant' (p. 63).

43 Mansuy, *Bachelard*, pp. 132–3.
44 *Repos*, p. 164.
45 *Eau*, p. 96.
46 ibid., p. 2. 'On pourrait distinguer deux imaginations: une imagination qui donne vie à la cause matérielle, et une imagination qui donne vie à la cause formelle'. See also Kaplan, 'Bachelard's philosophy', p. 6.
47 *Air*, p. 58. For Bachelard all images created by imagination manifest man's need to create his own world of being. Will becomes one with imagination in an absolute affirmation of human creativity: *Volonté*, pp. 20, 71; *Eau*, p. 117; *Repos*, p. 312; *PE*, p. 4; cf. Kaplan, 'Bachelard's philosophy of imagination', *Philosophy and Phenomenological Research*, pp. 9, 13, and Minkowski, *op. cit.*, p. 9.
48 For the best discussion of Bachelard's relation to Jung, see Mansuy, *Bachelard*, p. 9.
49 *Volonté*, p. 78.
50 *PE*, p. 80.
51 *Air*, pp. 283–4. See also 'Dans la fougue et la rutilance des images litéraires ... les mots ne sont plus de simples termes. La poésie fait ramifier le son du mot en l'entourant d'une atmosphère' (*Volonté*, p. 7). 'La Rêverie poétique ranime le monde des premières paroles...le dire du poète est fondation par la parole et dans la parole' (*PR* p. 2). See also Mansuy, *Bachelard*, p. 122 ff., Préclaire, *Poétique*, p. 46–51.
52 *Air*, p. 278; cf. *PE*, p. xix.
53 For Bachelard 'les formes ne sont pas des signes mais les vraies réalités' and man himself is nothing other than 'la parole de ce macro-anthrope qu'est le corps monstrueux de la terre' (*PR*, p. 161). Imagination is not therefore opposed to thought and language but their very inspiration: 'Connaître vraiment les images du verbe, les images qui vivent dans nos pensées, dont vivent nos pensées, donnerait une promotion naturelle à nos pensées. Une philosophie qui s'occupe du destin humain doit donc non seulement avouer ses images, mais s'adapter à ses images, combiner le mouvement de ses images' (*Air*, p. 302). For an interesting discussion on this subject, see Kaplan, 'Bachelard's philosophy', pp. 15–6; and M. Dufrenne (*Esthétique et Poétique*), p. 61.
54 *Air*, p. 302.
55 *Volonté*, p. 3.
56 *Air*, p. 14.
57 *PR*, p. 70.
58 Bachelard borrows this term from Ludwig Binzwanger, *Le Rêve et l'existence*, trans. J. Verdeux (Paris: Desclée, 1956); see particularly pp. 126 ff.
59 Quoted Préclaire, *Poétique*, p. 38.
60 *Air*, p. 90. Also Durand, *Structures*, p. 20 and Kaplan, 'Bachelard's philosophy', pp. 4–5.
61 See my chapter on 'The Hebraic imagination' in *The Wake of Imagination* (London: Hutchinson/University of Minnesota Press, 1988).
62 *Air*, p. 300. Why the material imagination is essential to dynamism: 'Ce qui est certain c'est que les rêveries matérielles changent la dimension de nos puissances. En éprouvant dans le travail d'une matière cette

109

curieuse condensation des images et des forces, nous vivrons la synthèse de l'imagination et de la volonteé' (*Volonté*, p. 24). Why the dynamic (that is, iconoclastic) is essential to the material: 'Seule un philosophie iconoclaste peut entreprendre cette lourde besogne: détacher tous les suffixes de la beauté, s'évertuer à trouver derrière les images qui se montrent, les images qui se cachent, aller à la racine même de la force imaginante' (*Eau*, p. 3). The dialectical imagination establishes a certain liaison between the material drive towards incarnation and the dynamic drive towards reincarnation; we shall return to this point in our conclusion.

63 'Le rêverie poétique nous donne le monde des mondes ... Elle est une ouverture à un monde beau. Elle donne au moi un non-moi qui est le bien du moi; le non-moi mien ... C'est ce non-moi qui me permet de vivre ma conscience d'être au monde' (*PR* p. 12). See also Préclaire, *Poétique*, p. 133. One can only regret at this point that Bachelard did not combine his dialectical phenomenology of imagination with the Husserlian notion of 'possibility'. Had he done so, he would have avoided the awkwardness and inevitable ontological contradictions involved in the positing of a dimension of being which is *before* being or *other* than being.

64 *PR*, p. 161. See also this notion of reciprocity, ibid., p. 148: 'Soudain le rêveur est rêveur de monde. Il s'ouvre au monde et le monde s'ouvre à lui.' Also *Eau*, p. 11: '[L'imagination] est un univers en émanation, un souffle odorant qui sort des choses par l'intermédiaire d'un rêveur'. For the best glosses on this topic, see Dufrenne, *Phénoménologie de l'expérience esthétique*, Paris: PUF, 1953, p. 197; E. Kaelin, *An Existentialist Aesthetic* (Madison, Wis.: University of Winsconsin Press, 1962), p. 360; Kaplan, 'Bachelard's philosophy', pp. 9, 10, 13, 20, 23 ff.

65 *PR*, p. 144.

66 *PE, p.* 7.

67 ibid., p. 200. See also M. McAllester, pp. 175–6.

68 *Repos*, p. 182.

69 *Volonté*, p. 343, and *Air*, p. 12. I am grateful to my Cerisy friend and colleague, Anne-Catherine Benchelah, for these references and observations.

70 *PE*, p. 12.

71 *Air*, p. 283.

Suggestions for further reading

Although every text by Gaston Bachelard on 'poetics' deals with the role of imagination in both art and everyday reverie, it is in his famous preface to *The Poetics of Space*, trans. M. Jolas (Boston, Mass.: Beacon Press, 1969) that he most clearly and consistently articulates his phenomenological approach to imagining. Unfortunately, much of Bachelard's work on the poetics of imagination still remains untranslated, but a useful concise anthology of selected texts in English is provided in *On Poetic Imagination*, ed. Colette Gandin (New York: Bobbs Merrill, 1971). Two informative secondary sources in English on Bachelard's overall contribution to a phenomenological poetics are E. Kaplan, 'Gaston Bachelard's philosophy of imagination' in *Philosophy and Phenomenological Research* (1972), and Mary McAllester, 'Bachelard twenty years on: an assessment' *Revue de littérature comparée*, no. 2 (1984).

4

The dialectical imagination (Merleau-Ponty)

The treatment of imagination to be found in the writings of Maurice Merleau-Ponty – the most celebrated French phenomenologist after Sartre – offers a *dialectical* approach to this enigmatic subject. Striving to accommodate the eidetic perspective of Husserl, the existential perspective of Sartre and the predominantly aesthetic perspective of Bachelard, Merleau-Ponty seeks a dialectical ontology of imagining, which he hopes will resolve some of the oppositions and aporias of his predecessors.

Merleau-Ponty understands 'dialectics' in both the traditional and modern senses of this term – in the *traditional* sense to the extent that his reflections on imagining constitute a 'dialogue' between the adversarial positions of his fellow-philosophers (in particular Husserl, Sartre, Heidegger and Bachelard); in the *modern* sense to the extent that his reasoning is deeply informed by the dialectical method advanced by Hegel and Marx. The Cartesian proclivity towards antithesis – which still haunts the Husserlian and Sartrean oppositions between immanence and transcendence, the imaginary and the real – is overridden by a Hegelian drive towards synthesis and synergy.

Between the visible and the invisible

Already in the thirties Merleau-Ponty and Sartre – like most young philosophers of their generation in Paris – had come under the influence of Alexander Kojève whose famous lectures on the *Phenomenology of Spirit* were delivered at the École des Hautes Études in Paris between 1933 and 1939. But, while Sartre inclined towards the antinomies of the Master–Slave struggle – as evinced in his hell-is-other-people analysis of intersubjective relations – Merleau-Ponty favoured the dialectical gestures of overlapping (*entrelacs*), enfleshment and chiasmus. This predilection for a dialectical rather than a dualist ontology led in turn to a preference for Bachelard's approach to the imaginary over Sartre's. The following passage from *The Visible and the Invisible* (1964) is revealing: 'For Sartre [the imaginary] is negation of negation, an order in which annihilation is applied to itself and consequently counts as a positing of being although it would absolutely not be its equivalent and although the least fragment of true, transcendent being immediately reduces the imaginary.' And he goes on to explain: 'Being and the imaginary are for Sartre "objects", "entities" – for me they are "elements" in Bachelard's sense, that is, not objects, but fields, subdued being, non-thetic being, being before being; and moreover involving their auto-inscription, their subjective correlative is a part of them – this is not coincidence but a dehiscence which knows itself as such.'[1]

Here Merleau-Ponty reveals a concern to rescue imagination from the alienated status with which Sartre endowed it, and to have it recognized as a fundamental expression of Being. He does not for a moment wish to suggest that the imaginary is but one thing in consciousness among others. Far from relapsing into the empiricist fallacy which saw the image as a faded perceptual thing in the mind, Merleau-Ponty, like his phenomenological colleagues, continually upheld the unique and irreducible intentionality of imagination. But he differed from his closest colleague – Sartre – in arguing that the fact that the image is an intentionality different from all other modes of being does not mean that it is a non-being or, worse, some sort of negative 'entity'. On the contrary, imagination may, he believed, boast of a privileged access to the hidden dimensions of Being – what in his later writings he terms 'the invisible'. This invisible, he says, can be imagined but it cannot be seen. It is not non-existent. It pre-exists *in* the *visible*:

This visible not actually seen is not the Sartrean imaginary: presence to the absent or of the absent. It is a presence of the immanent, the latent, or the hidden – something Bachelard understood when he said that each sense has its own imaginary.[2]

As soon as a positive ontological validity is ascribed thus to the imaginary, the way is open for an investigation of the particular *symbolique* of each realm of being. Every 'visible' dimension of being is for Merleau-Ponty correlatively connected to an invisible or imaginary dimension. In this sense, not only each 'element', 'nation', 'individual' or 'sense' may be regarded as having a unique form of imaginative intentionality, but even each major function of the human body. To recognize such a pluralism of imaginary regions is to humanize our understanding of ourselves. As Merleau-Ponty puts it in *Existence et dialectique* (1971), for example, reacting against the biological reductionism of behaviourist psychology:

> We refuse and have always refused to reduce the phallus to a part of the objective body as an organ of micturition and copulation, a power of causality governing a quantity of behaviours. What we have learned from our study of dreams, images, and behaviour and finally of the unique reverie of the body, is to discern an imaginary (*imaginaire*) of the phallus, a symbolic phallus, oneiric or poetic. It is not the utilizable, functional, prosaic body which explains man: on the contrary, the body is precisely human to the extent that it discovers its symbolic and poetic charge.[3]

Merleau-Ponty approaches the phenomenon of dreaming in a similar way. The dream, he declares, is a unique expression of one's corporeal ontology. As imaginary, it signifies a mode of being without a real and perceiving body; or, if one prefers, a mode of being 'with an imaginary body without weight'.[4] Thus understood, the imaginary is salvaged from its Sartrean role as a non-being which falsely lays claim to perceptual being (as in his theory of quasi-observation), and is acknowledged as a 'true *Stiftung* of Being of which the observation of the articulated body are special variants'.[5] There is, Merleau-Ponty suggests, a *fundamental* being of the body-subject which perdures throughout its many forms of expression, an invisible symbolizing foundation from which all our visible actions spring.

This Heideggerian view of imagination as an agent of fundamental ontology was in marked contrast to Sartre's existentialist account. And Sartre explicitly acknowledges as much in an interview in 1975: 'I believe there is a basic incompatibility', he declares, 'because behind his analysis Merleau-Ponty is always referring to a kind of being for which he invokes Heidegger and which I consider to be absolutely invalid. The entire ontology which emerges from the philosophy of Merleau-Ponty is distinct from mine. It is much more of a continuum ... I am not a continuist.'[6]

Each realm of being is marked, for Merleau-Ponty, by a *chiasmus* of visibility and invisibility. These chiasmic poles are not mutually

114

exclusive in the way that being and nothingness are for Sartre. For, though they may be said to constitute the unique worlds of perception and imagination respectively, they remain at all times founded in a dimension of Being more fundamental than both – and in the light of which both are seen to correspond. In other words, the imagination addresses an invisible meaning in the visible world and the world responds only because both participate in a common core of Being. It is precisely because of this cognate genesis that imagination may serve as an agent of creative dialogue rather than monologue. Above all else – and here we find the common source of Bachelard's and Merleau-Ponty's refutation of the Sartrean theory – imagination is dialogical. This point is made in the following classic, though characteristically dense, passage from *The Visible and the Invisible*:

> Meaning is *invisible*, but the invisible is not the contradictory of the visible: the visible itself has an invisible inner framework (*membrure*) and the in-visible is the secret counterpart of the visible – one cannot see it there and every effort to *see it there* makes it disappear, but it is *in the line* of the visible, it is its *virtual focus*, it is inscribed within it in filigree ... One cannot account for this double 'chiasmus' by the cut of the for-itself and the cut of the in-itself. A relation to Being is needed that would form itself *within Being*. This, at bottom, is what Sartre was looking for. But since for him there is no *interior* except me, and every *other* is exteriority, Being for him remains pure positivity, object, and the for-itself participates in it only through a sort of folly.[7]

Briefly stated, Merleau-Ponty wished to ground the Sartrean imagination (as pure for-itself) in some fundamental ontology, and thereby rescue it from the hell of its own self-negation. He sought to establish the real and the imaginary as two separate but corresponding realms: separate on the level of ordinary being, but corresponding – though never identical – on the level of fundamental Being. That his theory and terminology are extraordinarily close to that of Heidegger is undeniable; nor does Merleau-Ponty himself seek to deny it. In fact in the final pages of *The Visible and the Invisible* (posthumously published with working notes in 1964) he explicitly acknowledges his debt to his fellow-phenomenologist. This debt is nowhere more apparent than in his various attempts to formulate the ontology of the invisible as 'an explosion of Being which is forever', a 'universal dimensionality which is Being', an 'existential eternity – the eternal body'.[8] But the influence of Heidegger's fundamental ontology does not detract in the least from the originality of Merleau-Ponty's application of it to the question of the imaginary.

Art and dialectics

In *Eye and Mind*, the last study that Merleau-Ponty wrote before his death, he seeks to extrapolate a dialectical notion of imagination from an ontology of art. He begins by confirming Sartre's repudiation of the classical fallacy of the image as mere imitation. 'The word image', he says, 'is in bad repute because we have thoughtlessly believed that a design was a tracing, a copy, a second thing, and the mental image was such a design.' But if in fact it is nothing of the kind 'neither the design nor the painting belongs to the in-itself'.[9] Merleau-Ponty then proceeds explicitly to establish the basic difference between his and Sartre's ontological assessment of the imagination:

The picture and the actor's fantasy-imaginary are not devices to be borrowed from the real world in order to signify prosaic things which are absent. For the imaginary is much nearer to, and much farther away from, the actual – nearer because it is in my body as a diagram of the life of the actual ... farther away from the actual because the painting is an analogue or likeness only according to the body; because it does *not* present the *mind* with an occasion to rethink the constitutive relations of things; because, rather ... it offers to vision its inward tapestries, the imaginary texture of the real.[10]

The image, for Merleau-Ponty, is not just a ruse for making the absent present; it is a unique mode of expressing that hidden logos of lines, colours, gestures and textures which elicits our vision – much in the same way as marrow elicits the growth of a bone. Accordingly, he attempts to explicate Cézanne's puzzling credo that 'nature is in the inside' by outlining a certain dialectical interrelation between a secret visibility (that is, in-visibility) of the body and a corresponding secret visibility of things. 'Things have an internal equivalent in me,' Merleau-Ponty explains, 'they arouse in me a carnal formula of their presence.' Why, then, he asks, 'shouldn't these correspondences in their turn give rise to some external visible shape in which anyone else would recognize these motifs which support his own inspection of the world'?[11] The artist is he who fashions these correspondences into such visible shapes. Thus each artwork serves in some sense as a 'blueprint of the genesis of things'. Once completed, the work is capable of awakening those powers dormant in ordinary vision which Merleau-Ponty calls 'the secret of preexistence'.[12]

The artist breaks the skin of existence in order to lay bare the generating axis of its becoming. And, in so far as he is successful, his act of imaginative disclosure is reciprocated by an objective act of epiphany. The artist's vision is then much more than just a view upon the *outside*, a merely imitative relation with the world. 'The world no longer stands before him through representation,' Merleau-Ponty tells us, 'rather it is the artist to whom the things of the world give birth by a sort of concentration or coming-to-itself of the visible.'[13] Thus it is by reaching beneath the visual givens that the imaginative painter opens himself to the in-visible dialectic of Being:

> He paints ... because the world has at least once emblazoned in him the (invisible) cyphers of the visible ... [which] is both out there in the world and here in the heart of vision – the same, or if one prefers, a *similar* thing, but according to an efficacious similarity which is the parent, the genesis, the metamorphosis of Being in his vision.[14]

And Merleau-Ponty concludes from this that there must be a certain dialectical 'expiration and inspiration of Being, action and passion so slightly discernible' that it becomes impossible to distinguish between what paints and what is painted.

Developing the discovery by Husserl and Sartre of imagination as a *sui generis* mode of intentionality, Merleau-Ponty declares that the image can never be visible in the sense of a thing perceived. And he claims that this accounts, furthermore, for the spectator's inability to say exactly *where* the painting which he imaginatively intends actually is – in the world? in the eye of the mind? in both? It is, he suggests, 'more accurate to say that I see *according* to it or *with* it, than that I see *it*'.[15] The fact that the image is not a copy of visible reality does not necessarily mean, however, that it is its total negation. The painted image does not renounce, but rather redeems the visible by disclosing its in-visible genesis. Painting is the transmutation of a carnal surface into a certain carnal 'essence' – which in turn relates to its surface, not as a soul to a body or a Platonic form to matter, but as an inside to an outside. This is why, for Merleau-Ponty, the fact that one's gaze cannot situate the image of a painting does not mean that one must gaze at *nothing*. It is more correct to say that one gazes at 'the halos of Being'.[16]

Art's transcendence of reality is, for Merleau-Ponty, always grounded in a fundamental bedrock of Being which saves it from the verdict of nothingness. Though he frequently speaks of imagination as both a presence-in-absence and an absence-in-presence, it is always as an absence and a presence which *presuppose* Being. Imaginative vision is not, he points out, 'a certain mode of thought or presence to itself'; it is the 'means given me for being absent from myself, for being present at the fission of Being from the inside – the fission at whose termination, and not before, I come back to myself'.[17] The difference between this dialectical notion of presence-in-absence and Sartre's non-dialectical notion is made even more explicit in the following passage:

> Every visual something, individual as it is, functions also as a dimension, because it gives itself as the result of a dehiscence of Being. What this ultimately means is that the proper essence of the visible is to have a layer of invisibility in the strict sense, which it makes present as a certain absence.[18]

It should now be evident that Merleau-Ponty's dialectical notion of presence-in-absence as *invisibility*, no more signifies *nothingness* than does Bachelard's aesthetic notion of absence as otherness. Both phenomenologists availed themselves of the Sartrean term (absence) but invested it with a positive ontological status. It was, indeed, one of their common aims to root artistic imagination in a 'primordial ground' – and as a corollary to demonstrate its privileged access to the 'genesis' of things. The subsequent revelation of the imaginary as an invisible (Merleau-Ponty) and sur-real (Bachelard) dimension of Being led in both cases to the characterization of aesthetic imagination as an agency of dialogue: 'There is no break at all in this circuit: it is impossible to say that nature ends here and man or expression starts here. It is, therefore, mute Being which itself comes to show forth its own meaning.'[19]

118

By tracing the phenomenological discovery of the aesthetic image as intentional relation to its *positive* ontological ground, Merleau-Ponty and Bachelard declared the primary function of the imagination to be a dialogue between inside and outside, between the being that is in the world and the world that being is in: a reciprocity rooted in a fundamental Being which is in both. In this manner, Sartre's dualism of imagination and reality is dialectically transcended.

Art and politics

Merleau-Ponty's acknowledgement of a mutual rapport between the imaginary and the real enables him to relate art to politics without committing the folly of reducing one to the other. In *Adventures of the Dialectic* (1955), Merleau-Ponty puts forward a controversial explanation of Sartre's swing from the extreme of an a-political imagination in the thirties to a voluntaristic politics in the forties. Sartre's monistic reduction of politics to the imaginary was said to stem directly from its opposite – a naïve dualism between the imaginary and the political. Both these extremes arose, he argues, from the lack of any principle of dialectical mediation. Blind to the common symbolic life shared by both imaginative consciousness and political action, Sartre could only relate them – if at all – by collapsing one into the other.

Consequently, Sartre's transition from disengaged to engaged art constitutes a volte-face. It has no explanation other than Sartre's own wilful choice. Consistent with this voluntarist premiss, the imaginative consciousness takes itself for an omnipotent magician and reduces the world of action to a theatre. Sartre's subsumption of praxis into fantasy is what Merleau-Ponty, in a well-known phrase, called 'the myth of the mandarins which reunites the fantasy of total knowledge and pure action'.[20] Unwilling to accept delegation of the party's function, Sartre chose to delude himself that imaginative writing is equivalent to political action. To judge otherwise, as Merleau-Ponty recommends in a rebuke to Sartre, 'one must live in a universe where everything has meaning, politics as well as literature: literature and politics are really united to each other ... but as two divergent viewpoints on a single symbolic life or history'.[21]

Given this dialectical position, it is not surprising that Merleau-Ponty should so vehemently oppose Sartre's view that the imaginary and the moral are mutually exclusive. He rejected Sartre's conclusion to *The*

Psychology of Imagination that since 'beauty is a value applicable only to the imaginary, the negation of the world being its essential structure', it necessarily follows that it is 'stupid to confuse the moral and the aesthetic'.[22] But there is a further difficulty. Since moral value for Sartre is defined, above all, as freedom, and since imaginative consciousness is the essential pre-condition of a free consciousness, morality cannot do without the imaginary projections of consciousness which it ostensibly excludes. Moreover, since freedom is a project of imagination it is the product of the negation of the real, hence aa nothingness. And to say accordingly that the highest moral value (freeedom) is an imaginary nothingness, which human consciousness projects from itself as its ultimate goal, is to condemn morality – no less than aesthetics – to solipsism. In the pursuit of the Good, no less than in the pursuit of the Beautiful, existentialist man is, in the Sartrean view, condemned to be free; which means, in turn, condemned to himself alone (*solus ipse*).

Merleau-Ponty develops this critique of Sartre's phenomenology of imagination into a detailed debunking of his political philosophy in *Adventures of the Dialectic*, a work which resulted in a deep rift between the two former comrades and co-editors of *Les Temps modernes*. The starting-point of Merleau-Ponty's critique is that since Sartre's model of imagination made moral and political relationships with other human beings virtually impossible (since each individual can only express his own freedom by negating that of others) the single remedy left to him was to espouse a politics of revolutionary voluntarism, or what Merleau-Ponty calls 'Ultrabolshevism'.

Focusing most of his critical remarks on a series of articles enti-tled 'Les Communistes et la paix' which Sartre had written for *Les Temps modernes* between 1952 and 1954, Merleau-Ponty argues that Sartre's injunction to the proletariat to follow the party, regardless of circumstances, epitomizes his desire to annex history to the dictates of an élite consciousness. Sartre's politics of extreme pragmatism serves as a mask for extreme fictionalism. Moreover, Merleau-Ponty indicates how Sartre's division between an imaginative subjectivity (which is concerned with value) and an objective reality (which must be negated in favour of value) prompted him to consider history as devoid of any meaning other than the meaning given to it by the will of the party. Revolution is, for Sartre, then, nothing other than the 'decision' of consciousness to intervene in history. And since the objective material structures of history can furnish us with no directive (being pure *en-soi*) it is imperative that revolution be the spontaneous and unmediated action of the party. To mediate the absolute subjectivity of the party with external considerations would be to defeat its spontaneity. Thus Merleau-Ponty accounts for Sartre's view that the proletariat must do nothing to hinder or detract from this subjectivity: they must pledge full and unconditional allegiance to the decision of the party. The proletariat can only have meaning, in short, as the imaginary project of the party.

Merleau-Ponty goes on to argue that history has no value in itself for Sartre. It is we, or the party, who *imagine* this value in it. And so politics becomes thaumaturgy – a matter of magical *fiat*: but one, Merleau-Ponty insists, which would not even know what it is applied to 'if what was to be done was not simultaneously represented as an *imaginary end* which I choose'.[23] Revolution is therefore less a collective action than an arbitrary decree. Merleau-Ponty offers this severe summary:

Sartre used to say that there is no difference between imaginary love and true love because the subject, being a thinking subject, is by definition what he thinks he is. He could say accordingly that a historically 'true' politics is always an invented one, that only by a retrospective illusion is this politics seen to be prepared within the history where it intervenes, and that, in a society, revolution is *self-imagination*.[24]

Merleau-Ponty's dialectical view of the rapport between imagination and history seeks to repudiate this Sartrean account of politics as a magical power which, unable to transform history in fact, contrives to do so by fiat. It is precisely because Sartre drove a chasm between imaginative consciousness and reality, making value the exclusive prerogative of the former, that his politics degenerated into psychodrama. Political praxis is thus reduced to an imaginary action which tries to impose itself on things and suddenly returns to the unreal from which it was born: it becomes theatre.[25] According to this reading of Sartre's politics, imaginative 'spontaneity' is synonymous with the pure choice of the party; and the proletariat and the revolution appear as mere images in the party's consciousness, suspended above the fabric of history and inexplicable in terms of anything outside this consciousness. Thus the moment the proletariat disobeys the party it disobeys its own *raison d'être*; it ceases to exist. By draining history of all meaning, Sartre unrealized history and incarcerated himself in the *solus ipse* of imagination:

For him, to be committed is not to interpret and criticize oneself in contact with history; rather it is to recreate one's own relationship with history as if one were in a position to remake oneself from top to bottom; it is to decide to hold as absolute the meaning one invents for one's personal history and for public history; it is to place oneself deliberately in the imaginary.[26]

Merleau-Ponty proceeds to suggest that Sartre's theory of political commitment is really a transformation of the relationships of *action* into relationships of *contemplation*. It is, at best, action at a distance; a sort of politics by proxy. But such a politics is a complete denial of the fact that man is as much a creature of history as he is a product of his own imagination. There is simply no avoiding the truth that we are inextricably bound up in events of historical reality, born into certain situations for which we are in no way accountable. By making man's imaginative consciousness the sole source of value in the world, and by condoning no other relationship between imagination and reality than that of negation, Sartre condemned politics to impotence.[27] To operate on the basis of an ideal image of a future society is to blind consciousness to the complexities of the present historical condition. And worse: it leads ultimately to a politics of 'ultrabolshevism' where the immediate decision of the party and the unconditional obedience of the worker becomes the order of the day. On this account, Merleau-Ponty accuses Sartre's politics of 'oscillating from what one *sees* to what one *dreams* thereby contaminating the real with the imaginary and obscuring the harsh present under the haze of a fictitious future'.[28]

But Merleau-Ponty's condemnation of Sartre is not unequivocal. He admires Sartre's attempt to construe politics as the striving for some utopian-imaginary end which would challenge the present and make men responsible for the creation of a new world. His disagreement with Sartre stems from his dialectical conviction – nourished by Hegel and Marx – that this imaginary end cannot be totally unmindful of history. In other words, imagination can only become politically legitimate if it is understood not as a negation of history but as its dialectical complement. Such a dialectic would ensure that consciousness remain open to the complexities of reality and forsake solipsistic illusion. But, while Sartre frequently intuited the necessity of such a dialectical synthesis and continually employed a dialectical terminology, his fundamental dualism of the imaginary and the real rendered this unfeasible. He was condemned, by his own admission, to being a 'communist on his own'.[29] As Merleau-Ponty concludes:

> The end is the imaginary object that I choose. The end is the dialectical unity of the means, Sartre said elsewhere; and this would have happily corrected his abuse elsewhere of this notion, if he had not deprived himself, by rejecting dialectical thought, of the right of recourse to an open consciousness.[30]

Sartre admits in an obituary tribute to Merleau-Ponty that this philosopher's critique constituted for him the 'history lesson' which altered the train of his thought and prompted him to adopt a properly dialectical theory of politics.[31] *The Critique of Dialectical Reason* (1960) was the result of this conversion. In this work, Sartre attempted to marry the basic concepts of existentialism and Marxism by introducing the notion of Society as a mediating structure between individual freedom and historical necessity. Value is here redefined as a 'Concrete Universal' – that is, a synthesis between the concrete creative self and the universal world-situation which it strives to totalize.

From the perspective of a dialectical imagination, art and politics can converge to form a unity-in-distinction. Their distinctiveness as two principles of dialectical contrariety – art concerned with the emergence of the invisible, politics concerned with the organization of the visible – speaks for itself. On the other hand, their unity is to be understood in terms of a common symbolic life which subtends both. The ontological dimensions of this life were expounded by Merleau-Ponty in *The Visible and the Invisible* and *Eye and Mind*. While we have already outlined his ontological position in these works, it is necessary – if we are to complete the picture – to situate this within the general perspective of his phenomenological psychology, with particular reference to his key distinction between 'primordial' and 'secondary' expression.

Towards an ontology of style

In *The Structure of Behaviour* (1942) and, more important, *The Phenomenology of Perception* (1945), Merleau-Ponty advances the notion of a primordial expression by means of which the body-subject structures its experience in a movement towards equilibrium. This primordial structuring of the environment by an organism constitutes a certain

123

style. Style is like a fingerprint – it is possessed by all, but each in a unique way. Human existence may be considered a style which each person 'embodies' in the struggle to achieve an individual equilibrium within a global environment.

All styles, which range from sexual to artistic expression, succeed in dialectically uniting man's imaginative and perceptual intentionalities in a nexus of symbolic projection. For Merleau-Ponty, in contradistinction to Sartre, there is no quarrel between the claims of imagination and perception. Both share the common cause of investing the world with meaning.

In order to illustrate this primordial communion of the imaginary and the real, Merleau-Ponty chooses the act of love. He categorically rejects Sartre's alternative of sadism and masochism, declaring that the body in an act of love is a perfect synthesis of the form of expression and the feeling expressed. He compares the act of sexual communication here to a successful aesthetic expression – there is no distinction to be made between body (*en-soi*) and consciousness (*pour-soi*). Because of his discovery of an internal rapport between imaginative and perceptual expression, Merleau-Ponty can affirm that all of our actions are in some sense symbolic.[32] The corporeal, far from being opposed to the imaginary, is, he argues, its most effective mode of incarnation in the world. The body-subject, as the organ which carries meaning and value into the world, is the image made flesh. With this dialectic of the corporeal and the imaginary, Merleau-Ponty refutes the solipsism which vitiated Sartre's theory of intersubjective relations. 'There is no choice', he asserts, 'between the for-itself and the for-others . . . in the moment of expression, the other to whom I address my self, and myself in the act of expression, are linked without reserve.'[33]

Every individual has his or her own style – even if it be an improvisation on some more collective or popular style: for example, Dadaism, Beatlemania or Bogartism. And, to this extent at least, everyone is an artist. Whether this style be considered genuine artistry or consumer culture is a question which can only be decided at the level of what Merleau-Ponty calls *secondary expression*. Secondary expression, unlike the projective spontaneity of primordial expression, is reflective and critical. But it has no warrant to impose its secondary judgements upon primary experience. It seeks rather to make 'our reflections equal to the non-reflective life of consciousness'.[34]

Subjecting the whole question of style to scrutiny, Merleau-Ponty defines genuine art as the creative and original structuring of the world. Style becomes artifice, he says, only when it no longer serves as a means to communicate and becomes an end in itself. For this reason, he objects strongly to Malraux's apotheosis of subjective genius and continually reminds us that the imagination, too, must live and breathe 'in situation'. Genuine art is not the prerogative of the individualist visionary. It is an act of cultural communication between artist and public. Style should not be seen as something final – as Malraux and many Formalist critics have argued. It constitutes a primordial expression which epitomizes both a project of individual imagination and an interaction of this imagination with the universal history which grounds it. The modern movement in painting is a good expression of this double allegiance:

> Modern painting is concerned with quite a different problem from that of the return to the individual: the problem of knowing how one can communicate without the help of a pre-established Nature on which all of our senses are opened, how each of us is enmeshed in the universal by that which is most peculiar to ourselves.[35]

This 'universal', as Merleau-Ponty suggests in his later ontological writings, can only be understood in terms of a fundamental dehiscence of Being which links together the dialectical poles of the imaginary and the actual. And it is because of this universal event of Being that we can argue for a continuity between art and life. The painter or poet does not differ in any *qualitative* sense from fellow humans. He differs only in precision, coherence and consistency of expression. Merleau-Ponty's position thus serves to derogate the Romantic cult of genius and to emancipate the hidden artist in each one of us by demonstrating that our every gesture is constitutive of a primordially creative project. In short, the artist is nothing more nor less than the human subject writ large:

> The movement of the artist in tracing his arabesques in infinite matter serves to amplify, but also to continue, the simpler marvel of directed locomotion of simple grasping gestures ... We are interested in the expressive function of the human body which was already begun in the least act of perception, and which has since been amplified into painting and art. The field of pictorial meanings has been opened up since the time of man's first appearance in the world. And the first designs drawn on the walls of caves were able to establish a

tradition only because they reaped the benefits of another: that of perception.[36]

In a study entitléd 'Cézanne's Doubt', Merleau-Ponty reiterates Sartre's view that every artist calls for an 'enlivening' imaginer, that is, spectator or reader. Merleau-Ponty goes far beyond Sartre, however, in his declaration that this enlivening is grounds for the celebration of their common humanity. Reciprocity, not solipsism, is the predominant theme of Merleau-Ponty's aesthetic. He writes:

> The painter could only make an image. One must wait for that image to be animated by others. Then the work of art will have joined these separated lives; it will no longer exist solely in one of them like a tenacious dream or persistent delirium, or even in space as a colored canvas: it will inhabit several minds indivisibly, even presumably every possible mind, as a perpetual human acquisition.[37]

Whereas Sartre had maintained that the image teaches us nothing new – since it is a mere projection of consciousness containing nothing more than what consciousness already knew – Merleau-Ponty retorts that the artistic image is the greatest teacher of all. By means of it, hitherto opposed realms are synthesized in order to bring forth some totally novel dimension of Being. It is precisely, he says, because art installs us in a world whose significance is foreign to us that 'it teaches us to see and give food for thought as no analytical work can, since analysis never finds in its object anything other than what it has already put there'.[38]

Merleau-Ponty's aesthetic could be summarized, therefore, as a critical investigation (secondary expression) of the symbolizing intentionality (primordial expression) which any work of art – or, to a lesser extent, any human gesture – embodies in the form of a 'style' which mediates between symbolizer and spectator. In this way, he succeeds in obviating two major pitfalls of traditional aesthetics: (1) the *motivational fallacy* which reduces the whole aesthetic process to the artist's psychological motivation – and only part of this motivation at that, for the original purpose of the artist may be aborted in its actual expression; (2) the *affective fallacy*, which reduces the aesthetic enterprise to the emotional reaction it can provoke in its recipients. Both of these positions are erroneous in that each, taken alone, falsifies the essence of art as dialogue. From a dialectical standpoint only that motive of the artist is relevant which is 'embodied' in the style of the artwork. Similarly, only those feelings are relevant to the work which are sponsored by the phenomenal structures of the work itself – as creatively intended by the artist and recreatively intended by the spectator. In brief, art can only be adequately appreciated as a dialogical interaction between the imaginative intentionalities of creator and re-creator.[39] Because traditional theories tended to emphasize the subjectivity rather than the intersubjectivity of aesthetic experience they almost invariably ignored the social dimensions of art. But for Merleau-Ponty the phenomenology of art can only be properly understood in terms of a dialectic of relations ranging from the interpersonal to the political.

Conclusion

Merleau-Ponty has hit here upon the possibility of a solution to the epistemological puzzle which impaired the credibility of both Husserl's and Sartre's theories of imagination.

If in an act of imagination consciousness can create an object to fit the requirements of an essence, it is difficult to deny that imagination must have a prior knowledge of essences in order to create its objects. Both Husserl and Sartre wish to deny this conclusion; yet their undialectical division between the worlds of reality and irreality leave them with little alternative but to affirm it, that is, to contradict themselves. Merleau-Ponty offers a way out of this dilemma by pointing out that an essence is, in large part, a symbol of intersubjective existence – our being with others in the world. Essences are the implicit structures of primordial expression to be disclosed dialectically by means of a secondary form of expression, that is, eidetic reflection.[40] It would appear, in the final analysis, that Merleau-Ponty's thinking here is influenced by both Hegel's predilection for dialectical *aufhebung* and Heidegger's theory of the hermeneutic circle.

Merleau-Ponty brings imagination back to life by demonstrating that imagination never left real life in the first place. Imagination is not opposed to our everyday lived experience. Even the most ordinary instance of perception relies on imagination. Moreover, since the invisible essence of any object can never be exhausted in a single perspectival perception, its totality can only be anticipated by means of a proleptic imagining. This is very close to Husserl's notion of free variation; it differs, however, on the important point that Merleau-Ponty believes the essence to be primordially *given by Being* as well as constituted by consciousness.[41]

The world is full with the imaginary. Not, as Sartre maintained, because the imaginary is its negation, but because it is its expression. Even society itself is, in a fundamental sense, an incarnation of human imagining. Each institution, Merleau-Ponty affirms, is a symbolic system that human subjects incorporate into their behaviour as a certain style of conduct. And every individual imagination is charged accordingly by the symbols of society which surround it – as it in turn recharges these symbols with its own creativity. Neither is at the expense of the other. The watchword is *chiasmus*.

Because Husserl and Sartre held that the imaginary object intended by consciousness is always transcendent *of* consciousness and yet unrelated to real existence, they opened themselves to the criticism of having reduced art to the status of an idealist essence; or, in the instance of Sartre's theory of 'committed' art, to the status of voluntarist propaganda.[42] Since Merleau-Ponty's theory of art argues for a dialectical communion between the visible/perceptual and the invisible/imaginary, he eschews both the Husserlian–Sartrean danger of *idealism* and also its opposite extreme, *materialism* (which over-emphasizes the empirical or environmental qualities of the artwork).[43]

For Merleau-Ponty the imaginary is not a single act sequestered from reality; it is a vital process of communication whereby we pass beyond ourselves towards what is *other* than ourselves.[44] Merleau-Ponty shares this dialogical model of imagination with Bachelard, but he breaks new ground in his discovery of its social and political implications. Bachelard had jealously guarded the imaginary from all things political. The imagination could legitimately relate to the cosmic Thou but never with impunity to the It-world of politics. Merleau-Ponty overcame this bias, and showed that the symbolizing function of imagination was as operational in the political world as it was in the poetical. Once grounded in a dialectical phenomenology, art and politics could be acknowledged as successful double agents within the matrix of Being. As Merleau-Ponty concludes his *Adventures of the Dialectic*: 'Politics and culture are reunited not because they are completely congruent or because they both adhere to the event, but because the symbols of each order have echoes, correspondences and effects of induction in the other.'[45]

Notes

1 Merleau-Ponty, *Le Visible et l'invisible* (Paris: Gallimard, 1964); trans. A. Lingis as *The Visible and the Invisible* (Evanston, Ill.: Northwestern University Press, 1969), p. 267.
2 ibid., p. 245.
3 M. Merleau-Ponty, *Existence et dialectique*, (Paris: Presses Universitaires de France, 1971), p. 85. It is interesting to note that Rollo May, an American psychologist deeply influenced by phenomenology, and particularly the notion of intentionality, came to a similar recognition of the vital connection between the imaginary and the phallic. The imagination, he argues, in his book *Love and Will* (New York: Fontana, 1974), functions not just as a forger of surrogates, a symptom of frustration or an evasion into nothingness, but as an openness to hidden possibility: 'We can let our imaginations play on it [i.e. eros], dwell on it, turn it over in our minds, focus on it, "invite" the possibility of love in fantasy' (p. 282).
4 Merleau-Ponty, *Visible and the Invisible*, p. 262.
5 ibid., p. 263.
6 'An interview with J.-P. Sartre', published in P. A. Schipp (ed.), *The Philosophy of J.-P. Sartre* (La Salle, Ill.: Open Court, 1981), p. 43.
7 Merleau-Ponty, *Visible and the Invisible*, p. 215. This bears a conspicuous resemblance to the following passage from G. Bachelard's *L'Eau et les rêves: essai sur l'imagination de la matière* (Paris: Gallimard, 1938), p. 24: 'Les événements les plus riches arrivent en nous bien avant que l'âme s'en aperçoive. Et quand nous commençons à ouvrir les yeux sur le visible, déjà nous étions depuis longtemps adhérents à l'invisible.'
8 Merleau-Ponty, *Visible and the Invisible*, p. 265.
9 Merleau-Ponty, *L'Oeil et l'esprit* (Paris: Gallimard, 1964); trans. J. Edie as *Eye and Mind* in *The Primacy of Perception* (Evanston, Ill.: Northwestern University Press, 1964), p. 164.
10 ibid., p. 165.
11 ibid., p. 164.
12 ibid., p. 182.
13 ibid., p. 181.
14 ibid., p. 166.
15 ibid., p. 164.
16 ibid., p. 164.
17 ibid., p. 186.
18 ibid., p. 187.
19 ibid., p. 188.
20 M. Merleau-Ponty, *Les Aventures de la dialectique* (Paris: Gallimard, 1955); trans. J. Bien as *Adventures of the Dialectic* (New York, Heinemann, 1974), p. 239.
21 ibid., p. 201. See also E. Kaelin, *An Existentialist Aesthetic* (Madison, Wis.: University of Wisconsin Press, 1962) p. 145 (hereafter cited as *EA*).

22 J.-P. Sartre, *The Psychology of Imagination*, n.t. (New York: Citadel Press, 1948) p. 281. See A. Mezaros' discussion of the early Sartre's apathy towards all social and political questions, ' Jean-Paul Sartre: a critical tribute', in *The Socialist Register*, ed. R. Milliband (London: Merlin, 1975), pp. 40 ff. See also Iris Murdoch, *Sartre* (London: Fontana, 1953), pp. 100–4.

23 Merleau-Ponty, *Adventures of the Dialectic*, p. 196.

24 ibid., p. 132; cf. R. Rossanda, 'Sartre's political practice' in *The Socialist Register* (1975), p. 70: 'The rightness of a political direction of the subject, in fact, has only to measure itself against itself. This is where emerges what seems to us to be the abiding limitation of Sartre's thought, his purely *subjective* reading of Marx ... Paradoxically the root of his present pessimism, lies in what Sartre still shares with the Communist Parties: the lure of Leninist voluntarism, with its inevitable corollary of opportunist recriminations of betrayal by the leadership groups.'

25 Merleau-Ponty, *Adventures of the Dialectic*, p. 119.

26 ibid., p. 195. See here Sartre's statement to Camus, 'Réponse à Albert Camus', in *Les Temps modernes*, vol. 8 (1952), reprinted in *Situations IV* (Paris: Gallimard, 1964): 'The problem is not to ask whether history makes sense or not, and whether we should design to take part in it or not ... the problem is to try to give it the meaning which seems to us to be most right.' Also L. Spurling, 'Merleau-Ponty: adventures of the dialectic', *Journal of the British Society of Phenomenology*, vol. 6, no. 1, 1975), p. 63.

27 In response to this danger of political impotence – or solipsism writ large – Merleau-Ponty writes: '... solipsism would be strictly true only of someone who managed to be tacitly aware of his existence without being or doing anything, which is impossible since existing is being in and of the world' (*Phénoménologie de la perception*, Paris: Gallimard, 1945; trans. C. Smith, New York: Humanities Press, 1962, p. 361; hereafter cited as *PP*). Later in the same work Merleau-Ponty states that Sartre's view of the other as a mere object is 'nothing but an insincere modality of others' (p. 448). Similar critiques of Sartre's political solipsism are made by A. Mezaros, 'Jean-Paul Sartre: a critical tribute', p. 34; and H. Marcuse, 'Sartre's existentialism', in *Studies in Critical Philosophy* (London: New Left Books, 1972), pp. 175–6.

28 Merleau-Ponty, *Adventures of the Dialectic*, p. 167. Merleau-Ponty expresses his disapproval of this contamination of reality by imagination more indulgently later in the book when he writes: 'There are two distinct ways of going to the universal – one, the more direct, consists in putting everything into words; the other consists in entering into the game in all its obscurity and creating there a little bit of truth by sheer audacity. One cannot therefore reproach the writer with a professional defect when he tries to see everything and restricts himself to *imaginary* action.' For by doing so, Merleau-Ponty goes on, 'He maintains one of the components of man. But he would be quite mistaken if he thought he could thus glue together the two components and move to political action because he

looks at it' (p. 178). He comments: 'If the Marxist revolution was only a *general idea* there would be nothing to say against this play of the imaginary and the real' (p. 167). But for Merleau-Ponty it is not just a general idea, it is a practical concern of history.

29 Quoted in R. Rossanda, 'Sartre's political practice', p. 72.

30 Merleau-Ponty, *Adventures of the Dialectic* p. 137. Compare with Marcuse, 'Sartre's existentialism', p. 176: 'The ontological foundation of Sartre's existentialism frustrates its efforts to develop a philosophy of the concrete human existence ... Sartre's concepts are, in spite of his dialectical style and the pervasive role of negation, decidedly undiluted.' For another, similar critique of the relationship between imagination and history in Sartre see L. Krieger 'History and existentialism in Sartre', in *The Critical Spirit* (Boston, Mass.: Beacon Press, 1967), p. 250: 'Since the imaginative consciousness must grasp reality in order to deny it, we are left with the apparent paradox that what Sartre calls "human reality" is constituted by the faculty which constitutes the unreal. Since, moreover, the imaginary is for Sartre a "fact" and he confers on it the status of existence – "unreal existence" – an unstated generic notion of being underlies the two-dimensional existence. It was this tendency of Sartre's art and imagination to slide over into reality which explains his tenuous *attraction* to the history he denies.'

31 Sartre, 'Merleau-Ponty', *Situations IV*, p. 247; and also p. 255.

32 *PP*, p. 193: 'On this side of the conventional means of expression which manifest my thoughts to another only because within him there is a meaning assigned to each symbol and which, in this sense, does not produce a veritable communication, one must recognise a primordial operation of signifying in which the thing expressed does not exist outside of the expression itself and in which the signs used themselves induce outward a meaning.' More often than not, in fact, Merleau-Ponty used the word 'symbol' where Bachelard and Sartre would have used 'image'. This is so, I would suggest, first, because Merleau-Ponty tended to work within a linguistic framework and, second, because he did not wish to have his theory confused with Sartre's solipsistic one.

33 M. Merleau-Ponty, in *Les Temps modernes*, vol. 8, (1952), p. 82.

34 *PP*, pp. x–xi. See also Kaelin, 'A new direction in phenomenological philosophy', in *EA*, p. 208.

35 Merleau-Ponty, in *Les Temps modernes* vol. 8, (1952), p. 129. Also *EA*, p. 274–5.

36 ibid., p. 76.

37 M. Merleau-Ponty, 'Cézanne's doubt', in *Sens et non-sens* (Paris: Nagel, 1948), p. 37; cf. *Les Temps modernes*, vol. 8, (1952), p. 85. Also M. Dufrenne *Phénoménologie de l'expérience esthétique* (Paris: Presses Universitaires de France, 1953), pt 3, ch. 5; and R. Ingarden, 'A phenomenological aesthetics', *Journal of Aesthetics and Art Criticism*, vol. 23 (1974), p. 528.

38 Merleau-Ponty, in *Les Temps modernes*, vol. 8 (1952), p. 86.

39 On this point, see *EA*, pp. 332–3; M. Natanson, 'Toward a phenomenology of the aesthetic object', in *Literature, Phenomenology and the Social*

Sciences (The Hague: Nijhoff, 1962) pp. 83–5; Dufrenne, *Esthétique et Philosophie*, pp. 59–61.

40 *PP*, p. xi.

41 See Dufrenne, *Phénoménologie de l'expérience esthétique*, pp. 440 ff; *EA*, pp. 368 ff; Natanson, 'Toward a phenomonology', p. 97; Paul Ricoeur, *Finitude et culpabilité*, Paris: Aubier, 1960, p. 20; L. Binzwanger, *La Science des rêves*, p. 116.

42 See *EA*, pp. 531–2.

43 As advocates of a 'materialist' aesthetic, see Susan Sontag or Terry Eagleton. Notable exponents of an 'Idealist' aesthetic would include Kant, Croce, Collingwood and Hegel.

44 By extension, dialectical phenomenology ensures that the image is a communiqué to the other rather than a mirage of the self, that is, communication not negation. On this point, see *EA* pp. 364–5, and Dufrenne, *Phénoménologie de l'expérience esthétique*, pp. 443 ff. Both of these phenomenologists endorse three principal tenets derived from Merleau-Ponty's aesthetic: (1) that the aesthetic image is a primordial structure; (2) that the unity of aesthetic communication (between artist and audience) constitutes the unity of the aesthetic object; and (3) that imagination works in the form of a dialectical intentionality which uses an 'indirect language' to communicate to the public at large. Both, however, tend to prejudice their case by introducing a Kantian critical method instead of a presuppositionless phenomenological one. Indeed, in so far as their work remains phenomenological, it remains so in the form of an elaborate critical commentary on Merleau-Ponty rather than an original contribution. In fact, one could say that the main thrust of both works is to refute the 'idealist-dualist' premises of Sartre's phenomenology of imagination in favour of Merleau-Ponty's dialectical one: see *EA*, pp. 368 ff., and Dufrenne, *Phénoménologie de l'expérience esthétique*, pp. 276 ff.

45 Merleau–Ponty, *Adventures of the Dialectic*, p. 201.

Suggestions for further reading

Merleau-Ponty – unlike fellow French phenomenologists Sartre and Bachelard – did not devote any specific work, or set of works, to imagination. His main commentaries on the role of the imaginary are to be found scattered through *The Phenomenology of Perception*, trans. C. Smith (London/New York: Routledge/Humanities Press, 1962), and *The Visible and the Invisible*, trans. A. Lingis (Evanston, Ill.: Northwestern University Press, 1965). His polemical critique of Sartre's 'politics of the imaginary' is contained in a chapter entitled 'Sartre and Ultra-Bolshevism' in *Adventures of the Dialectic*, trans. J. Bien (New York: Heinemann, 1974). And his most comprehensive, if sometimes opaque, contribution to a phenomenology of art is doubtless *Eye and Mind*, trans. J. Edie in *The Primacy of Perception* (Evanston, Ill.: Northwestern University Press, 1964). The most impressive comparative analysis of the respective theories of imagination advanced by Sartre and Merleau-Ponty is E. Kaelin, *An Existentialist Aesthetic* (Madison, Wis.: University of Wisconsin Press, 1962).

5

The hermeneutical imagination (Ricoeur)

> Are we not ready to recognise in the power of imagination, no longer the faculty of deriving 'images' from our sensory experience, but the capacity for letting new worlds shape our understanding of ourselves? This power would not be conveyed by images, but by the emergent meanings in our language. Imagination would thus be treated as a dimension of language.
>
> (From 'Metaphor and the central problem of hermeneutics', in Paul Ricoeur, *Hermeneutics and the Human Sciences*, 1981, p. 181)

Most phenomenological accounts of imagination concentrated on its role as *vision*, as a special or modified way of *seeing* the world. Imagination is thus defined in terms of its relation to perception, be it positive or negative, continuous or discontinuous. Husserl describes the act of imagining as a 'neutralized' mode of seeing, Sartre as an 'unrealized' mode of quasi-seeing, and Merleau-Ponty as a dialectical counterpart of the visible.

This privileging of the visual model is no doubt related to the primary role granted to 'description' in the phenomenological method. With the hermeneutic turn in phenomenology, this privilege is significantly revised. As one moves from description to interpretation, from *Wesensschau* to *Verstehen*, the imagination is considered less in terms of 'vision' than in terms of 'language'. Or, to put it more exactly, imagination is assessed as an indispensable agent in the creation of meaning in and through language – what Paul Ricoeur calls 'semantic innovation'.

Ricoeur provides us with the most impressive example of such a hermeneutics of imagination. While his early works – *Freedom and*

Nature (1950) in particular – conformed to the descriptive conventions of eidetic phenomenology, the publication of *The Symbolism of Evil* in 1960 introduced a 'hermeneutic' model of analysis which opened up the possibility of a new appreciation of the linguistic functioning of imagination. This was to be the first of a number of works in which Ricoeur would explore the creative role of imagination in language – be it in the guise of symbols, myths, poems, narratives or ideologies. The following study proposes to isolate some of the key steps in Ricoeur's hermeneutic exploration of imagination – an exploration which, it should be noted at the outset, is less systematic than episodic in nature. Ricoeur's tentative and always provisional probing of a poetic hermeneutic of imagination represents, I believe, the ultimate, if discreet, agenda of his philosophical project. That, at least, is the hypothesis that guides my reading of his work below – my own hermeneutic wager regarding his hermeneutic wager.

The link between imagination and language had been hinted at by phenomenological thinkers prior to Ricoeur. Bachelard's suggestive remarks about a linguistic imagination in *The Poetics of Reverie* already pointed in this direction – while not actually delivering any comprehensive or coherent theory. But the most decisive prelude to Ricoeur's hermeneutic reformulation of imagining was surely Martin Heidegger's analysis of the Kantian concept of 'transcendental imagination' in *Kant and the Problem of Metaphysics* (1929) – a 'destructive' rereading of *The Critique of Pure Reason* from the point of view of an existential hermeneutic. As I have already devoted considerable attention to the Heideggerian interpretation of transcendental imagination in previous works – *Poétique du Possible* (1984) and *The Wake of Imagination* (1988) – suffice it to say briefly here that Heidegger's controversial reading opened the way for a hermeneutic re-examination of imagining. This entailed a radical enlargement of the range of application traditionally accorded to the term 'imagination' – including ontological considerations of action, time and language. But, so doing, it also posed disconcerting questions for the inherited metaphysical conceptions of Being. Referring to Kant's claim for a 'pure productive imagination', independent of experience, which first renders experience possible, Heidegger explains that Being must henceforth be understood as a temporal horizon of human existence (*Dasein*). 'The imagination', he writes, 'forms in advance and before all experience of the object, the aspect in the pure form (*Bild*) of time and precedes this or that particular experience of an object.' And he adds: 'As a faculty of intuition, imagination is formative in the sense that it produces a particular image. As a faculty not dependent on objects of intuition, it produces i.e. forms and provides, images. This "formative power" is at one and the same time receptive and productive (spontaneous). In this "at one and the same" is to be found the true essence of the structure of imagination.'[1] Moreover, since for Heidegger receptivity is identified with sensibility and spontaneity with understanding, imagination can now be ultimately understood as the source of all human knowledge – or, as Kant put it, the 'common root' of the two stems of sensible and intelligible experience. But the subversive implications of this discovery were, Heidegger argues, to prove intolerable for Kant – who revised his initial claims in the second edition of *The Critique of Pure Reason* – and for subsequent metaphysicians who stubbornly clung to the traditional divide of knowledge into sensation (the empirical-corporeal-aesthetic) and understanding (the analytic-logical-conceptual).

The fact is, however, that Heidegger himself does not develop these insights under the heading of a new hermeneutic of *imagination*. When he speaks of imagination he does so exclusively in the Kantian context. And the fact that its functions are subsumed, in Heidegger's other works, into the more generic and 'fundamental' term *Dasein* means effectively that a hermeneutics of imagining is ultimately abandoned in favour of a hermeneutics of existence in general. Though the parallels remain highly instructive, we would have to await the later works of Paul Ricoeur for a properly hermeneutical treatment of imagination. What is indisputable is that Heidegger's rereading of the Kantian concept of imagination blazed the trail for the subsequent hermeneutic acknowledgement of imagination as a pathway leading to, rather than away from, the truth of being.

The fact, however, that the term 'hermeneutic' did not feature in the post-Heideggerian phenomenologies of imagination up to Ricoeur did not, as we saw, prevent the analyses of imagining proposed by Sartre, Merleau-Ponty and Bachelard from registering the influence of Heidegger's radical ontological concerns.[2] But the first phenomenologists after Heidegger actually to espouse a hermeneutic method in name as well as in deed were Hans-Georg Gadamer in Germany and Paul Ricoeur in France. With respect to a hermeneutic of imagining, which specifically concerns us here, it was Ricoeur who made the most incisive intervention. Gadamer, though much preoccupied with problems of art, creativity and aesthetics, has not yet, to my knowledge, addressed the cooncept of imagination directly or comprehensively; it is, for example, only mentioned in two brief passages of his *opus magnus, Truth and Method* (1960), and these both refer to Kant's treatment of this term.[3] This may have been due to a strategic resolve on Gadamer's part to avoid identification with the German Idealist and Romantic movements – characterized by the extravagant claims made for the 'productive imagination' by thinkers such as Schelling, Fichte and Jacobi. Or it could have been prompted by a fidelity to his two main philosophical mentors – Hegel and Heidegger – both of whom sublated the formative (*bildende*) and projective (*entwerfende*) powers of imagining into more inclusive concepts such as *Geist* or *Dasein*. Either way, Gadamer's conspicuous omission of any substantial hermeneutic treatment of imagination *per se* accounts for my present omission of him (apart from occasional references) in this work. It is my view that Ricoeur's hermeneutic discussion of the imaginative function – ranging from *Le Symbolique du mal* (1960) and *La Métaphore vive* (1975) to *Temps et récit* (3 vols, 1983–5), *Ideology and Utopia* (1986) and *Du texte à l'action* (1986) – represents the singlemost direct reorientation of a phenomenology of imagining towards a hermeneuties of imagining.

The linguistic imagination

In so far as hermeneutics is concerned with multiple levels of meaning, it is evident that images can no longer be adequately understood in terms of their immediate *appearance* to consciousness. Replacing the visual model of the image with the verbal, Ricoeur – like Bachelard – affirms the more *poetical* role of imagining: that is, its ability to say one thing in terms of another, or to say several things at the same time, thereby creating something *new*. The crucial role played by imagination in this process of 'semantic innovation' was to become one of the abiding concerns of Ricoeur's later philosophy.

The problem of semantic innovation remained unresolved for Sartre who, as noted, argued in *L'Imaginaire* that imagination was condemned to an 'essential poverty'. The imaginary could not teach us anything new since it was held to be a 'nothingness' projected by consciousness. The cognitive content of an image presupposed our prior contact with the perceptual world (from which all our knowledge arises). The imaginary world, for Sartre, is a *negation* of the perceptual world. It is not a simultaneous juxtaposing of two different worlds which produces a new meaning, as Ricoeur would hold.

137

Before proceeding to a more detailed account of Ricoeur's own original contribution to the philosophy of imagination, it may be useful first to cite Ricoeur's critical summary of the available theories of images and imagining. In an essay entitled 'L'imagination dans le discours et dans l'action' in *Du texte à l'action* (1986), Ricoeur adverts to the problematic and often confused nature of modern philosophies of the image. He argues that the radical equivocity at the very heart of the imaginative activity has led to a series of rival, and often mutually exclusive, accounts. These accounts are located by Ricoeur in terms of two opposite axes. On the one hand, they explain the process of imagining in terms of the *object*: a typical example of this being Hume's empiricist account of the image as a faded trace of perception, a weakened impression preserved and represented in memory. Towards this pole of explanation gravitate the theories of the *reproductive* imagination. On the other hand, we find theories which explain our imaginative activity in terms of the *subject*, that is, in terms of a human consciousness that is fascinated or freed by its own images. An example of this latter theory would be the German Idealist and Romantic accounts of the *productive* imagination from Kant and Schelling to the existentialist descriptions of Sartre in *L'Imaginaire*. But this basic distinction between the reproductive and productive roles of imagination does not resolve the aporetic nature of our inherited understanding of imagining. Ricoeur extends the problematic horizons of this debate as follows:

> The productive imagination, and even the reproductive to the extent that it comprises the minimal initiative concerning the evocation of something absent, operates ... according to whether the subject of imagination is capable or not of assuming a critical consciousness of the difference between the real and the imaginary. The theories of the image here divide up along an axis which is no longer noematic but noetic, and whose variations are regulated by degrees of belief. At one end of the axis, that of a non-critical consciousness, the image is confused with the real, mistaken for the real. This is the power of the lie or error denounced by Pascal; and it is also, *mutatis mutandis*, the *imaginatio* of Spinoza, contaminated by belief for as long as a contrary belief has not dislodged it from its primary position. At the other end of the axis, where the critical distance is fully conscious of itself, imagination is the very instrument of the critique of reality. The transcendental reduction of Husserl, as a neutralization of existence,

is the most complete instance of this. The variations of meaning along this second axis are no less ample than the above. What after all could be in common between the *state of confusion* which characterizes that consciousness which unknown to itself takes for real what for another consciousness is not real, and the *act of distinction* which, highly self-conscious, enables consciousness to posit something at a distance from the real and thus produce the alterity at the very heart of existence?

Such is the knot of aporias which is revealed by an overview of the ruins which today constitute the theory of imagination. Do these aporias themselves betray a fault in the philosophy of imagination or the structural feature of imagination itself which it would be the task of philosophy to take account of?[4]

Ricoeur appears to answer yes to both parts of the question. The 'fault', in other words, of most philosophies of imagination to date has been their failure to develop a properly hermeneutic account of imagining in terms of its most basic structural feature of semantic innovation.

The adoption of hermeneutics – as the 'art of deciphering indirect meanings' – acknowledges the *symbolizing* power of imagination. This power, to transform given meanings into new ones, enables one to construe the future as the 'possible theatre of my liberty', as a horizon of hope. The implications of this approach are crucial. The age-old antagonism between will and necessity (or, in Sartre's terms, between *l'imaginaire* and *le réel*) is now seen to be surmountable. 'We have thought too much', observes Ricoeur, 'in terms of a will which submits and not enough in terms of an imagination which opens up.'[5]

Ricoeur's preference for a semantic model of imagination over a visual one makes possible a new appreciation of this properly creative role of imagination. If images are *spoken* before they are *seen*, as Ricoeur maintains, they can no longer be construed as quasi-material residues of perception (as empiricism believed), nor indeed as neutralizations or negations of perception (as eidetic phenomenology tended to believe). Ricoeur's privileging of the semantic functioning of images illustrates his conviction that the productive power of imagination is primarily verbal. The example of a verbal metaphor in poetry epitomizes the way in which imagination conjoins two semantic fields, making what is predicatively impertinent at a literal level into something predicatively pertinent at a new (poetic) level. Or to use Ricoeur's graphic phrase:

'Imagination comes into play in that moment when a new meaning emerges from out of the ruins of the literal interpretation.'[6]

Taking up Aristotle's definition of a good metaphor in the *Poetics* (1495a: 4–8) as the apprehension of *similarity*, Ricoeur points out that what is meant here is not similarity between already similar ideas (for such a role would be redundant) but similarity between semantic fields hitherto considered *dissimilar*. It is the 'semantic shock' engendered by the coming together of two different meanings which produces a *new* meaning. And imagination, Ricoeur claims, is precisely this power of metaphorically reconciling opposing meanings, forging an unprecedented semantic pertinence from an old impertinence. So that if one wants to say with Wittgenstein, for example, that imagining is a 'seeing-as' (seeing one thing in terms of another) this is only the case in so far as the linguistic power of conjoining different semantic fields is already at work – at least implicitly.

This is a decisive point. Ricoeur claims that what matters in imagination is less the *content* than the *function* of images. This specific function is understood here both in terms of an intentional projection of possible meanings (the phenomenological–hermeneutic model) and a schematizing synthesis of the many under the guise of the same (the Kantian model). It is this twin function of projection and schematism which accounts for imagination as 'the operation of grasping the similar in a predicative assimilation responding to a semantic clash between dissimilar meanings'.[7] Ricoeur thus links the productive power of language and that of imagination. For new meanings to come into being they need to be spoken or uttered in the form of new verbal images. And this requires that the phenomenological account of imagining as *appearance* be supplemented by its hermeneutic account as *meaning*.

Imagination can be recognized accordingly as the act of responding to a demand for new meaning, the demand of emerging realities to *be* by *being said* in new ways. And it is for this reason that Ricoeur frequently invokes Bachelard's famous phrase that 'a poetic image, by its novelty, sets in motion the entire linguistic mechanism. The poetic image places us at the origin of the speaking being.'[8]

A poetic imagination is one which creates meaning by responding to the desire of being to be expressed. It is a Janus facing in two directions at once – back to the being that is revealed and forward to the language that is revealing. And at the level of language itself it also does double duty, for it produces a text which opens up new horizons of meaning for the reader. The poetic imagination liberates the reader into a free space of possibility, suspending the reference to the immediate world of perception (both the author's and the reader's) and thereby disclosing 'new ways of being in the world'.[9] The function of 'semantic innovation' – which is most proper to imagination – is therefore, in its most fundamental sense, an *ontological* event. The innovative power of linguistic imagination is not some 'decorative excess or effusion of subjectivity, but the capacity of language to open up new worlds.'[10] The function of imagination in poetry or myth, for example, is defined as the 'disclosure of unprecedented worlds, an opening onto possible worlds which transcend the limits of our actual world'.[11]

To account for this phenomenon of ontological novelty, Ricoeur's hermeneutics of imagination looks beyond the first-order reference of empirical reality – which ordinary language discourse normally entails – to a second-order reference of possible worlds. A hermeneutic approach to imagination thus differs from a structuralist or existentialist one in its concentration on 'the capacity of world-disclosure yielded by texts'. In short, hermeneutics is not confined to the *objective* structural analysis of texts, nor to the *subjective* existential analysis of the authors of texts; its primary concern is with the *worlds* which these authors and texts open up.[12]

An understanding of the possible worlds uncovered by the poetic imagination also permits a new understanding of ourselves as beings-in-the-world. But, for Ricoeur, the hermeneutic circle precludes any short cut to immediate self-understanding. The human subject can only come to know itself through the hermeneutic detour of interpreting signs – that is, by deciphering the meanings contained in myths, symbols and dreams produced by the human imagination. The shortest route from the self to itself is through the images of others.

The hermeneutic imagination is not confined, however, to circles of *interpretation*. By projecting new worlds it also provides us with projects of *action*. In fact the traditional opposition between *theoria* and *praxis* dissolves to the extent that 'imagination has a projective function which pertains to the very dynamism of action.'[13] The metaphors, symbols or narratives produced by imagination all provide us with 'imaginative variations' of the world, thereby offering us the freedom to conceive of the world in other ways and to undertake forms of action which might lead to its transformation. Semantic innovation can thus point towards social transformation. The possible worlds of imagination can be made real by action. This is surely what Ricoeur has in mind when he says that there can be 'no action without imagination'. We shall return to this crucial aspect of Ricoeur's argument in our discussion of the 'social imagination' below.

The symbolic imagination

Having outlined the key features of Ricoeur's hermeneutic account of imagination, I now propose to take a more systematic approach by examining four categories which broadly correspond to consecutive phases in the later philosophy of Paul Ricoeur: (1) *The Symbolic Imagination*; (2) *The Oneiric Imagination*; (3) *The Poetic Imagination*; (4) *The Social Imagination*.

The publication of *Le Symbolique du mal* in 1960 marked Ricoeur's transition from a phenomenology of will to a hermeneutics of symbol. It signalled a departure from descriptive phenomenology, as a reflection on intentional modes of consciousness, towards the hermeneutic conviction that meaning is never simply the intuitive possession of a subject but is always mediated through signs and symbols of our intersubjective existence. Henceforth an understanding of consciousness would involve an interpretation of culture.

In *The Symbolism of Evil*, Ricoeur shows that a rigorous interpretation of the founding myths of Western culture (for example, Adam, Prometheus, Oedipus) enables us to disclose the symbolic relation of the human subject to meaning. Suspending the conventional definition of myth as a 'false *explanation* by means of fables', Ricoeur attempts to recover myth's genuinely *exploratory* function. Once we accept that myth cannot and does not provide us with a scientific account of the way things really are, we can begin properly to appreciate its creative role as a *symbolizing* power.

What is a symbol for Ricoeur? A symbol is a double intentionality, wherein one meaning is transgressed or transcended by another. As such, it is a work of imagination which enables being to emerge as language (signification) and, by extension, as thought (interpretation). Whence Ricoeur's famous hermeneutic maxim 'Le symbole donne à penser'. There are three principal categories of symbol examined by Ricoeur: *cosmic, oneiric* and *poetic*.

(*a*)   Cosmic symbols refer to a human's primary act of reading the sacred *on* the world. Here the human imagination interprets aspects of the world – the heavens, the sun, the moon, the waters – *as* signs of some ultimate meaning. At this most basic level, the symbol is both a thing and a sign: it embodies and signifies the sacred at one and the same time.[14] Or, to put it in another way, when dealing with cosmic symbols the imagination reads the things of the world as signs, and signs as things of the world. As such, the symbolic imagination is already, at least implicitly, *linguistic*. Ricoeur makes this clear in the following passage from *Freud and Philosophy*: 'These symbols are not inscribed *beside* language, as modes of immediate expression, directly perceptible visages; it is in the universe of discourse that these realities take on a symbolic dimension. Even when it is the elements of the world that carry the symbol – earth, sky, water, life – it is the word (of consecration, invocation or mythic narrative) which *says* their cosmic expressivity thanks to the double meaning of the *words* earth, sky, water, life' (that is, their obvious literal meaning as reference to things *and* their ulterior meaning, for example, water as a symbol of renewed spiritual life). Ricoeur can thus affirm that the 'expressivity of the world comes to language through the symbol as double meaning'.[15] For a cosmic symbol – like any other kind – occurs whenever 'language produces composite signs where the meaning, not content to designate something directly, points to another meaning which can only be reached (indirectly) by means of this designation'.[16] Illustrating this linguistic property of symbols, Ricoeur comments on the phrase from the Psalms, 'The skies tell of the glory of God', as follows: 'The skies don't speak themselves; rather, they are spoken by the prophet, by the hymn, by the liturgy. One always needs the word to assume the world into a manifestation of the sacred (hierophany).'[17] And here he cites the view of the structural anthropologist Dumézil that 'it is under the sign of the *logos* and not under that of *mana* that research in the history of religions takes its stand today' (preface to M. Éliade, *Traité d'histoire des religions*).

(*b*)   In the second category of symbols – the oneiric or dream image – we witness a shift from the cosmic to the psychic function of imagination. Here Ricoeur talks of complementing a phenomenology of religious symbols (à la Éliade) with a psychoanalysis of unconscious symbols. To this end, he invokes the works of Freud and Jung who investigated links between the symbols of the individual unconscious and symbols as 'common representations of the culture or folklore of humanity as a whole'.[18] Ricoeur spells out the rapport between cosmic and oneiric symbols as follows: 'To manifest the "sacred" *on* the "cosmos" and to manifest it *in* the "psyche" are the same thing ... Cosmos and psyche are two poles of the same "expressivity": I express myself in expressing the world.'[19] It is precisely this expressive function of the psychic or oneiric image which establishes its intimate relation to language. As Ricoeur remarks, dream images must be 'originally close to words since they can be told, communicated.'[20]

(c) The third modality of symbols – the 'poetic imagination' – completes the double 'expressivity' of cosmos and psyche. It is here that the creative powers of imagination are most evident and receive explicit acknowledgement from Ricoeur. In fact it is only in this third category that Ricoeur (in *The Symbolism of Evil*) uses the term 'imagination' in any systematic sense. It is the poetical perspective, he argues, which enables us to draw back from both the religious images of cosmology and the dream images of psychoanalysis, disclosing the symbolic function of the image *per se* in its nascent state. In poetry, Ricoeur maintains, the symbol reveals the welling-up of language – 'language in a state of emergence' – instead of regarding it in its hieratic stability under the protection of rites and myths as in the history of religion, or instead of deciphering it through the resurgences of a suppressed infancy.[21] In this sense, the poetical is the epitome of the symbolic imagination.

Ricoeur insists, however, that these three levels of symbolism are not unconnected. The structure of poetic imagination is also that of the dream as it draws from fragments of our past and future; and it is also at bottom that of hierophanies which disclose the heavens and the earth as images of the sacred. In all three instances what is at issue is not the image-as-representation but the image-as-sign. Ricoeur returns to this crucial distinction again and again. In *The Symbolism of Evil* he does so in terms of a differentiation between the static image as 'portrait' and the dynamic image as 'expression'. In *Freud and Philosophy* he uses the opposition *image-representation* and *image-verb*. But, whatever the particular formulation, what Ricoeur is concerned with is a critique of the representational model of the image as a mere negation of perceptual reality. This critique is levelled most explicitly at Sartre.

The following passage from the introduction to *The Symbolism of Evil* makes this clear: 'It is necessary firmly to distinguish imagination from image, if by image is understood a function of absence, the annulment of the real in an imaginary unreal. This image-representation, conceived on the model of a portrait of the absent, is still too dependent on the thing that it makes unreal; it remains a process for *making present* to oneself the things of the world. A poetic image is much closer to a word than to a portrait.'[22] To be fair to Sartre, however, one would have to recall that, while most of his examples of the 'unrealizing' function of imaging are drawn from visual representation (picturing Peter in Berlin, the portrait of King Charles, and so on), he does go to pains to establish the image as a dynamic act of consciousness rather than a quasi-perceptual thing in consciousness. But, that said, it is true that he, like Husserl before him, fails adequately to grasp the fact that signification and imagination are not two opposed modes of intentionality but are inextricably related through their common belonging to language. It is for this reason that Ricoeur clearly prefers the position of Bachelard, which he approvingly cites: 'The poetic image becomes a new being of our language, it expresses us in making us that which it expresses.'[23]

The essential point to retain from Ricoeur's hermeneutic analysis of the three kinds of symbol – cosmic, oneiric and poetic – is that they all find expression in a *linguistic* imagination. This is stated most succinctly in *Freud and Philosophy* when Ricoeur affirms that 'it is always in language that the cosmos, that desire, and that the imaginary, come into words'.[24]

There is no doubt that *The Symbolism of Evil* concentrates on the first category of symbol – the cosmic. This initial phase of the hermeneutic project is described by Ricoeur as a 're-enactment in sympathetic imagination' of the foundational myths where Western man sought to communicate his first experiences of the cosmos. Myths are understood as symbolic stories – or, to be more precise, as 'species of symbols developed in the form of narration and articulated in a time and a space that cannot be co-ordinated with the time and space of history and geography'.[25] This hermeneutic act of sympathetically re-imagining the cosmic images of our foundational myths demands that Ricoeur abandon the original phenomenological dream of a 'philosophy with-out presuppositions'. Indeed, it presupposes that which descriptive phenomenology often tended to ignore – language. The hermeneutics of symbols must begin from a full language, that is, from the recognition that before reflection and intuition *there are already symbols*. 'It is by beginning with a symbolism already there', as Ricoeur notes, 'that we give ourselves something to think about.'[26]

This hermeneutic task of recovering language in its symbolic full-ness is, for Ricoeur, a singularly modern one. It is precisely because language has become so formalized, transparent and technical in the contemporary era that the need is all the greater to rediscover lan-guage's inventive powers of symbolization. This is not a matter of nostalgia for a lost Atlantis. It is a task animated by the 'hope for a re-creation of language'.[27] And it also involves a critical project. For it is only by demythologizing the abuses of myth (as a false explanation of reality) that we can remythologize our contemporary language – restore to it the poetic and symbolic powers of imagi-nation. 'The dissolution of the myth as (false) explanation is the necessary way to restoration of the myth as symbolism,' writes Ricoeur. If demythologization is the possible gain of modern attention to objec-tive truth, this should not prevent the positive hermeneutic task of reunifying the various fields of meaning by renewing 'contact with the fundamental symbols of consciousness'.[28] In short, we need to combine the critical gesture of modernity with the symbolizing gesture of myth if we are to develop an adequate hermeneutic of human imagination. Instead of adopting the reductive approach of an 'alle-gorical' reading – which would seek to uncover a disguised message beneath the image-symbols of myth – Ricoeur advances a hermeneutic imagination which would, on the contrary, 'start from the symbols and endeavor to promote the meaning, to form it, by means of crea-tive interpretation'.[29] This is, I suspect, what Ricoeur has in mind when he suggests that it is by 'interpreting that we can hear again'.

The oneiric imagination

Whereas Ricoeur concerned himself in *The Symbolism of Evil* with one particular field of symbols – those related primarily to mythic accounts of evil – in *Freud and Philosophy* he enlarges the inquiry to analyse the 'epistemology of the symbol' as it manifests itself in the desires of the unconscious.[30] The dream image shows, in exemplary fashion, how we can say things other than what we are ostensibly saying; how behind direct meanings there are indirect ones. Because of this double intentionality, symbols are what make 'poets of every dreamer'.[31]

The poet is the dreamer writ large. And what is important here is the suggestion that symbols are essentially 'image-words' which traverse 'image-representations'. Imagination is not simply a 'power of images' to represent absent objects. The visual images of dreams are sensory vehicles for verbal images which transcend them and designate *other* meanings than the literal ones. Thus psychoanalysis recognized that dream images call forth narrative interpretation. It is precisely because dreams – like myths and poems – operate according to a depth language of double meanings that they can be recounted and deciphered. Dreams want to tell themselves. They give rise to speech, to narration, to thought. The dreamer feels closed off in a private world until the dream is recounted. And this power of recounting is exemplified, for Ricoeur, in the poetic imagination which exposes the 'birth of the word such as it was buried within the enigmas of . . . the psyche'.[32]

But, if poetry represents the positive pole of dreams, dissimulation represents its negative pole. The basic hermeneutic lesson to be gleaned from dreams, according to Ricoeur, is that images can serve to *mask* as well as to disclose meanings. The work of dream images provides ample evidence of the fact that the symbolic levels of sense are far more complex and oblique than the traditional models of analogy and allegory would allow. Along with Marx and Nietzsche, Freud was to champion a modern *hermeneutics of suspicion*, alert to the distorting and falsifying potential of images. Each of these three 'masters of suspicion', as Ricoeur calls them, approached images as devices for concealing hidden motivations. For Nietzsche this was the will to power, for Marx class struggle, and for Freud the neurotic repression of desire. The last developed the method of psychoanalysis, accordingly, as a means of detecting the censoring function of dream images – the primary function of this method being to 'disclose the variety of elaborate procedures which interpose between apparent and latent meanings'.[33]

Psychoanalysis calls for the hermeneutic function of critical interpretation by showing how images are not innocent, how they conceal as well as reveal meaning, how they deform as well as disclose intentions. It is the double texture of dream images – the internal transgression of one meaning by another – that invites our critical interpretation. Or, as Ricoeur puts it, 'every *mythos* carries a latent *logos* which demands to be exposed – where someone dreams . . . another rises up to interpret'.[34]

But, if psychoanalysis promotes a hermeneutics of *suspicion*, it also points towards a hermeneutics of *affirmation*. While the former examines how images disguise meanings drawn from our private or collective past, by means of an 'archaeological' reference back to an experience which precedes them, the latter shows how dream images can open up new dimensions of meaning by virtue of a 'teleological' reference to new worlds of possibility. Because desire is the basic motivation of all such dream images, as Freud argued, these images are ways of *saying* this desire. And they do this either by dissimulating it in other guises or by expressing a passion for possibilities not yet realized.

In so far as this second option is concerned, the desire of dream images invents a future and thus aspires to a condition of creation, *poiesis*, poetry. It generates a surplus of meaning (*surcroît du sens*).[35] And this surplus is proof of a level of meaning which is irreducible to a retrospective correspondence between the image of one's dream and a literal event of one's past experience. Or, as Bachelard put it, 'you cannot explain the flower by the fertilizer'. It is this productive power of images – which Freud recognized in the *eros* of dreams – which ensures that any adequate hermeneutic of imagination must extend beyond an 'archaeology of the unconscious' to include both a 'teleology of desire' and an 'eschatology of the sacred'.

In *The Conflict of Interpretations* (1969), Ricoeur elaborates on this dual function of the hermeneutic imagination – as *recollection* and *projection*. He writes: 'We may fully comprehend the hermeneutic problem if we are able to grasp the double dependence of the self on the [symbolic images of the] *unconscious* and the *sacred* – since this dependence is only made manifest through the modality of symbolism. In order to illustrate this double dependency, reflection must humble consciousness and interpret it through symbolic significations, rising up from *behind* or in *front* of consciousness, *beneath* or *beyond* it. In short, reflection must include an archaeology and an eschatology.'[36]

Ricoeur argues, moreover, that prophecy needs demystification. By unmasking the falsifying function of certain dream images, with the help of a psychoanalytic model of 'suspicion', we may find ourselves in a better position to restore aspects of these images as 'signs of the sacred'. Without the hermeneutic detour of suspicion we would not be able to discriminate between those images which are merely a 'return of the repressed' (in Freud's phrase) and those which serve as symbols of an eschatological horizon of possibility. But it is rarely a simple matter of discriminating between regressive images on the one hand and progressive images on the other. Every utopian image contains an archaic element and vice versa. Images of the mythic past are often used to allude prophetically to an *eschaton* still to come. And the eschatology of imagination is always, as Ricoeur puts it, a creative repetition of its archaeology. 'The progressive order of symbols is not external to the regressive order of phantasms. In plunging into the archaic mythologies of the unconscious new signs of the sacred rise up.'[37]

A critical hermeneutic of imagination, for Ricoeur, is one which demystifies the dissimulating property of phantasms in order to release the symbolizing power of images. Idols must be unmasked so that symbols may speak. And an additional reminder which hermeneutics receives from psychoanalysis is that the images of the unconscious are charged with multiple associations which are irreducible to the level of a one-to-one conceptual correspondence. They provoke rational interpretation; but the rational interpretation can never exhaust them. For, even when infantile or archaic images are deciphered in terms of their regressive reference to the past, there always remains a *surplus* which points towards an inexhaustible creativity of meaning. This is where Ricoeur locates his wager that new meanings *can* emerge, that things as they are *can* change. 'Liberty according to hope', he writes in *The Conflict of Interpretations*, 'is nothing other when understood psychologically, than this creative imagining of the possible.'[38]

It is this double axis of archaeological and eschatological reference which signals the failure of all theories which seek to reduce the oneiric imagination to a system of speculative reason. We are reminded that there is always more to imagination than has ever been dreamed of in our philosophies. Moreover, it is due to this *excess* of imagination over reason that symbols call forth a multiplicity of meanings which in turn give rise to a multiplicity of readings – psychoanalytic (Freud), religious (Éliade), philosophical (Hegel). This is why a hermeneutic of imagination culminates not in absolute knowledge but in an endless conflict of interpretations.

The poetical imagination

Having concentrated on a hermeneutics of mythic and oneiric symbols in his three major works of the sixties – *The Symbolism of Evil, Freud and*

Philosophy and *The Conflict of Interpretations* – Ricoeur devoted much of his attention in the seventies and eighties to the 'poetical' expressions of imagination. This more recent phase of Ricoeur's hermeneutic project includes *The Rule of Metaphor* (1975) as well as his three-volume *Time and Narrative* (1984–5). Ricoeur comments on this phase as follows: 'In *The Rule of Metaphor* I try to show how language could extend itself to its very limits forever discovering new resonances within itself. The term *vive* in the French title *La Métaphore Vive* is all important, for it was my purpose to demonstrate that there is not just an epistemological and political imagination, but also, and perhaps more fundamentally, a *linguistic imagination* which generates and regenerates meaning through the living powers of metaphoricity.' And of his three-volume study of narrative he adds: '*Time and Narrative* develops this inquiry into the inventive power of language. Here the analysis of narrative operations in a literary text, for instance, can teach us how we formulate a new structure of "time" by creating new modes of plot and characterization ... how narrativity, as the construction or deconstruction of paradigms of story-telling, is a perpetual search for new ways of expressing human time, a production or creation of meaning.'[39]

In *The Rule of Metaphor*, as in other works, Ricoeur deals with imagination in a fragmentary rather than systematic fashion. It is, as it were, a hidden prompter guiding and motivating his delivery without ever occupying centre stage in the process of explication. Describing the innovative power of metaphorical imagination in terms of the ability to establish similarity in dissimilarity, Ricoeur points out that he has now progressed from an analysis of the creative tension between meanings in words (symbols) to that between meanings in sentences (metaphors). Or, to put it in another way, in metaphor the productive unit is no longer the *word* but the *sentence*. It is at the level of the sentence that metaphor expresses the power of imagination to create a new semantic unit out of two different ideas. 'It is in the moment of the emergence of a new meaning from the ruins of literal predication that imagination offers its specific mediation.'[40]

In this context Ricoeur tenders one of his most useful formulations of the distinction between verbal and non-verbal imagination. Borrowing Kant's terminology, he identifies the former with the productive imagination and the latter with the reproductive. 'Would not imagination have something to do with the conflict between identity and difference?' he asks. And he makes it clear that he is not speaking here of 'imagination in its sensible, quasi-sensual aspect' – the *non-verbal* imagination. On the contrary, he argues that the 'only way to approach the problem of imagination from the perspective of a semantic theory, that is to say on a verbal plane, is to begin with productive imagination in the Kantian sense, and to put off reproductive imagination or imagery as long as possible. Treated as a schema, the image presents a verbal dimension; before being the gathering-point of faded perceptions, it is that of emerging meanings.' Placing himself thus in the camp of Kant rather than of Hume, Ricoeur goes on to explain that the metaphor works in the same way as the schema in so far as it functions as 'the matrix of a new semantic pertinence that is born out of the dismantling of semantic networks caused by the shock of contradiction'. The metaphoric function of imagination involves a verbal aspect to the extent that it involves 'grasping identity within differences', establishing the 'relatedness of terms far apart' in such a way that they confront each other rather than fuse together. This schematism of metaphor 'turns imagination into the place where the figurative meaning emerges in the interplay of identity and difference'.[41]

And yet the imagination needs images. Without any visual aspect, the verbal imagination would remain an invisible productivity. So what remains to be demonstrated is the sensible moment of metaphoric imagination. And this is where Ricoeur calls for a (phenomenological) psychology of *seeing-as* to complement a semantics of creative *saying*. If the productive imagination were confined to a purely verbal innovation, it would cease to be *imagination*. Ricoeur seeks accordingly to graft a psychology of the imaginary on to a semantic theory of metaphor. 'Seeing-as' provides a key as the sensible aspect of poetic imagination. It holds sense and image together in an intuitive manner. It selects from the quasi-sensory mass of imagery, producing a certain semantic order. And it can also work contrariwise to bring conceptual meaning to intuitive fullness, as in the example of reading: 'The *seeing as* activated in reading ensures the joining of verbal meaning with imagistic fullness. And this conjunction is no longer something outside language since it can be reflected as a relationship. *Seeing as* contains a ground, a foundation, this is precisely, resemblance.' Ricoeur can thus conclude that seeing-as plays the role of a schema which unites the *empty* concept and the *blind* impression: 'Thanks to its character as half thought and half experience, it joins the light of sense with the fullness of the image. In this way, the non-verbal and the verbal are firmly united at the core of the image-ing function of language.'[42]

But the metaphorical imagination not only combines the verbal and the non-verbal; it also produces a new meaning by confronting a literal with a figurative sense. This *tensional* theory of metaphor is most obvious in the case of a living metaphor such as Hopkins's 'Oh! The mind has mountains', where a literal *is not* (the reader knows that literally the mind does not have mountains) is accompanied by a metaphorical *is*. This power to transform contradiction into new meaning is evident in the metaphorical function of seeing x as y – for while we know x is not y, at a literal level, we affirm that it *is* it, at an imaginative level. Metaphor is living by virtue of the fact that it introduces the spark of imagination into a 'thinking more' (*penser plus*).[43] And this thinking more – which is at root a saying-seeing more – attests to the curious paradox that the 'concept of imagination, in the context of a theory of metaphor centred around the notion of semantic innovation' is also a 'logic of *discovery*'.[44]

Having brought his semantic theory of imagination to its limits – to the frontier of exchange between *saying* and *seeing as* – Ricoeur invokes once again Bachelard's phenomenology of imagination as an avenue to explore the ontological depths of this interaction between the verbal and non-verbal: 'Bachelard has taught us that the image is not a residue of impression, but an aura surrounding speech ... The poem gives birth to the image'; the poetic image 'is at once a becoming of expression and a becoming of our being. Here expression creates being ... one could not meditate in a zone that preceded language.'[45] The poetic image thus points to the very 'depths of existence' where 'a new being in language' is synonymous with a 'growth in being' itself. It is because there is poetical imagination that words dream being.

The hermeneutic analysis of imagination's role in the metaphorical play of language leads Ricoeur to the ontological paradox of *creation-as-discovery*. 'Through the recovery of the capacity of language to create and recreate, we *discover* reality itself in the process of being *created* ... Language in the making celebrates reality in the making.'[46] Ricoeur can thus conclude that 'the strategy of discourse implied in metaphorical languages is ... to shatter and to increase our sense of reality by shattering and increasing our language...with metaphor we experience the metamorphosis of both language and reality'.[47] At this point in his reflections on metaphor Ricoeur approximates to the Aristotle of the *Poetics*, for whom it was vain to ask whether 'the universal that poetry "teaches", already existed *before* it was *invented*. It is as much found as invented.'[48]

In *Time and Narrative*, Ricoeur develops some of these ontological implications of 'metaphorical' reference. He shows how poetical language – be it lyrical or narrative – reveals a capacity for non-descriptive reference which exceeds the immediate reference of our everyday language. While poetical reference suspends literal reference and thereby appears to make language refer only to itself (as the structuralists argued), it in fact reveals a deeper and more radical power of reference to those ontological aspects of our being-in-the-world that cannot be spoken of *directly*. *Seeing as* thus not only implies a *saying as* but also a *being as*. Ricoeur relates this power of poetic imagination to redescribe and reinvent being to the narrative power of 'emplotment' (*mise-en-intrigue*). Borrowing François Dagognet's term *iconic augmentation*, he points out that the role of the image or *Bild* is to bring about an increase in the being of our world impoverished by quotidian routine. 'We owe a large part of the enlarging of our horizon of existence to poetic works. Far from producing only weakened images of reality – shadows, as in the Platonic treatment of the *eikon* in painting or writing (*Phaedrus* 274e–77e) – literary works depict reality by *augmenting* it with meanings that themselves depend upon the virtues of abbreviation, saturation and culmination, so strikingly illustrated by emplotment.'[49]

Ricoeur here rejoins the ontological hermeneutics of Heidegger and Gadamer which, in contradistinction to Romantic hermeneutics, aims less at restoring the author's intention than at making explicit the movement by which the text unfolds a world in front of itself.[50] The poetical imagination at work in a text is one which augments my power of being-in-the-world: '. . . what is interpreted in a text is the proposing of a world that I might inhabit and into which I might project my ownmost powers.'[51] Ricoeur thus places the referential capacity of narrative works under those of poetic works in general. For if the poetic metaphor redescribes the world, 'poetic narrative resignifies the world in its temporal dimension to the extent that narrating, telling, reciting is a way of remaking action following the poem's invention'.[52]

Every *historical narrative* borrows from this imaginative power of redescription since, as a 'reference through traces', 'the past can only be reconstructed by the imagination'.[53] But it is clearly in *fictional narrative* that the productive power of human imagination to configure and refigure human time is most dramatically evident. Presupposed by both historical and fictional narrative, however, is the pre-narrative capacity of human imagination to act in the world in a symbolically significant manner. For human being-in-the-world in its most everyday sense – as Kant and Heidegger realized – involves a process of *temporalization* which makes our present actions meaningful by interpreting them in terms of a recollected past and a projected future. This capacity of temporal interpretation is none other than that of the transcendental imagination. Ricoeur can thus claim:

> What is resignified by narrative is what was already presignified at the level of human acting. Our preunderstanding of the world of action ... is characterized by the mastering of a network of intersignifications constitutive of the semantic resources of human acting. Being-in-the-world according to narrativity is being-in-the-world already marked by the linguistic practice leading back to this preunderstanding. The iconic augmentation in question here depends upon the prior augmentation of readability that action owes to the interpretants already at work. Human action can be oversignified, because it is already presignified by all modes of its symbolic articulation.[54]

It is in his analysis of the configurative function of narrative, however, that Ricoeur most explicitly identifies the role of productive imagination. By narrative configuration he means the temporal synthesis of heterogeneous elements – or, to put it more simply, the ability to create a plot which transforms a sequence of events into a story. This consists of 'grasping together' the individual incidents, characters and actions so as to compose a unified temporal whole. The narrative act of emplotment, which configures a manifold into a synthesis, enacts what Kant defined as the productive power of transcendental imagination. As a power of grasping the many under the rules of the same, the narrative imagination is one which introduces recollection and repetition into a linear sequence of events (natural time), thus making it into a recapitulative story (narrative time): 'In reading the ending in the beginning and the beginning in the ending, we also learn to read time itself backwards, as the recapitulation of the initial conditions of a course of action in its terminal conditions.'[55]

In this manner Ricoeur translates the schematism of imagination from the metaphorical act to the larger scenario of the narrative act. He extends his analysis of the functioning of the poetical imagination from the unit of the *word* (symbol) and the *sentence* (metaphor) to that of the *text* as a whole (narrative). 'We ought not to hesitate', he says,

> in comparing the production of the configurational act to the work of the productive imagination. This latter must be understood not as a psychologizing faculty but as a transcendental one. The productive imagination is not only rule-governed, it constitutes the generative matrix of rules. In Kant's first *Critique*, the categories of the understanding are first schematized by the productive imagination. The schematism has this power because the productive imagination fundamentally has a synthetic function. It connects understanding and intuition by engendering syntheses that are intellectual and intuitive at the same time. Emplotment, too, engenders a mixed intelligibility between what has been called the point, theme or thought of a story, and the intuitive presentation of circumstances, characters, episodes, and changes of fortune that make up the denouement. In this way we may speak of a schematism of the narrative function.[56]

This analysis of the schematizing function of narrativity brings us to one of the most problematic issues of *Time and Narrative* – the relationship between *tradition* and *innovation*. Imagination, once again, comes to the rescue by operating in a double capacity. In so far as it secures the function of recollecting and reiterating types across discontinuous episodes, imagination is plainly on the side of tradition. But, in so far as it fulfils its equally essential function of projecting new horizons of possibility, imagination is committed to the role of semantic – and indeed ontological – innovation. As soon as one recognizes the schematizing and synthesizing power of imagination at work in narrative, the very notions of tradition and innovation become complementary. Thus Ricoeur can claim that the term tradition must be understood not as the 'inert transmission of some already dead deposit of material but as the living transmission of an innovation always capable of being reactivated by a return to the most creative moments of poetic activity'.[57] So interpreted, tradition can only survive, can only pass itself on from one generation to the next, by fostering innovation in its midst. The function of tradition plays a role analogous to that of narrative paradigms: they not only constitute the grammar that directs the composition of new works but they also do not and cannot eradicate the role of *poiesis* which in the last analysis is what makes each work of art different, singular, unique – an 'original production, a new existence in the linguistic kingdom'.[58]

The reverse is equally true. If tradition cannot survive without innovation, neither can innovation survive without tradition. Once again we see it is imagination which plays this reciprocal role. 'Innovation remains a form of behaviour governed by rules,' writes Ricoeur. 'The labour of imagination is not born from nothing. It is bound in one way or another to the tradition's paradigms. But the range of solutions is vast. It is deployed between the two poles of servile application and calculated deviation, passing through every degree of rule-governed deformation.'[59] While myth, folk-tale and traditional narratives in general gravitate towards the first pole, the more modern and post-modern exercises in narrative tend towards deviation. And so we find that the *nouveau roman* becomes a form of *anti-roman* where the very notions of narrative configuration and synthesis seem redundant. But this idea of a total suspension of tradition, in favour of unfettered deviation, is one strongly contested by Ricoeur. 'The possibility of deviation is inscribed in the relation between sedimented paradigms and actual works,' he claims. 'Short of the extreme case of schism, it is just the opposite of servile application. Rule governed deformation constitutes the axis around which the various changes of paradigm through application are arranged. It is this variety of applications that confers a history on the productive imagination and that, in counterpoint to sedimentation, makes a narrative tradition possible.'[60]

In short, the schematizing function of productive imagination involves both *tradition* and *innovation*. And this dual function of imagination as a poetic creation of the new by reference to the old is not just a property of writing but also and equally of *reading*. Indeed, Ricoeur goes so far as to claim that in many contemporary works it is the imaginative task of the reader to complete the narrative sketched out and often even deliberately fragmented by the written work: 'If emplotment can be described as an act of the productive imagination, it is insofar as this act is the joint work of the text and reader.' For it is the reading, which accompanies the interplay of the innovation and sedimentation of paradigms, that schematizes emplotment. 'In the act of reading, the receiver plays with the narrative constraints, brings about gaps, takes part in the combat between the novel and the anti-novel, and enjoys the pleasure that Roland Barthes calls the pleasure of the text.'[61] Taking the example of Joyce's *Ulysses* as a narrative full of holes and indeterminacies, Ricoeur concludes that such a text serves as an added invitation to the creative power of the reader's imagination: 'It challenges the reader's capacity to configure what the author seems to take malign delight in defiguring. In such an extreme case, it is the reader, almost abandoned by the work, who carries the burden of emplotment.'[62]

Conclusion: the social imaginary

It is at this final stage of narrative imagination – the reader's reception of the text – that the hermeneutic circle returns to the world of action. The act of reading is the ultimate indicator of the 'refiguring of the world of action under the sign of the plot'. Narrative plots are not, of course, confined to literature. Ricoeur is well aware of this. There is a whole set of collective stories and histories which need not bear the signature of any individual author, and which exercise a formative influence on our modes of action and behaviour in society. This is what Ricoeur calls the 'social imaginary'. And this 'social imagination is constitutive of social reality itself'.[63] Ricoeur examines it under two limit ideas – *ideology* and *utopia*.

In his *Lectures on Ideology and Utopia* (1986), Ricoeur spells out the similarities and differences of these two pivotal functions of our 'social imaginary'. Though both constitute sets of collective images which motivate a society towards a certain mode of thinking and acting, ideology tends towards 'integration' (preserving a sense of shared identity) while 'utopia' works in the opposite direction of rupture (introducing a sense of novelty, difference, discontinuity). In the fifteenth lecture Ricoeur explains the basic contrast thus:

> On the one hand, imagination may function to preserve an order. In this case the function of the imagination is to stage a process of identification that mirrors the order. Imagination has the appearance here of a picture. On the other hand, though, imagination may have a disruptive function; it may work as a breakthrough. Its image in this case is productive, an imagining of something else, the elsewhere. In each of its three roles, ideology represents the first kind of imagination; it has a function of preservation, of conservation. Utopia, in contrast, represents the second kind of imagination; it is always the glance from nowhere.[64]

In the eighteenth lecture Ricoeur elaborates on this distinction between ideology as image-picture and utopia as image-fiction. While 'all ideology repeats what exists by justifying it, and so gives a picture of what is ... Utopia has the fictional power of redescribing life'. Once again Ricoeur combines the Kantian distinction between reproductive and productive imagination with the phenomenological distinction between imaging as a 'neutralizing' of perception and as a 'free variation' of possibilities. On this count, Ricoeur clearly places the utopian function on the side of the productive and free imagination, affirming its power not only as a critique of ideology (in so far as it distances us from what is given) but also as a projection of possible social worlds. As he argues in the first lecture, utopia 'has a constitutive role in helping us rethink the nature of our social life'. It is, at best, the 'fantasy of an alternative society and its exteriorization *nowhere*' which can enable utopia to operate as one of the most formidable contestations of what is.

Every society participates in a socio-political *imaginaire*. This represents the ensemble of mythic or symbolic discourses which serve to motivate and guide its citizens. The 'social imaginary' can function as an *ideology* to the extent that it reaffirms a society in its identity by recollecting its 'foundational symbols'. Thus Soviet society remembers its October revolution, Britain its 'glorious revolution', the United States 1776, France 1789, Ireland 1916, and so on. And non-revolutionary societies may recall their originating myths and legends to ensure a similar sense of ideological continuity. This use of a 'social imaginary' as an ideological recollection of sacred foundational acts often serves to integrate and legitimate a social order. It is particularly conspicuous during moments of cultural or political revival. But it can also give rise to 'a stagnation of politics' where each power simply repeats the stereotypical images of an anterior power by way of consolidating its status. In such instances, one finds that 'every prince wants to be Caesar, every Caesar wants to be Alexander, every Alexander wants to Hellenise an Oriental despot'.[65] By ritualizing and codifying its experiences in terms of idealized self-images, recollected from the past, a society provides itself with an ideological stability: a unity of collective imagination which may well be missing from the everyday realities of that society. Thus, while Ricoeur readily acknowledges that every culture constitutes itself by telling stories of its own past, he warns against the ideological abuses attendant upon such a process of imaginative restoration. 'The danger is that this reaffirmation can be perverted, usually by monopolistic elites, into a mystificatory discourse which serves to uncritically vindicate or glorify the established political powers. In such instances, the symbols of a community become fixed and fetishized; they serve as lies.'[66]

It is at this point that *utopia* as an adversarial visage of the 'social imaginary' comes into play. Where ideology sponsored reaffirmation, utopia introduces rupture. Images of utopia remain suspicious of ideological power. They challenge the consensus of tradition and point towards an 'elsewhere', a 'no-place', a society that is 'not yet'. But dangers can enter in here also. As soon as a utopian imaginary relaxes its critical guard, it can establish itself as a new orthodoxy in its own right – its future images becoming just as dogmatic as the ideological images of the past it ostensibly seeks to dismantle. Moreover, if the social imaginary of utopia becomes too far removed from the society it is proposing to liberate, it runs the risk of a total schism which ultimately degenerates into repression. It is with this in mind that Ricoeur warns against a 'dangerously schizophrenic utopian discourse which projects a static future without ever producing the conditions of its realization'.[67] This can happen, for example, with the Marxist-Leninist notion of utopia if one announces the final 'withering away of the state' without taking the necessary measures to make such a goal realizable. In such instances, the utopian imaginary functions as a future completely cut off from the experience of past and present – a 'mere alibi for the consolidation of the repressive powers that be'. Thus, instead of demystifying the abuses of ideology, utopia can serve as a mystificatory ideology in its own right – justifying the oppressions of today in the name of some unattainable liberties of tomorrow. Ricoeur concludes accordingly that the two faces of the social imaginary – the ideological and the utopian – are indispensable to each other. 'Ideology as a symbolic confirmation of the past and utopia as a symbolic opening towards the future are complementary.'[68] Once cut off from each other, they fall into extreme forms of political pathology: the one incarcerating us in the past, the other sacrificing us to the future.

Ricoeur here rejoins Herbert Marcuse's view that all authentic utopias are grounded in recollection.[69] Critique, he recalls, is also a tradition – one reaching back indeed to the biblical narratives of exodus and resurrection or to the Greek narratives of Socratic defiance.[70] We may witness this in a genuine theology of liberation, for example, which gives direction to the utopian projection of a future by grounding it in the gospel memories of sharing and in the actual experiences of communal solidarity. The biblical promise of a kingdom thus serves as an image which reconnects the future with the past – with tradition, in the best sense of the word, as an ongoing narrative project, as a possibility which demands to be realized. 'The promise remains unfulfilled until the utopia is historically realized; and it is precisely the not-yet-realized horizon of this promise which binds men together as a community, which prevents utopia detaching itself as an empty dream.'[71]

The same applies, needless to say, to a philosophy of emancipation. To be genuine such a philosophy must seek to bring together the utopian 'horizon of expectation' with our actual 'field of experience'. If the modern idea of progress divorces itself from the inherited narratives of tradition and the concrete experience of the present, it becomes pathologically devoid of meaning. The universal loses contact with the actual. Expectancy becomes dissociated from existence. The *ought* floats free from the *is*. Whereas the grand narratives of Christianity and Marxism provided intermediary steps leading from a past of bondage to a future of emancipation, we now appear bereft of such universal stories of historical continuity. 'We don't seem to believe in these intermediaries any more,' observes Ricoeur. 'The problem today is the apparent impossibility of unifying world politics, of mediating between the polycentricity of our everyday political practice and the utopian horizon of a universally liberated humanity. It is not that we are without utopia, but that we are without *paths* to utopia. And without a path towards it, without concrete and practical mediation in our field of experience, utopia becomes a sickness.'[72]

By the same token, ideology as a system of pre-established paths laid down by past tradition is equally sick if not directed towards some future goal or utopia. That is why we require, perhaps more than ever, the schematizing function of a productive 'social imagination' capable of mediating between these two sundered realms of past and future. By bringing the two faces of the 'social imaginary' together – establishing a dialogue between the narratives of ideology and utopia, between experience and expectancy – Ricoeur's hermeneutic enterprise highlights the indispensable role of imagination in the contemporary world. 'An urgent task today is to preserve the tension between tradition and utopia. The challenge is to reanimate tradition and bring utopia closer.'[73]

That this task of creative imagination is central to Ricoeur's overall hermeneutic itinerary, albeit most explicit in his later work on the social imaginary, is acknowledged by the author himself in this revealing statement of his fundamental philosophical project:

Despite appearances, my single problem since beginning my reflections has been creativity. I considered it from the point of view of individual psychology in my first works on the will, and then at the cultural level with the study on symbolisms. My present research on the narrative places me precisely at the heart of this social and cultural creativity, since telling a story ... is the most permanent act of societies. In telling their own stories, cultures create themselves ... It is true that I have been silent from the point of view of practice, but not at all at the theoretical level, because the studies I have already published on the relation between ideology and utopia are entirely at the centre of this preoccupation.[74]

Is this not testimony to the hypothesis, observed in our presentation throughout, that Ricoeur's ultimate wager remains a hermeneutics of creative imagination?

Postscript

Strangely, most recent contributions to a radical hermeneutic of culture – be it Vattimo's *The End of Modernity: Nihilism and Hermeneutics in Postmodern Culture* (1986), Palmer's *Hermeneutics* (1969), Lyotard's *Instructions païennes* (1977) or Caputo's *Radical Hermeneutics* (1977) – fail to profit from Ricoeur's pivotal research. Heidegger and Gadamer still remain, for all these figures, the dominant figures of the contemporary hermeneutic debate. The present chapter hopes to have addressed in some way the temporary eclipse of Ricoeur's hermeneutics of imagination. By underscoring the original import of Ricoeur's adumbration of a new poetics of imagining – conjoining the virtues of an ontological hermeneutic à la Heidegger/Gadamer and a critical hermeneutic of ideology à la Habermas – I endeavour to restore to its rightful place what I believe to be one of the most incisive and fruitful moments of the hermeneutic debate. Ricoeur's analyses of the symbolizing and narrating imagination, and its attendant expressions in the 'social poetry' of ideology and utopia, demand consideration in any serious discussion of a radical hermeneutics of imagining.

I would like to think of this study as contributing, in some measure, to the ongoing hermeneutic project of devising a new poetics of imagination – a poetics most suggestively sketched out by Ricoeur and already filled in, to different intents or purposes, by the recent work of Vattimo, Caputo, Lyotard, Tracy and, especially, Gary Madison in his *Hermeneutics and Postmodernity* (1989).[75] Every poetics of imagining serves to supplement the work of imagination itself – a work in perpetual process, which began with the birth of humankind and will not cease until we cease. Thinking poetically, acting poetically or dwelling poetically are all modalities of imagining poetically. They are all ways of realizing the *possibilities* of what we are. As the poet Emily Dickinson wrote: '... possibility is the fuse lit by the spark of imagination.'

Notes

An earlier version of this chapter appeared in D. Rasmussen and P. Kemp (eds), *The Narrative Path: Paul Ricoeur* (Cambridge Mass.: MIT Press, 1989).

1 Martin Heidegger, *Kant and the Problem of Metaphysics* (1929), English trans. J. Churchill, (Bloomington, Ind.: Indiana University Press, 1962), pp. 140, 149. Heidegger comes close to a hermeneutics of imagination in this work, as does H.-G. Gadamer in *Truth and Method* (1960). However, both thinkers offer more of a commentary on the Kantian theory of transcendental imagination than a distinctively hermeneutic development of it as attempted by Ricoeur. I examine Heidegger's interpretation of Kant's theory of imagination in *The Wake of Imagination* (London/Minneapolis: Hutchinson/University of Minnesota Press, 1988), pp. 189–95, 222–4. Other useful and more detailed readings of the Heideggerian interpretation of the Kantian imagination include W. J. Richardson's *Heidegger: From Phenomenology to Thought* (The Hague: Nijhoff, 1963), and Calvin O. Schrag, *Heidegger and Cassirer on Kant*, *Kantstudien*, vol. 58 (1967), pp. 87–100. See also Hannah Arendt's reading of the Kantian imagination in *Kant's Political Philosophy* (Chicago, Ill.: University of Chicago Press, 1982), pp. 79–89.

2 This concern is markedly absent, for example, from such 'Husserlian' phenomenologies of imagination as Eugen Fink's *Vergegenwärtigung und Bild* (1930), Maria Saraiva's *L'Imagination selon Husserl* (1970) or Edward Casey's *Imagining: A Phenomenological Study* (1977) – works which concentrate on a rigorous application of phenomenological method to comparative descriptions of perceptual and imaginative intentionalities.

3 There is one tantalizing passage in Gadamer's essay, 'The Universality of the hermeneutical problem' (1966) where the author touches on the central role of imagination in hermeneutic inquiry: 'It is imagination (*Phantasie*) that is the decisive function of the scholar. Imagination naturally has a hermeneutical function and serves the sense for what is questionable. It serves the ability to expose real, productive questions, something in which, generally speaking, only he who masters all the

methods of his science succeeds' (*Philosophical Hermeneutics*, Berkeley, Calif.: University of California Press, 1976, p. 12). Unfortunately, Gadamer does not develop this insight, though there are some additional hints in his essay 'Intuition and vividness', in *The Relevance of the Beautiful* (Cambridge: Cambridge University Press, 1986), pp. 157–69.

4 Paul Ricoeur, 'L'imagination dans le discours et dans l'action', in *Du texte à l'action* (Paris: Éditions du Seuil, 1986), pp. 215–16.

5 Ricoeur, 'Herméneutique de l'idée de Révélation', in *La Révélation* (Brussels: Facultés Universitaires Saint-Louis, 1977), p. 54.

6 Ricoeur, 'L'imagination dans le discours et dans l'action', pp. 213–19.

7 ibid.

8 G. Bachelard, *Poetics of Space*, trans. Maria Jolas (Boston, Mass.: Beacon Press, 1964), p. xix. Cited by Ricoeur in *The Rule of Metaphor*, trans. R. Czerny (Toronto: University of Toronto Press, 1977), pp. 214–15.

9 Paul Ricoeur, 'Myth as the bearer of possible worlds', in Richard Kearney (ed.) *Dialogues with Contemporary Continental Thinkers* (Manchester: Manchester University Press, 1984), pp. 44–5. See also my 'Note on the hermeneutics of dialogue' in the same volume, pp. 127–33; and Paul Ricoeur's 'The hermeneutical function of distanciation', in *Hermeneutics and the Human Sciences* (Cambridge: Cambridge University Press, 1981), pp. 139 ff.

10 Ricoeur, 'Myth as the bearer of possible worlds', p. 44.

11 ibid., p. 45.

12 ibid.

13 Ricoeur, 'L'imagination dans le discours et dans l'action'. See also Theoneste Nkeramihigo's discussion of Ricoeur's theory of imagination in *L'Homme et la transcendance selon Paul Ricoeur* (Paris: Le Sycamore, 1984), pp. 241–4.

14 Paul Ricoeur, *The Symbolism of Evil* (Boston, Mass.: Beacon Press, 1969), pp. 10–11.

15 Paul Ricoeur, *De l'interprétation: essai sur Freud* (Paris: Éditions du Seuil, 1965), pp. 23–4; English trans. *Freud and Philosophy: An Essay on Interpretation* (New Haven, Conn.: Yale University Press, 1970).

16 ibid., p. 24.

17 ibid., p. 25.

18 Ricoeur, *Symbolism of Evil*, p. 12.

19 ibid., pp. 12–13.

20 ibid., p. 13.

21 ibid., p. 14.

22 ibid., p. 13.

23 ibid.

24 Ricoeur, *De l'interprétation*, p. 25. But to say that a symbol is always a sign – or a mode of linguistic signification – is not to say that every sign is a symbol. The sign always stands for something (idea, meaning, object, person); but a symbol contains a double intentionality – it can aim at two or more meanings at the same time. This is evident in the ability of poetic language (to take the paramount example) to have at least 'two thinks at a time', as Joyce once remarked. Symbolic images have a literal meaning

and a secondary analogical meaning. Thus, to take Ricoeur's example from *Symbolism of Evil*, the biblical image of somebody being 'defiled' refers both to the *literal* function of this image as a sign of physical uncleanliness and to its *symbolic* allusion to man's impure or deviant relationship to the sacred. The literal meaning of a stain points beyond itself to the existential condition of sinfulness which is *like* a stain. As Ricoeur puts it: 'Contrary to the perfectly transparent technical signs, which say only what they want to say in positing that which they signify, symbolic signs are opaque, because the first, literal, obvious meaning itself points analogically to a second meaning which is not given otherwise than in it' (p. 15). It is because there is no *direct* discourse for the confession of evil that symbolism becomes the privileged means of expression. In other words, the experience of evil is always conveyed by means of expressions (for example, stain, rebellion, straying from the path, bondage and so on) borrowed from the field of everyday physical existence which refer *indirectly* to another kind of experience – our experience of the sacred. Ricoeur concludes accordingly that symbolic images are 'donative' in that a primary meaning gives rise to a secondary one which surpasses the first in its semantic range and reference.

Further to clarify what he means by symbol, Ricoeur contrasts it to allegory. While an allegory relates one meaning directly to another, without residue or ambiguity, a symbol works by enigmatic suggestion or evocation – it designates a surplus of meaning which exceeds the obvious one. Allegories have one meaning, symbols two or more.

25 Ricoeur, *Symbolism of Evil*, p. 18.
26 ibid., p. 19.
27 ibid., p. 249. 'There is no pure philosophy without presuppositions,' Ricoeur argues. 'A hermeneutic meditation on symbols starts from speech that has already taken place ... its first task is from the midst of speech to remember; to remember with a view to beginning' (pp. 348–9).
28 ibid., p. 351.
29 ibid.
30 Ricoeur, *De l'interprétation*, p. 23. Ricoeur tightens his definition of the symbolic image by distinguishing it from two competing models, one too expansive, the other too restrictive. The restrictive definition – which Ricoeur equates with the Platonic and Neoplatonic model of formal analogy – reduces the symbol to a one-to-one correspondence between pre-existing meanings. This relation of proportional correspondence between meanings can be assessed from *without* at a purely intellectual level. It thus ignores the inner creative power of symbolism to generate a surplus of meaning within itself – a semantic surplus which calls for interpretation in order to make sense of the new meaning, a second meaning which emerges from the first (ibid., pp. 26–7). The expansive definition, by contrast, equates the symbolic function with the function of mediation in general – that is, with the function of human consciousness to construct a universe of meaning ranging from perception to language. This expansive model was given common currency by Ernst Cassirer, whose three-volume *The Philosophy of Symbolic Forms* was published in the fifties.

According to this model, the symbolic (*das Symbolische*) designates the basic precondition of all modes of giving meaning to reality. For Cassirer the symbolic refers to the universal activity of 'mediating' between consciousness and reality, an activity which operates in art, religion, science, language, etc. Ricoeur's objection to this expansive definition is that in including all mediating and objectifying functions under the title of 'symbolism' the concept of symbol becomes so amplified as to refer both to real and imaginary worlds, that is, to virtually *everything*. So doing, Cassirer appears to dissolve the distinction – so fundamental to hermeneutics – between univocal and multivocal expressions. Ricoeur insists, on the contrary, on a strict hermeneutic division between different fields of meaning – the field of signification in general (which Cassirer equates with the symbolic) and the more specific field of double or multiple meanings – where a literal meaning calls forth other meanings. It is only this latter field which, Ricoeur argues, deserves the designation 'symbolic' proper to hermeneutics. In short, the symbolic image is one which says something more than what it appears to say. It opens up an indirect or oblique meaning on the basis of a direct one – thus provoking the hermeneutic activity of *interpretation*. Hermeneutics is devoted to the specific investigation of symbolic images which contain 'the relation of one level of meaning to another' (ibid., p. 22).

31   ibid., p. 24.
32   ibid., p. 28.
33   ibid., p. 26.
34   ibid., p. 24. Ricoeur remarks here on the suggestiveness of the Greek term *enigma* – 'The enigma does not block [hermeneutic] intelligence but provokes it: there is something to unfold, or unwrap in the symbol' (ibid., p. 26). It is precisely the double meaning, the intentionality of a second sense in and through a primary sense, which solicits critical interpretation. It is because dream images involve an internal transgression of one meaning by another that Ricoeur concludes that hermeneutic interpretation belongs organically to the hermeneutic process.
35   ibid., p. 27.
36   Paul Ricoeur, *Le Conflit des interprétations* (Paris: Éditions du Seuil, 1969); English trans. *The Conflict of Interpretations* (Evanston, Ill.: Northwestern University Press, 1974), pp. 328–9.
37   ibid., p. 328.
38   ibid., p. 399.
39   Ricoeur, 'The creativity of language', p. 17.
40   Paul Ricoeur, 'The function of fiction in shaping reality', *Man and World*, vol. 12, no. 2 (1979), p. 130. Quoted in G. Taylor, introduction to P. Ricoeur *Lectures on Ideology and Utopia* (New York: Columbia University Press, 1986), p. xxviii.
41   Paul Ricoeur, *The Rule of Metaphor* (London: Routledge, 1978), pp. 199–200.
42   ibid., pp. 207–8.
43   ibid., p. 303.
44   ibid., p. 22 and 'Imagination in discourse and action', in *Analectica Husserliana* 7 (1978), ed. A.-T. Tymieniecka, Boston: D. Reidel, 1978.

45 Ricoeur, *Rule of Metaphor*, p. 215, quoting Bachelard, *Poetics of Space*, p. xix. Ricoeur goes on to quote a further passage from Bachelard (p. xx) later in *Rule of Metaphor*, p. 351: 'The essential newness of the poetic image poses the problem of the speaking being's creativeness. Through this creativeness the imagining consciousness proves to be, very simply, very purely, an origin. In a study of the imagination, a phenomenology of the poetic imagination must concentrate on bringing out this quality of origin in various poetic images.'

46 Paul Ricoeur, 'Poetry and possibility', *Manhattan Review*, vol. 2, no. 2 (1981), pp. 20–1.

47 Paul Ricoeur, 'Creativity in language', in C. Regan and D. Stewart (eds), *The Philosophy of Paul Ricoeur* (Boston, Mass.: Beacon, 1973), pp. 122–33 (quoted in G. Taylor, in *Lectures*).

48 Ricoeur, *The Rule of Metaphor*, p. 306 (quoted in G. Taylor, *Lectures*, p. xxxii).

49 Paul Ricoeur, *Time and Narrative* (Chicago, Ill.: University of Chicago Press, 1984), p. 80.

50 ibid., p. 81.

51 ibid., p. 81.

52 ibid., p. 81.

53 ibid., p. 82. See also Ricoeur's discussion of the role of imagination in historical narrative, pp. 183–8. Here Ricoeur explores the analogy between narrative emplotment, which is 'a probable imaginary construction', and the equally 'imaginary constructions' of 'probabilist' theories of historical causation as proposed by Max Weber or Raymond Aron (for example, Aron's statement in *Introduction to the Philosophy of History* that 'every historian, to explain what did happen, must ask himself what might have happened'; see also Weber: 'In order to penetrate the real causal relationships, we construct unreal ones'). But while Ricoeur argues for a certain continuity between narrative explanation and historical explanation, in so far as both deploy imagination to construct unreal relationships, he also acknowledges a discontinuity: 'historians are not simply narrators: they give reasons why they consider a particular factor *rather than some other* to be the sufficient cause of a given course of events ... Poets produce, historians argue' (*Time and Narrative*, p. 186)

54 ibid., p. 81.

55 ibid., p. 67.

56 ibid., p. 68. Ricoeur's hermeneutic reading of this schematizing-temporalizing-productive power of imagination, as first outlined by Kant in the first edition of *The Critique of Pure Reason* (1781), bears interesting parallels to Heidegger's reading in *Kant and the Problem of Metaphysics* (1929), pp. 135–49, 177–92; and to the analyses of two of Heidegger's most brilliant students in Freiburg in the late 1920s, Hannah Arendt (*Kant's Political Philosophy*, 1982, pp. 78–9) and Herbert Marcuse (*Eros and Civilization*, 1955, pp. 174 ff.).

57 Ricoeur, *Time and Narrative*, p. 68.

58 ibid., p. 69.

59 ibid., p. 70.
60 ibid.
61 ibid., p. 77.
62 ibid.
63 Paul Ricoeur, *Lectures on Ideology and Utopia*, ed. G. Taylor (New York: Columbia University Press, 1986), lecture 1.
64 ibid., lecture 15, quoted by G. Taylor in his illuminating introduction to which I am indebted, p. xxviii.
65 Paul Ricoeur, 'Science and ideology', in J. B. Thompson (ed.), in *Hermeneutics and the Human Sciences* (Cambridge: Cambridge University Press, 1981), p. 229.
66 Paul Ricoeur, 'The creativity of language', p. 29.
67 ibid., p. 30.
68 ibid. For a more detailed and comprehensive analysis of this relationship, see Ricoeur's *Du texte à l'action* and particularly the section entitled 'L'idéologie et l'utopie: deux expressions de l'imaginaire social', pp. 379–92. This also means for Ricoeur that a hermeneutics of the 'mytho-poetic core of imagination' requires to be complemented always by a critical 'hermeneutics of suspicion'. See G. Taylor's introduction to Ricoeur's *Lectures on Ideology and Utopia*, p. xxxiii.
69 Herbert Marcuse, *The Aesthetic Dimension* (Boston, Mass.: Beacon Press, 1978), p. 73.
70 Paul Ricoeur, 'Hermeneutics and the critique of ideology', in Thompson, *Hermeneutics and the Human Sciences*, p. 99.
71 Ricoeur, in *Dialogues*, p. 30.
72 ibid., p. 31. See also Ricoeur's adjudication of the Habermas–Gadamer debate in 'Hermeneutics and the critique of ideology'; his discussion of Reinhart Kosselek's theory of history as a dialectic between 'experience' and 'expectancy' in *Temps et récit, III* (Paris: Éditions du Seuil, 1985), pp. 301–13, and finally his attempts to reconcile the ideological and utopian expressions of the 'social imaginary' in *Du texte à l'action*, pp. 213–37 and 379–93. See also my own commentaries on Ricoeur's hermeneutics of the social imaginary: 'Religion and ideology: Paul Ricoeur's hermeneutic conflict', *Irish Philosophical Journal*, vol. 2, no. 1 (1985), pp. 37–52; 'Myth and the critique of ideology', in *Transitions* (Manchester: Manchester University Press, 1988), pp. 269–84; and 'Between tradition and utopia', in D. Wood (ed.), *Narrative and Interpretation: The Recent Work of Paul Ricoeur* (London: Routledge, 1991).
73 Paul Ricoeur, *Le Monde* interview, Paris, 7 February, 1986.
74 Paul Ricoeur, 'L'histoire comme récit et comme pratique', interview with Peter Kemp, *Esprit*, no. 6, Paris, June 1981, p. 165. George Taylor provides a brief, lucid and, to my knowledge, unprecedented summary of the role of imagination in Ricoeur's work in his introduction to *Lectures on Ideology and Utopia*, pp. xxvii–xxxv; see also the concluding notes, 39 and 47, to G. B. Madison's *The Hermeneutics of Postmodernity* (Bloomington, Ind.: Indiana University Press, 1988), pp. 194–5, where he also acknowledges the central role played by imagination in Ricoeur's

overall hermeneutic project. He cites the two following passages where Ricoeur himself adverts to this central role. The first is from Ricoeur's 'retrospective' text 'On interpretation' published in A. Montefiore (ed.) *Philosophy in France Today* (Cambridge: Cambridge University Press, 1983), p. 184:

> The imagination can justly be termed productive because, by an extension of polysemy, it makes terms, previously heterogeneous, *resemble* one another, and thus homogeneous. The imagination, consequently, is this competence, this capacity for producing them in spite of ... and thanks to ... the initial difference between the terms which resist assimilation. (p. 184).

Ricoeur interestingly remarks on how from this point of view the act of understanding 'consists in grasping the semantic dynamism by virtue of which, in a metaphorical statement, a new semantic relevance emerges from the ruins of the semantic non-relevance as this appears in a literal reading of the sentence. To understand is thus to perform or to repeat the discursive operation by which the semantic innovation is conveyed' (ibid.).

The second quotation is from Ricoeur's text 'Metaphor and the central problem of hermeneutics', in his *Hermeneutics and the Human Sciences*, ed. and trans. J. B. Thompson (Cambridge: Cambridge University Press, 1981), p. 181:

> Allow me to conclude [the preceding discussion of metaphor] in a way which would be consistent with a theory of interpretation which places the emphasis on 'opening up a world'. Our conclusion should also 'open up' some new perspectives, but on what? Perhaps on the old problem of the imagination which I have carefully put aside. Are we not ready to recognise in the power of imagination, no longer the faculty of deriving 'images' from our sensory experience, but the capacity for letting new worlds shape our understanding of ourselves? This power would not be conveyed by images, but by the emergent meanings in our language. Imagination would thus be treated as a dimension of language. In this way, a new link would appear between imagination and metaphor. We shall, for the time being, refrain from entering this half-open door.

75 Gary Madison's *Hermeneutics and Postmodernity* (Bloomington, Ind.: Indiana University Press, 1989) is the most significant exception to the general eclipse of Ricoeur's hermeneutics of imagination, acknowledging the importance of his work for the current debate on postmodern hermeneutics and culminating with some suggestive reflections on 'The philosophical centrality of imagination: a postmodern approach'.

Suggestions for further reading

Ricoeur's hermeneutic account of imagination is fragmented over several works. Although such an account is implicit in major texts like *The Symbolism of Evil* (Boston, Mass.: Beacon Press, 1969), *Freud and Philosophy* (New Haven, Conn.: Yale University Press, 1970) and *The Rule of Metaphor* (Toronto: Toronto University Press, 1977), it is in more recent essays that Ricoeur explicitly outlines the centrality of imagination in his overall hermeneutic project – in particular, 'Metaphor and the central problem of hermeneutics' in *Hermeneutics and the Human Sciences*, ed. and trans. J. B. Thompson (Cambridge: Cambridge University Press, 1981); 'Imagination in discourse and action', *Analectica Husserliana*, vol. 7, no. 3 (1978); and 'On interpretation', in A. Montefiore (ed.) *Philosophy in France Today* (Cambridge: Cambridge University Press, 1983). Suggestive, if cursory, glosses on Ricoeur's hermeneutic theory of imagination are to be found in George Taylor's lucid introduction to Ricoeur's *Lectures on Ideology and Utopia* (New York: Columbia University Press, 1986) and Gary Madison's conclusion to *Hermeneutics and Postmodernity* (Bloomington, Ind.: Indiana University Press, 1989).

6

The post-modern imagination

A labyrinth of mirrors

We now inhabit what cultural critics increasingly call the 'post-modern' age. In this final chapter, I propose to explore some of the implications of the advent of post-modernism for our hermeneutic understanding of images and imaging. Indeed, this question is of added relevance when one considers that post-modern culture is frequently referred to as a 'civilization of the image' (a phrase coined by Roland Barthes).

The role of the image in post-modern culture is essentially one of *parody*. By this is meant that the image no longer refers primarily to some 'original', situated outside itself in the 'real' world or inside human consciousness. Devoid of any fixed reference to an origin, the image appears to refer only to other images. The post-modern image circulates in a seemingly endless play of imitation. Each image becomes a parody of another which precedes it ... and so on. The idea of an 'authentic' image is thus subverted – as is evident in the practice of pastiche which informs contemporary forms of representation.

In this context, one might argue that the pre-modern model of the image as *mirror* (as in book 10 of Plato's *Republic*, for example) and the modern model as *lamp* (as in German Idealist and Romantic notions of *Einbildungskraft*) give way to the post-modern model of a *circle of looking glasses* – each one reproducing the surface images of the other in a play of infinite multiplication.[1] This interplay of self-multiplying mirror images without depth or interiority is a recurring preoccupation of not only post-modern thinkers like Derrida and Barthes, but also of a wide variety of contemporary writers, artists and film-makers.

In this chapter, I consider some recent hermeneutic attempts to respond to this post-modern crisis of the image. But, first, I offer a summary account of the post-modern subversion of our accredited notions of imagination.

(a)

The post-modern paradigm of parody threatens the modern view of the image as a unique invention of a unique human subject. The term 'post-modern' first gained common currency in architecture in the mid-seventies: it designated a shift away from the modernist International Style of Le Corbusier and Mies van der Rohe, with its emphasis on utopianism and novelty, towards a 'radical eclecticism' of pseudo-historical forms.[2] In literary criticism in the seventies and eighties the term 'post-modern' has been used to refer to a growing body of texts – ranging from Beckett and the *nouveaux romans* to Pynchon and Eco – which illustrate the 'death of the author' (as controlling origin or intention) and the 'birth of the reader' (as free play of interpretation). Here writing becomes a reflection of the very process of writing. The text disintegrates into an endless self-mirroring of the impossibility of authorial creation. Fiction swallows its own tail, as dramatically illustrated in Beckett's title *Imagination Dead Imagine*.

The visual arts have also witnessed the emergence of the post-modern movement. This is manifest in the erosion of the modernist belief in artists as an élite avant-garde committed to the salvation of humankind. The modernist distinction between high art and popular culture disappears, as pop images parody the classic images of the great works of art (for example, Martin Sharp's pop poster of Van Gogh, Robert Ballagh's cutout reproductions of revered masterpieces by David and Velázquez, Larry Rivers's take-off of Rembrandt's 'Dutch Masters'). And the reverse is equally the case: post-modern works of art often mimic images taken from the world of popular culture, particularly the mass-media culture of television and advertising – for example, Warhol's spoof seriographs of Marilyn Monroe, Jackie Kennedy and Coca-Cola bottles. Here the modernist claim that the artist is an extraordinary genius who creates extraordinary images is shattered by the multiple reproduction of fake images. And this parodic reduction of eternal art to ephemeral artifice is exemplified in Warhol's brazen boast that if Picasso, the modernist artist *par excellence*, could produce four thousand masterpieces in a lifetime he (Warhol) could reproduce as many in a day! In short, post-modern culture speaks of a 'Society of Spectacle' where there is no new image under the sun – only images of images of images . . .

The term 'post-modern' was quickly taken up by philosophers. Here it initially became synonymous with those structuralist and post-structuralist currents of thought which disputed the primacy of the humanist imagination as ultimate source of meaning. The idealist and existentialist arguments for the centrality of the autonomous imagination have, since the sixties, run the gauntlet of critical suspicion. Indeed, so vehement has this dismantling process been that one sometimes wonders if it is still possible to speak meaningfully of a post-modern imagination at all. Several contemporary critics dismiss the very notion of creative imagination as an ideological ruse of Western bourgeois humanism – little more than an 'effect' of language play, a ludic mirage of signs.

If the post-modern aesthetic could be said to mirror post-modern society – its commodified images tailored to the consumer demands of late capitalism – then post-modern thought may be seen as an articulation of post-modern aesthetics. In thinkers such as Jean-François Lyotard, Gianni Vattimo and Julia Kristeva, who explicitly invoke the term 'post-modern' – as well as in thinkers such as Derrida, Lacan, Foucault, Baudrillard and Barthes, who do not – one can detect four main refusals which define a post-modernist theory. First, the refusal of an imagining subject as transcendental origin of meaning (the thesis of modern idealists from Kant and Schelling to Husserl and Sartre). Second, the refusal of the universalizing grand narratives of history (as propagated by the modernist avant-garde who saw history as a Leap into the New, an onward march of time leading to universal Progress and Emancipation). Third, the refusal of the modern project of Truth (the ideology of a totalizing identity or Sufficient Reason which seeks to unify the limitless plurality of meanings that make up our language and our world). And, finally, as mentioned above, the refusal of the hallowed modernist opposition between the High Art of authentic images and the Mass Culture of electronically reproducible copies.[3]

The contemporary Italian author Italo Calvino captures the essential climate of post-modernity when he speaks of an 'intellectual turning point' where the

> notion of man as the subject of history is finished – the antagonist who has dethroned man must still be called man, but a man very different from what he was before. Which is to say, the human race of the 'big numbers' in exponential growth all over the planet; the explosion of the big cities; the ungovernability of society and economy, whatever system they belong to; the end of economic and ideological Eurocentrism; and the claiming of full rights by outcasts, the repressed, the forgotten, and the inarticulate. All the parameters, categories, and antitheses that we once used to define, plan, and

172

classify the world have been called into question. And not only those most closely linked to historical values, but even the ones that seemed to be stable anthropological categories – reason and myth, work and existence, male and female – and even the polarity of the most elementary combinations of words – affirmation and negation, above and below, subject and object'.[4]

(b)

One of the sources of the suspicion of imagination in much post-modern thought derives from the structuralist and, more particularly, post-structuralist argument that it is not the subject who speaks language, but language which speaks the subject. Thus Lacan, for example, argues that the *imaginary* is a narcissistic *illusion*: the self's project of an *imago* of self-sufficiency or self-completion. This Imaginary Order – deriving from the 'mirror stage' when the infant first intimates some sense of self-identity in its own reflection – leads to a fetishistic cult of the ideal self. This can only be overcome in the direction of a social relation of intersubjectivity, when the *imago* is dissolved into what Lacan calls the *symbolic* order of language which functions as unconscious desire for the other.

> The Imaginary Order includes the field of phantasies and images. It evolves out of the mirror stage, but extends into the adult subject's relationships with others. The prototype of the typical imaginary relationship is the infant before the mirror, fascinated with his own image. Adult narcissistic relationships ... are extensions of the infantile situation. The Imaginary Order also seems to include pre-verbal structures, for example, the various 'primitive' phantasies uncovered by the psychoanalytic treatment of children, psychotic and perverse patients.[5]

This idea that the modern notion of the autonomous ego – shared by idealists and existentialists alike – is a false 'imaginary' construct is taken up by a number of other structuralists. Althusser applies the Lacanian category of the Imaginary to ideology in general, interpreting this in the Marxist sense of *false consciousness*. The individual subject, says Althusser, is an imaginary construct of the modern bourgeoisie. While it claims to be a sovereign *subject of* freedom, it is in reality *subject to* an ideological apparatus which determines its mode of consciousness. Althusser describes the imaginary accordingly as a 'structure of misrecognition'. A structuralist approach to the unconscious, such as Lacan's, can be of great benefit to the Marxist critique of ideology in that it reveals that the 'human subject' is not an 'ego centred on consciousness but a "de-centred" process' constituted by a structure which has no centre, either, except in the imaginary misrecognition of the *ego*, that is, in the ideological formations in which it *recognizes* itself.[6] Althusser concludes that ideology is an 'imaginary assemblage' which fosters the falsehood that human beings are free subjects when they are in fact products of a structural causality of social formation which they do not consciously choose or control. The only answer to this ideological mystification is a new Marxist science which will replace man's 'imaginary relationship to the real' with 'knowledge' of the real.[7]

If Althusser and his followers applied the structuralist critique of the *imaginary* to ideology, Roland Barthes applies it to literature. Once again the ideal of an autonomous imagination is de-centred and de-psychologized. The death of God is now supplemented by the death of the author. The Romantic theory of the imagination as a quasi-divine expression of some transcendental subject, the creation of new meaning out of nothing, is replaced by a post-modern concept of parody. The idea of an original imagination is revealed to be no more than an 'effect' of the endless *intertextuality* of language itself. The imagination of the author, says Barthes, is not the origin but the side-product of 'multiple writings entering into mutual relations of parody'.[8] Far from originating images, the author imitates them. He is supplanted by the reader who re-creates rather than creates, mimics rather than invents, copies rather than initiates. 'The text is a tissue of innumerable quotations,' Barthes explains,

> drawn from the innumerable centres of culture. Similar to Bouvard and Pécuchet, those eternal copyists, at once sublime and comic, and whose profound ridiculousness indicates precisely the truth of writing, the writer can only imitate a gesture that is always anterior, never original. His only power is to mix writings, to counter the ones with the others, in such a way as never to rest on any one of them. Did he wish to *express himself*, he ought at least to know that the inner 'thing' he thinks to 'translate' is itself only a ready-formed dictionary, its words only explainable through other words, and so on indefinitely.

There is no question here – in contrast to phenomenological theories – of the imaginary expressing some inner intentionality of consciousness or some outer life of world. On the contrary, says Barthes: 'Life never does more than imitate the book, and the book itself is only a tissue of signs, an imitation that is lost, infinitely deferred.'[9]

The later Barthes is not content, however, to confine his post-modern analysis of writing to experimental literary texts. He generalizes the concept of textuality until it approximates, at some points, to the Lacanian/Althusserian model of an *ideological imaginary*. This he calls the 'mythical', in keeping with his structuralist critique of bourgeois myths in *Mythologies* (1957). He now seems to suggest indeed that *all* of language is inherently 'mythical' and that there is, consequently, no real hope of getting *outside* the post-modern labyrinth of the imaginary. 'The mythical', he claims, 'is present everywhere sentences are turned, stories told, from inner speech to outer conversation, from newspaper article to political sermon, from novel to advertising image – all utterances which could be brought together under the Lacanian concept of the *imaginary*'.[10] But if language is thus equated with the mythical status of the imaginary, how can we talk of a critical writing which would expose the falsifications of ideology (as the Barthes of *Mythologies* proposed)? The answer appears to be that we cannot.

The upshot of such readings is that human imagination is a highly duplicitous concept. 'The whole topic of "imagination" is vexed in radical theory', as a recent commentator argues, for many post-modern theorists, especially those influenced by radical French Marxism, 'regard imagination as a mystified and mystifying bourgeois notion, a romantic way of concealing the real roots of creativity which reach down not into some dark inner world but into that ideology which it is the radical critic's task to demystify'.[11]

(c)
Michel Foucault and Jacques Derrida have also contributed to the post-modern debate on the imaginary without actually endorsing the terms 'structuralist', 'post-structuralist' or 'post-modern'. In his critical commentaries on paintings by Magritte ('This Is Not a Pipe') and Warhol ('Campbells Soup Tins'), and in his analysis of Borges fictions in the opening of *The Order of Things*, Foucault speaks of a new kind of language which transgresses the 'boundaries of all imagination'.[12] In sharp contrast to the ideal *utopias* of the Romantic imagination – which aspired towards a harmony of understanding and reality – these post-modern imaages constitute *heterotopias* whose very otherness 'desiccates speech and dissolves our myths'. As such, they shatter the

limits of the transcendental imagination and bring human language and thought to the threshold of their impossibility. Hence the sense of dislocation we experience before Magritte's picture of a pipe with the caption 'This Is Not a Pipe'. The conventional rapport of image to origin *(resemblance)* is supplanted by a post-modern model of *similitude*, where the image refers only to other images: 'Magritte skirts the base of affirmative discourse on which resemblance calmly reposes, and he brings pure similitudes and non-affirmative verbal statement into play within the instability of a disoriented volume and unmapped space ... similitudes multiply of themselves, refer to nothing more than themselves ... the "This is a pipe" silently hidden in mimetic representation has become the "This is not a pipe" of circulating similitudes.'[13] And in the case of Andy Warhol's seriographs of consumer icons – such as soup-tins, Coca-Cola bottles or the faces of superstars – the reproductions are no more than parodies of advertising images. In other words, the very idea of an irreplaceable model disappears completely: '... by means of similitude relayed indefinitely along the length of a series, the image itself, along with the name it bears, loses its identity. Campbell, Campbell, Campbell, Campbell.'[14] Foucault's verdict seems to be that the demise of man also implies the demise of imagination – understood as a creative source of unique images. In the wake of imagination, we still have images. But these images are not inventions of a sovereign human subject, they are copies of copies of copies ... For Foucault, the productive imagination, like 'man' who supposedly possessed it, is itself but a modern invention which has now been erased – 'like a face drawn in sand at the edge of the sea'.[15]

But it is Derrida, arguably, who most rigorously assaults the modern claims for a productive imagination. Borrowing Mallarmé's metaphor of the *lustre* – a multifaceted network of glass reflectors – Derrida seeks to deconstruct the humanist notion of the imagination as a lamp projecting light from a single source of creativity. Commenting on the Mallarméan text, *Mimique*, in the second part of *Dissemination* (1972), he argues that the creation of a supposedly original model is in fact a mime of a mime of a mime ... The ideal of transcendental production is swallowed up in endless reproduction. But this is mimetic reproduction with a difference – it is devoid of any original presence which it might be said to represent. Derrida's text mirrors Mallarmé's text which mirrors a booklet written about the mime which in turn mirrors the mime of *Pierrot Murderer of His Wife*; but this mime itself mimics nothing that comes before or after the mimodrama. 'There is no simple reference,' as Derrida explains. 'It is in this that the mime operation does allude, but alludes to nothing, alludes without breaking the mirror, without reaching beyond the looking glass.'[16] In this phenomenon of a mimesis without origin, a mimicry which imitates nothing, we find a fitting emblem of post-modern depthlessness: 'We enter a textual labyrinth panelled with mirrors.'[17]

According to this scenario, there is no longer an original light, deriving from the God-Sun of Platonism or from the imagination-lamp of humanism. There is only a circling of reflections without beginning or end – the 'mirror of a mirror ... a reference without a referent, without any first or last unit, a ghost that is the phantom of no flesh, wandering about without a past, without any death, birth or present'.[18] Derrida is compelled to conclude that there can no longer be a *decidable* distinction between image and so-called reality. The mimicry which parodies itself also deconstructs itself. It is 'at once image and model, and hence image without model, without verisimilitude, without truth or falsity, a miming of appearance without concealed reality, without any world behind it'.[19] After imagination, there is no reality. Only the limitless play of pastiche.

Towards a post-modern hermeneutic of imagination

The crisis of the post-modern image has not always led, however, to declarations of the 'death of imagination'. Alongside the apocalyptic reading which tends to construe the imaginary as mere imitation of imitations – a mirrorplay of simulacra (Baudrillard) – there has arisen a hermeneutical reading. This second reading, more in keeping with the theoretical thrust of my own work, continues to apply itself to the challenges and undecidabilities of post-modern culture, including the famous 'linguistic turn'. But, rather than seeing the concept of imagination subsumed into an endless play of arbitrary signifiers, this post-modern hermeneutic strives to reconnect the texts of imagination to the human and historical contexts in which they emerge. The imaginary is here no longer seen as a fetish of false consciousness, a mere effect of linguistic systems, nor indeed as a modification of perception; it is recognized as a mode of discourse where *someone actually says something to somebody about something*. In short, a post-modern hermeneutic of imagination relocates the crisis of creativity in the context of a world which is refigured or prefigured by our imaginings. The apocalypse of floating signifiers is reconnected once again to the discourse of a life-world of affectivity and event. This does not mean a return to a foundational ontology or epistemology – which would seek to anchor our images in decidable categories of knowledge or being. What it does mean is that the imaginary is now recognized as a process which relates to something or somebody *other* than itself.

We already saw in our last chapter how Ricoeur's hermeneutic theory related the world of the imaginary to fictional and historical narratives – and by extension to the world of human action. This hermeneutic of a responsive imagination – in the sense of an imagination which responds to the world it both refigures and prefigures through the process of semantic innovation – was most explicitly formulated in Ricoeur's writings on the 'social imaginary' in *Du texte à l'action* (1986). But Ricoeur does not confront the challenge of postmodernity head-on. The lived world to which the narrative imagination relates is left historically vague and undefined. Occasional efforts have been made by a number of contemporary philosophers, however, to address the hermeneutic problem of a post-modern imagination. And amongst this number I would count recent works by David Tracy, Julia Kristeva, Jean-François Lyotard and Gianni Vattimo.

(a)

In *Plurality and Ambiguity* (1987), an analysis of the problem of interpretation in the post-modern scenario of multiple meaning, David Tracy refuses the temptation to 'ground' imagination by returning to some intuitive model of images (be it empirical or transcendental). Instead, he develops Ricoeur's textual account of the productive imagination: 'Any contemporary theory of the imagination', he writes, 'cannot be based on earlier scientific interpretations of images as disposable substitutes for presently absent but readily available perceptions. An adequate theory of the imagination also needs to be rescued from the dismissal of the imaginative as merely fanciful, as happens in attacks on rhetorical language as a disposable ornament of scientific and literal discourse.' A full theory of the text, Tracy concludes, 'linked to a theory of the productive imagination does not yet exist in the fully explanatory form needed. But whether or not a full theory of the imagination is ever developed, one thing is clear: Readers are able to use all the existing theories of composition, genre, and text along with some implicit theory of the productive imagination.'[20]

This restoration of the productive imagination to a central role in textual discourse implies, of course, a parallel restoration of its role in social discourse. Rejecting the 'ideology of the absolute text' – as promoted by certain strands of structuralist and post-structuralist theory – a radical hermeneutics of imagination re-establishes the link between text and history. Thus, as hermeneutics reveals the linguistic character of imagination it simultaneously reveals the historical character of language. There is no question here of incarcerating imagination in a prison-house of signifiers. To rediscover imagination as discourse, and vice versa, is 'to explore language as a reality beyond individual words in the dictionary, beyond both synchronic codes *(langue)* and individual use of words *(parole)*; it is to rediscover society and history'.[21]

A hermeneutic analysis of post-modern images does not, therefore, signal a return to the isolated and embattled imagination of existentialism. On the contrary, it recognizes that the images of any creative human subject are inextricably tied up with images of a collective social intersubjectivity – that is, the 'social imaginary' of ideology and utopia. In this manner, a critical hermeneutics articulates an alternative model of imagination to the one promoted by existentialism and structuralism. Beyond the extremes of sovereign subjectivity (where imagination reigns supreme) and anonymous linguistic systems (where imagination is merely one signifier amongst others afloat in a differential play of signs), post-modern hermeneutics charts an intermediary course. It advances a discourse of semantic interaction between different kinds of meaning – subjective and systematic, surface and hidden, obvious and indirect, conscious and unconscious, literal and figurative, emancipatory and distorting. Consequently, 'to acknowledge that language is discourse is to admit the need for ethical and political criticism of the hidden, even repressed, social and historical ideologies in all texts, in all language as discourse, and, above all, in all interpretations'.[22]

As related to the post-modern debate on the 'demise of man', such a critical hermeneutics steers a middle passage between the Scylla of existentialist humanism and the Charybdis of deconstructive anti-humanism. While the former chooses to ignore the post-modern challenge by simply reinstating the autonomous human imagination at the centre of the universe, the latter seeks to dethrone the humanist ego as an imaginary construct. This, at least, is Lacan's position. And it is one endorsed by several structuralist and post-structuralist thinkers – such as Lévi-Strauss when he argues that 'the ultimate goal of the human sciences is not to constitute but to dissolve man'; or Derrida when he claims that what is most necessary for us today is to think 'an end of man which would not be organized by a dialectics of truth and negativity'.[23]

A hermeneutic critique of the Civilization of the Image in which we live would seek to formulate a concept of the imaginative interpreter as one who is neither the 'effect' of a structural play of signifiers nor the self-sufficient origin of all sense. The hermeneutic circle means this, if it means anything: the only creative imagination still credible in our post-modern age is one which knows that the shortest root from self to self is through the images of *others* – that is, the discourse of a social and cultural imaginary:

> The idea that man understands himself only by interpreting the signs of his humanity hidden in literatures and cultures calls for no less radical a transformation of the concept of subject as of that of cultural text. For one thing, the indirect understanding of oneself implied by the hermeneutic act rejects the intuitionism of a philosophy founded on the *cogito*, with its claim to constitute itself in self-sufficiency and consistency, and attests the dependence of its meaning on the meaning of what it understands outside itself. For another thing, comprehension of a text does not end with discovering the codes that make up its structures but with revealing the *image of the world*, the mode of being, towards which it points. But this revelation is in turn only the counterpart of the dethroning of the subject who takes the roundabout route via the world of signs (and images) in order to understand himself. Thus the hermeneutic circle marks the simultaneous abandonment of the notions of *system* and of *subject*.[24]

The conclusion of such a radical hermeneutic is that a post-modern imagination is one which has no choice but to recognize that it is unfounded *(sans fondements)*. It no longer seeks an ontological foundation *in itself* as transcendental subject, or *outside itself* in some timeless substance. But it does not, for all that, necessarily find itself without purpose. This task always remains: to interpret the images of the other and to transfigure one's own image of the world in response to this interpretation.

(b)

If there is to be a credible philosophical response to the crisis of imagining – so dramatically staged by post-modern culture and theory

– it is, I have been suggesting, most likely to come from a *radical hermeneutics*. I understand this in the sense of John Caputo when he speaks of the need for a 'cold' or 'post-modern' hermeneutics: one capable of registering radical deconstructive readings of the imaginary while refusing, the while, to surrender the basic hermeneutic conviction that imagining – like all modes of human activity – is invariably related to our understanding of our being-in-a-world (itself inseparable from the interpretation of language).[25] The bottom line of all hermeneutics – cold or hot, deconstructive or existential – is that language is a process where *someone says something to someone about something*.

The main difference between hot and cold hermeneutics is that, while the former believes in interpreting the signs of existence so as to restore us to an original or lost metaphysical meaning (as epitomized by the Romantic and Idealist variations of hermeneutics which preceded Heidegger), the latter commits us to an appreciation of the irreducibly non-foundational 'otherness' of meaning. Radical (or cold) hermeneutics always keeps a 'watchful eye for the ruptures and the breaks and the irregularities in existence'. Where the traditional metaphysics of presence tried to make things look easy by putting the 'best face on existence', radical hermeneutics seeks to remain faithful to the difficulties and complexities of our existence, both lived and imagined. But, if it does write 'from below' about those dimensions of the imaginary that cannot be stabilized in terms of decidable metaphysical concepts, it does not abandon us 'to the wolves of irrationality, moral licence and despair'. The aim of a radical hermeneutics of the imaginary is not to surrender to nihilism and anarchism but to discern an alternative poetics of imagining capable of responding to the post-modern crisis of culture. The point is to make imagining possible, not impossible, in a contemporary climate of thought often hostile to it – or, to quote Caputo once again, 'to face up to the difference and difficulty which enter into what we think and do and hope for, not to grind them to a halt'.[26]

We have seen above how such a radical hermeneutics of imagining has been warranted by the recent writings of Ricoeur and his disciples – and, in particular, the critical hermeneutic readings of the 'social imaginary' as narratives of ideology and utopia. But these are not isolated examples. Apart from my own modest efforts to develop a critical hermeneutics of the imaginary,[27] there have been a growing number of critiques of the post-modern imaginary in recent years which could broadlly be described as 'hermeneutic'. Three of the most significant of these are to be found in the later writings of Gianni Vattimo, Jean-François Lyotard and Julia Kristeva. Kristeva relates the contemporary crisis of the imaginary to interpretations of the melancholic 'affects' of the unconscious. Lyotard relates the crisis to narratives of ethical–aesthetical resistance (or what he calls 'dissensus'). While Vattimo offers analysis of the modernity/post-modernity debate in terms of the narrative imaginary of myth. Despite their different assessments of the legacy of phenomenological hermeneutics – Vattimo explicitly celebrates it, Lyotard and Kristeva tend to challenge it – each of these post-modern thinkers has come to share the basic hermeneutic conviction that language does involve *someone saying something to someone else*. In other words, they all subscribe to the view that texts are primarily *discourses relating to the other*, rather than merely parodies of their own linguistic processes. The *mise-en-abîme* of linguistic self-reflexivity thus translates into an ethical *mise-en-question* of the self in relation to the other. I offer below a brief discussion of each of these three thinkers – Vattimo, Kristeva and Lyotard.

(c) Vattimo

Vattimo and Lyotard are two Continental thinkers explicitly identified with post-modern theory. While others vehemently denounce post-modernity as an endless cycle of parody and pastiche, mimicking the fetishistic logic of late capitalism, Vattimo and Lyotard attempt to discern some of its more enabling features.

Vattimo, for example, argues in *The End of Modernity: Nihilism and Hermeneutics in Postmodern Culture* (1988) that post-modernity is to be welcomed in so far as it endorses a certain practice of 'fragile thought' *(pensiero debole)*. By this he means a thinking which renounces the modern temptation – from Descartes and Spinoza to Hegel and Marx – to totalize the plurality of our human discourses in a single system or foundation. Post-modern thinking, by contrast, would be expressly *fragile* to the extent that it refuses to reduce the complex multiplicity of our cultural signs and images to a systematic synthesis. It resists appeals to ultimate grounds – theological, ontological or anthropological – which presume to resolve the 'conflict of interpretations' that makes up our contemporary culture; it declines all recourse to an absolute origin *(arche)* or end *(telos)*.

As becomes clear in his radical rereadings of his acknowledged mentors, Heidegger and Gadamer, Vattimo celebrates the advent of a non-foundational and tentative mode of thinking. He welcomes this unleashing of the metaphysical understanding of Being into a circular hermeneutic play of signs and images. The age of technology, he acknowledges, is not avoidable or surpassable. So, instead of resorting to nostalgia for some lost golden age, or naïvely crediting the inevitability of millennial progress, Vattimo recommends a 'post-modern art' of ludic imagining.

Thus might the 'Idolatry of the New' – predicated upon the Romantic cult of genial creation – be replaced by a non-fanatical and non-presumptuous play of 're-creation'. The modern philosophy of the transcendental ego is gently supplanted by a post-modern self which refuses to apologize for the 'feebleness of its own identity'. At its best, post-modernity cultivates and honours the 'casual role of the self'.[28] It releases us into an anti-foundational hermeneutic where a circular interplay of interpretations is an aesthetic liberty to be affirmed rather than feared.

In a text entitled 'Myth and the fate of secularization', Vattimo reflects on the implications of such a post-modern hermeneutics for our appreciation of mythic imagination. Observing that the modern ideal of philosophy – as a rigorous science based on essential foundations – is no longer tenable, Vattimo argues that not every dream of the past bequeathed to us by our cultural traditions is to be abandoned. He maintains that 'myth' may be an aesthetic category of thought which could survive the modern *hermeneutics of suspicion* bent on demythologizing its 'false consciousness' in the name of Rational Progress.

But Vattimo is quick to caution against any attempt to reappropriate myth in terms of some putative aboriginal innocence. In the concluding section of his text, entitled 'Myth and the postmodern', he suggests that the most fitting response to our present-day experience of myth would be to realize that 'our relationship to myth, once demythization itself has been shown to be a myth, will not be restored to some *original* state, but will remain marked by this very experience'. A theory of the presence of myth in contemporary culture must take this as its point of departure.[29] The post-modern paradox of imagination – mythic, aesthetic or social – is the following: 'to know that one is dreaming and yet to continue dreaming'.[30]

A post-modern hermeneutic of the mythic imaginary, therefore, would be one which abandons all pretence to legitimize myth in terms of metaphysical or scientific foundations, while retaining myth as a secular interplay of multifaceted meanings; an interplay which dramatizes our cultural memories and traditions as historical interpretations rather than idolizing them as timeless dogmas. The post-modern 'overcoming' of myth which Vattimo counsels – drawing from, but also surpassing, the Heidegger–Gadamer model of hermeneutic *Verwindung* – proposes to salvage myth in the transposed form of an ironically distanced or diluted reinterpretation. By not taking itself too seriously (that is, literally), myth can be taken seriously once again. Whence the curious paradox: it is precisely when the modern cult of 'demythization' is itself unmasked as a myth (an Enlightenment myth of absolute Reason) that the mythic imaginary can recover its legitimacy. But this legitimacy resides in the very acknowledgement of the *limits* of myth – its inherent modesty and *faiblesse* as an experience of truth. The weakness of myth is its strength. Its disclaimer to absolute truth is its claim to partial truth – the only kind we, as finite historical interpreters, can ever presume to possess. The critical moment of the 'demythization of demythization can be considered accordingly as the true and proper moment of transition from the modern to the postmodern'.[31] Vattimo spells out the radical implications of this argument for a post-modern hermeneutic of the imaginative subject as follows:

> After radical demythization, the experience of truth simply can no longer be the same as before, for there is no longer any apodictic evidence of the kind in which thinkers, during the era of metaphysics, sought to find a *fundamentum absolutum et inconcussum*. The postmodern subject, when it turns toward itself and searches its consciousness, is confronted not by the certainty of the Cartesian *cogito*, but by the *intermittences du coeur* described by Proust, the *récits* produced by the mass media, or the mythologies rediscovered by psychoanalysis. It is precisely this experience that the return of myth in our culture and in our language tries to capture, certainly not that of a mythical primitive culture uncontaminated by modernization and rationalism. Only in this sense – through a weakening of the notion of truth – can myth be understood to point towards the overcoming of the opposition between rationalism and irrationalism, and to open a possible new direction for contemporary thought.[32]

But can such a post-modern hermeneutic of myth be applied to the more general problem of our Civilization of the Image? In *The End of Modernity*, Vattimo outlines arguments in favour of a post-modern approach to art which go some way to answering this question. In contrast to the modernist ideology of the New – with its futurist idioms of progressivism or pessimism – the post-modern imagination bears witness to the 'dissolution of the value of the new'.[33] This drift towards secular dissolution is present at all levels of post-modern society; but it is most conspicuous, Vattimo holds, in the aesthetic imaginary of contemporary culture. 'Caught up in the phantasmagoric play (Adorno's phrase) of consumer society and the technological media, the arts have lived without any metaphysical mask (that is, without any seeking after a supposed authentic foundation of existence).' And so, he maintains, 'the (aesthetic) experience of the value of novelty itself is in a way more pure and visible than in science or technology (still bound, in some degree, to the values of truth and of use): with this aesthetic experience, the value of the new, radically unveiled, has lost all foundational value and any possibility of being valuable again'.[34]

This crisis of faith in the New, as evidenced most conspicuously in post-modern art, also discloses a crisis of the Future. What we are confronting in the contemporary imaginary is an emphatic alteration in our inherited ways of experiencing time and history. It is surely no accident, Vattimo observes, that works such as Joyce's *Ulysses* and *Finnegans Wake* are themselves reflections of the problematic experience of temporality which arises when we abandon the naïve belief in the linear progress of so-called 'natural time'.[35] Vattimo sees here a positive concept of *post-history* emerging, which has nothing to do with the Spenglerian obsession with decline. The modernist belief in the inevitability of 'artistic revolutions' is coming undone; it is being dismantled *(sfondamento)* as but one other, if terminal, variation on the old metaphysical hankering after new foundations and origins. And as the foundation stones of the modernist edifice are being prized loose Vattimo discerns the opportunity of an alternative path of dialogue emerging between poetics and philosophy – between the kind of post-modern theory of literature advanced by Ihab Hassan in *The Dismemberment of Orpheus* (1971) and the kind of post-modern theory he himself, amongst others, is promoting – a path committed to the problematic, but not impossible, 'overcoming of metaphysics'.[36]

Such a dialogue between post-modern poetry *(Dichten)* and thought *(Denken)* in turn opens up the possibility of a post-modern *ethics*. Post-modernism, understood in Vattimo's sense of a non-foundational non-functionalist theory of interpretation, solicits an ethical task of remembering *(An-denken)* that is not a simple repetition of tradition but its joyous re-creation *(fruizione)*. Such remembering emancipates

tradition from servile conformism, transposing it into a historical transmission of overtures to possible modes of being-in-the-world. Or, to put
it in our own terms, we would say that a post-modern *poetics of the possible* entails an *ethics of the possible*.[37] Here we are concerned not with
an 'ethic of commands', predicated upon abstract and unconditional
imperatives, but an 'ethic of goods' devoted to practices of concrete
historical experience. 'The rememoration of the spiritual forms of
the past, or even more so their savouring and reliving in aesthetic
terms, does not so much prepare for something else as contain in
itself an effect of emancipation. Maybe it is on such a basis that a
postmodern ethics could oppose itself to the still metaphysical ethics
of "development", of growth and of novelty considered as the ultimate
value.'[38]

The development of a radical hermeneutics – in the wake of Nietzsche,
Heidegger, Gadamer and Ricoeur – means that a properly post-modern
method of interpretation can no longer simply involve a reprise of
meanings from the past, but must remain alert to the contemporary
phenomenon of 'con-fusion' which characterizes knowledge as it circulates in our technological media of communications. Here we encounter
a hermeneutic detour where meanings become so disseminated that
the metaphysical nostalgia for a unified system of foundational truth
is forsworn.[39] In its place we find a 'weak ontology' where, rather
than seeking absolute grounds as bulwarks against the streams of
multiple meaning which epitomize our Civilization of the Image, we
endeavour to 'discover and prepare for the appearance of the *chances*,
ultra- and post-metaphysical, of our planetary technology'.[40] The end
of metaphysics thus corresponds with the world-image of technology
(die Gestell) – a global imaginary where the traditional metaphysical
distinctions between subject and object, reality and representation,
are contaminated if not dissolved. Vattimo concludes on a typically
paradoxical note of optimistic pessimism:

With the loss of these determinations, man and Being enter an order
of oscillation *(schwingend)*, which we ought, I suggest, imagine as
a world of 'alleviated' reality – in the sense of a world less neatly
divided into the true and the fictive, information and image: a world
of total mediation like the one we now inhabit to a large degree. It is
in such a world that ontology becomes *effectively* hermeneutic, and
that the metaphysical notions of . . . reality and of truth-foundation
lose their credibility. In such a situation, we should, I believe, speak of

a 'fragile ontology' as the one possibility of moving beyond metaphysics – in the sense of an acceptance-convalescence-distortion which has nothing to do with the activity of critical surpassing which characterizes modernity. It may well be here that post-modern thinking will find its *chance* of a new beginning – faintly, *faiblement*, new.[41]

(d) Kristeva

Julia Kristeva is another Continental thinker who approaches the post-modern imaginary from a hermeneutic perspective. Her controversial distinction between the *semiotic* and the *symbolic* was already a token of her dissent from the post-structuralist maxim that there is nothing beyond the text *(Il n'y a pas de hors texte)*. By *semiotic* Kristeva understands those 'representations of affects' – informed by the primary processes of unconscious displacement and condensation – which *precede* all verbal representations *(Wortvorstellung)*. The *symbolic*, by contrast, comprises 'representations tributary to the system of language'. Kristeva identifies the semiotic with the affects of the maternal body, or *chora*, which resist the categorizations of identity, unity and position, and consequently cannot be defined in any determinate language system. She equates the symbolic process, on the other hand, with the paternal language of grammar, syntax and law. The subject of discourse is, for Kristeva (echoing Lacan), a 'split subject': a radical heteronomy belonging to both the semiotic *chora* and the symbolic order of signification.[42]

It is precisely because the subject of discourse is thus divided that Kristeva has become increasingly engaged in a psychoanalytic hermeneutic bent on exploring the 'melancholic imaginary' which, she believes, epitomizes the subject's 'affective' experience of inner contradiction and loss. In a revealing text entitled 'On melancholic imagination' she spells out her theoretical preoccupation. While the imaginary expresses itself through discourse, it derives from a semiotic order of 'affects' which 'cannot be understood on the basis of a linguistic model deploying verbal signs as signifiers and signifieds'.[43] The experience of melancholy holds the key to this semiotics of the imaginary. It is the other side of eros. Or as Kristeva puts it: 'Melancholy is amorous passion's somber lining.'[44] The passion to unite with the other itself presupposes the melancholic experience of separation from the other. The imaginary originates in despair – the affect of utter loss. All imagination for Kristeva is, in the first and last instance, an expression of melancholy:

Rather than seeking the meaning of despair (which is evident or metaphysical), let me admit that there is no meaning aside from despair. The child-king becomes irremediably sad before proffering his first words: it is being separated from his mother, despairingly, with no going back, that makes him decide to try to recuperate her, along with other objects, in his *imagination* and later, in words. The semiology interested in the degree zero of symbolism is unfailingly led to pose itself questions concerning not only the amorous state but also its somber corollary – melancholy. Thereby to recognize, in the same movement, that if no writing exists that is not amorous, *nor does an imagination exist that is not, manifestly or secretly, melancholic.*[45]

Just as the erotic imaginary arises from the impossible mourning of the lost (maternal) object, the religious imaginary arises from the death of God – and the consequent inability to mourn this loss. Melancholy is thus affirmed in religious doubt – Kristeva cites the dead Christ of Holbein's painting which so fascinated Dostoyevsky in *The Idiot*. The melancholic humour of imagination is particularly acute in 'epochs of crisis', such as our own, which are witnessing the collapse of religious and political ideals. 'In times of crisis', writes Kristeva, 'melancholy imposes itself, lays down its archaeology, produces its representations . . .'[46] But here we confront a baffling paradox. The same melancholic imagination which finds creative expression in art and literature – as illustrated by Kristeva in her compelling analyses of works by Dostoyevsky and Duras in *Soleil noir: dépression et mélancholie* – seems to be the very opposite of that melancholic stupor which stifles artistic expression. Kristeva states her puzzlement in the following passage which combines the idioms of Merleau-Ponty and Lacan to original effect:

I find myself here before an enigmatic chiasmus that will not cease to preoccupy me: if loss, mourning, absence set the imaginary act in motion and permanently fuel it as much as they menace and undermine it, it is also undeniable that the fetish of the work of art is erected in disavowal of this mobilizing affliction. The artist is melancholy's most intimate witness and the most ferocious combatant of the symbolic abdication enveloping him . . . Until death strikes and suicide imposes its triumphant conclusion upon the void of the lost object . . .[47]

The melancholic imagination is not a reverie of vengeance towards the lost other (introverted into the self, as Freud and Klein believed); it is rather the experience of a 'fundamental lack' which defines the human subject as an 'incomplete, empty and wounded primitive ego'.[48] The imaginary is to be taken therefore as the most archaic expression of a wound that cannot be adequately named or symbolized in verbal language; it precedes every identification with an external agent (subject or object). Accordingly, the self-suffering, or even suicidal, imagination that one finds described in so much contemporary literature is not some 'camouflaged act of war' against the lost other; it is an end in itself, a sorrow that has become its own object for want of any other – 'a reuniting with sorrow and, beyond it, with that impossible love, never attained, always elsewhere; such as the promise of the void, of death'.[49]

The imaginary first arises, then, at the pre-linguistic stage when the child is still a 'pre-subject' – an *in-fans* in the literal sense of one unable to speak who receives and responds to the radical affects of loss. But if the imaginary is to cope with this affect of loss it must express itself 'by entering into the world of signs and creation'.[50] This entry into the symbolic strives to replace that which is lacking with signs which would be equivalents, substitutes. The human self thus sets itself up as a subject in its own right, normally identifying with a father-figure who compensates for the loss by denying the importance of the lost maternal object. So the newly constituted subject can thereby presume to mask its own split self: 'No I haven't lost anything: I evoke, I signify: through the artifice of signs and for myself, I bring into existence that which has separated itself from me'.[51]

But this 'manic' gesture of self-affirmation, which Kristeva defines as the upper half of depression, can in certain aesthetic circumstances actually work towards a 'sublimation solution to the crisis'.[52] Instead of allowing us to remain permanent victims of the polar divide between the affectivity of the imaginary and the signification of the symbolic, artistic or religious discourse can often point to other ways of expressing the melancholic dilemma. Kristeva writes:

Aesthetic – and, in particular, literary – creation, as well as religious discourse in its imaginary fictional essence, proposes a configuration of which the prosodic economy, the dramaturgy of characters and the implicit symbolism are an extremely faithful semiological representation of the subject's battle with symbolic breakdown. This

189

literary or religious representation is not an *elaboration* in the sense of 'becoming conscious' of the inter- and intrapsychic causes of moral pain. In this it differs from the psychoanalytic path that proposes for itsellf the dissolution of this symptom. However, this literary (and religious) representation possesses a real and imaginary efficacy that, concerned more with catharsis than elaboration, is a therapeutic method utilized in all societies throughout the ages.[53]

It is, however, in *Soleil noir: dépression et mélancolie* (1987) that Kristeva offers what is perhaps her most arresting account to date of the cathartic function of the aesthetic–religious imaginary. Discussing the recurrence of images of 'forgiveness' in Dostoyevsky's writing – what she calls *l'imaginaire du pardon* – Kristeva notes how the primary drives of *eros* and *thanatos* may be transformed *(poiein)* into a work of art. Citing the particular example of Raskolnikov in *Crime and Punishment*, Kristeva points out that the 'gravity' of pardon – which genuine aesthetic experience as well as genuine theology have realized – enables one to traverse the depths of abjection and suffering in order to 'name' it and ultimately arrive at a psychic renaissance. As such, the *imaginaire du pardon* presents itself as a therapeutic counterpart to *paranoia*. Raskolnikov's trajectory is an example of someone 'passing through melancholy, and even terrorist nihilation, before ultimately achieving that state of *recognition*, which is also a state of *renaissance*'.[54]

The *imaginaire du pardon* represents the transposition of destructive experience into aesthetic form. This has the impact of a *mise-en-acte*, a shaping, a making, a *poiesis*.[55] The therapeutic potential of this imaginary lies in the fact that it provides our affective experience of darkness and humiliation with the representational form of a work: a work which – be it musical, visual or literary – has not yet been transposed into the symbolic order of explanation. In other words, it operates at the transitional level of an 'art' which is still in contact with the *chora* of the body's wounded emotions – emotions which precede the verbal intelligence of logical understanding. But precisely as an aesthetic mid-way, this ambivalent *imaginaire* of sense and non-sense can act as midwife for an eventual translation into symbolic comprehension (for example, the 'talking cure' of psychoanalysis). In being able to play this dual role of linking us to both the *real* order of incomprehensible suffering and the *symbolic* order of understanding, the *imaginaire du pardon* enables the suffering body to undergo a transmutation – or a 'trans-substantiation' to use a more equivocal aesthetico-religious term employed by Joyce as well as by Kristeva herself. The decisive therapeutic potential of the *imaginaire du pardon* is that it introduces the subject (be it the artist or anyone who identifies with an aesthetic imaginary) to the possibility of another meaning *(sens)*. It opens us to the promise of an *other* – *le père aimant, imaginaire* – who may listen, speak, comprehend, absolve, deliver us back to ourselves as subjects of a 'second life'.[56]

Creative writing *(écriture)* exemplifies a certain enigmatic zone situated between the semiotic order of corporal 'affects' and the symbolic order of signifying 'effects'. 'At the frontiers of emotion and acts, writing arises through the surpassing of affectivity toward the effectivity of signs.' But this surpassing is no mere negation or obliteration. 'It serves as vehicle for the affects without repressing them,' explains Kristeva, 'it proposes a way of sublimating them, transposing them for an other in a third relation, imaginary and symbolic. And it is because it is pardon that writing is transformation, transposition, translation.'[57]

There are four main ways outlined by Kristeva in which the melancholic imagination may find expression: (1) through *mania*, born of paranoia, as the outer lining of despair; (2) through *religion*, as the sublimation of suffering, a process whereby the idiot may become a saint, the criminal a prophet, the victim a visionary; (3) through *artistic creation* which integrates both the manic and religious options, establishing less obsessional, more enabling relations between ourselves and others; (4) through *psychoanalysis* as a long discourse re-enacting and dissolving the transferential bond and thus, also, serving as an apprenticeship for living beyond despair.[58]

All four options register the 'hiatus of subjectivity' which constitutes the essence of the melancholic imagination. And, as such, they illustrate Kristeva's wish to establish a model of significance *(signifiance)* which permits us to appreciate how the logical word of discourse, supported by an infra-linguistic (semiotic) order of representations, can resonate at the affective level of our bodily experience. What is being espoused here is an imaginary order 'where the word can at every moment profoundly touch and affect the living flesh'.[59]

The semiotic *chora* which makes up the melancholic imaginary is acutely felt in much post-modern literature. Concluding a detailed analysis of *nouveaux romans* by Marguerite Duras which epitomize *une maladie de la douleur*, Kristeva proffers comments on the complex relationship between the modern and post-modern imaginary. As a literature of malady, Duras' writing reflects the deep sense of dereliction evident in the crisis of modernity; but it equally lays claim to a transhistorical dimension of experience. As a literature of limits, the elliptical language of its characters – in addition to recurring evocations of a void informing our *maladie de la douleur* – bears witness to the breakdown of words when confronted with the unnameable. Unlike Mallarmé who sought to translate the 'nothing' of silence into a music of words, Duras' insistence on the inescapability of the suffering which the 'nothing' affects produces a whiteness of meaning (*une blancheur du sens*) which in turn reproduces in us, her readers, the troubling 'affect' of malaise. But how does such writing face the post-modern condition? Says Kristeva:

Modern from an historical and psychological point of view, this writing finds itself today confronted with the postmodern challenge. Henceforth it is a matter regarding the 'sickness of suffering' as a moment in the *narrative synthesis* which is capable of importing into its complex whirlpool philosophical meditations as well as erotic defenses or pleasurable distractions. Postmodernity is closer to the *comédie humaine* than to the *malaise abyssal*. Has not hell itself, as explored to the last bitter detail in the post-war literature, not lost its infernal inaccessibility to become our daily lot, transparent, almost banal – a 'nothing' – just like our 'truths' henceforth visualized and televised, in short, not as secret as all that ...? Today the desire for comedy comes to re-cover – without ignoring – the scruple of this truth without tragedy, this melancholy without purgatory ... A new world of love is trying to surface in the eternal return of historical and mental cycles. The artifice of seeming replaces the winter of our discontent; the rending amusement of parody replaces the whiteness of *ennui*. And vice versa. In short, truth makes its way just as well in the mirrorings of factitious pleasures as it is able to affirm itself in the mirror play of pain. Does not the very wonder of the psychic life not reside after all in these alternations between protection and fall, laughter and tears, sun and melancholy?[60]

A further question is this: Is it possible that our post-modern culture might produce works capable of engendering in us a new *imaginaire de la comédie* – one which might resolve, however tentatively, the opposition between the *imaginaire de la mélancolie* and the *imaginaire du pardon* (the two poles of modern literature exemplified by Duras and Dostoyevsky)? Is it not such a possibility that a post-modern author like Milan Kundera has in mind when he identifies the wisdom of fiction as a 'spirit of humour' – an 'art which came into the world as an echo of God's laughter'?[61]

This prospect of a positive post-modern imagination is explored by Kristeva herself in a number of recent works. In a text entitled *In the Beginning Was Love: Psychoanalysis and Faith* (1987), she argues that the end of therapy is not the moment of paranoid selfhood – exemplified in the statement 'I am alone, hence I am the Creator' – but in the advent of a certain 'playfulness of spirit', a moment which comes *after* the period of disillusionment. The attitude here is that if one is indeed alone, like no other person, one is also inhabited by a perpetual sense of the other – as exemplified in the statement 'I am someone else, I cannot say who. There are things that cannot be said, and I am entitled to play with them so that I can understand them better.'[62] It is in this second moment of imaginative play that perversions may be tamed, neuroses allayed. In coming to know and own my desires imaginatively I am freer to love others or delude myself at my own risk. 'Gravity becomes frivolity that retains its memory of suffering and continues its search for truth in the joy of perpetually making a new beginning.'[63]

But gravity can only be transformed into frivolity in a *liberating* way if we have first witnessed the 'resurrection of imagination'. This is why the ultimate priority of a post-modern therapy according to Kristeva is 'to reawaken the imagination and to permit illusions to exist'.[64] Restoring imagination to its full therapeutic value already signals a departure from the Freudian rationalism which held that the end of analysis was the demise of imagination and the birth of reason.

Analysis now takes imagination as both its means and its end. It takes it as *means* in so far as therapeutic discourse is essentially determined by the mnemonic techniques of free association. This process (well documented by Freud himself) is essentially a work of imagination in that the speaking analysand, no less than the listening analyst, works by enticements, subterfuges, approximations, hints and guesses. The amorous discourse of the analysand is an act of imagining irreducible to a scientifically rational interpretation (that is, the attitude which would dismiss it as nothing but a projective fantasy or hysterical identification – though it may be that in part). On this point, the

Freudians who construe the unconscious as an exclusively linguistic system to the virtual elimination of a *positive* imaginary stand rebuked. 'By emphasizing only the *verbal substance* of the transference, without highlighting the fact that it involves not just play-acting but, initially at least, mystification, we miss the imaginary aspect of psychotherapy.' But it is precisely because analytic discourse is not definitively fixed by verifiable rational arguments that it is able, 'as a discourse of the imagination', to work on three levels at once – as representations of words; as representations of things; and as semiotic traces of emotions. Without this third level of physical efficacy and affectivity (where the imaginary plays its primary role) our desires obtain no real impact.[65]

But the imaginary is not just a psychoanalytic means; it is also an *end*. The analytic truth woven out of the rapport between analysand and analyst, between the teller and the interpreter of tales, is a 'narrative fiction'. The destabilized subject becomes stabilized in and through the creation – and conscious assumption – of a new imaginary, playfully free yet always mindful of its prior incarceration. The most decisive factor in such therapy is the imaginary meaning established between analysand and analyst. And whether what the analysand tells the analyst actually happened or not is ultimately of little importance if, through the imaginary narrative, it is possible for the analyst to grasp the logic of the fantasies. The purpose of analysis, therefore, is not to terminate imagination but to restore its role as free play. So that if it is necessary to demystify certain *imagos* of the self – as self-sufficient and sovereign cogito – it is equally necessary to recall imagination to its Heraclitean vocation of 'acting like a child, of playing'.[66] This is the most healing lucidity, after all the idols of dogmatic 'truth' have been toppled – that imagining is not merely a means towards an end, but an end in itself. We become confident of our own desires as we enact the transfer beyond narcissism towards the other. For to acknowledge our imaginary discourse, the discourse of loving play, is to acknowledge the discourse of the other in us.

In this respect, Kristeva actually speaks of an *ethical* dimension to imagination. She equates ludic imagination with love. 'The speaking being', as she puts it, 'opens up to and reposes in the other.'[67] This presupposes our readiness not only to order and keep accounts of the unconscious but also to play with it, to take pleasure in it, to live it. We recognize accordingly that side by side with ourselves as knowing subjects we exist as subjects who derive our meaning from an alterity which transcends and overwhelms us. In an essay entitled

Postmodernism? (1980), Kristeva calls this alterity the 'unnameable' – something revealed to the imagination as unsayable, unrepresentable, uncanny, *unheimlich*.[68] Self-discovery is now seen as inseparable from the discovery of the other in us. And the ultimate knowledge gained from the imaginary play of desire is that there is always a residue of unconscious unknowability which forever escapes our conscious designs. It is this very residue, moreover, which serves to remind us that human desire is limited, finite, subject to the ethical imperative that the self is answerable to the other. Kristeva describes this ethical moment of self-discovery in the face of the other as follows:

> Once he has recognized his desire he acquires a new desire for (self-)knowledge; the 'new' man recognizes that he is caught in the toils of an unconscious logic, even though he can grasp the nature of that logic on a conscious level. Besides calculating knowledge we have a discourse that encompasses both allusion and illusion – displacements born of the interminable quest for an adequate fit between 'meaning' and 'object'. This is the realm of imagination, play, and possibility, where even calculation becomes renewal and creation. At the very heart of our rationality, psychoanalysis refuses to be confined within the narrow bounds of rationalism. Inwardly it veers toward metaphysics, yielding not only maximal lucidity but also a sacrifice of lucidity for which one need not feel any guilt. Has desire, the ultimate sign of subjectivity, therefore triumphed? The self has also subordinated itself to the other for the sake of a necessary, if temporary, tie ... It is the height of nihilism to claim, in the name of the rights of man – or superman – rights over life itself. The analyst takes another view, he looks forward to the ultimate dissolution of desire (whose spring lies in death), to be replaced by relationship with another, from which meaning derives ... Only the meaning that my desire may have for an other and hence for me can control its expansion, hence serve as the unique, if tenuous, basis of a morality.[69]

Faced with the discovery that our desire is inhabited and inhibited by the other, we have two alternatives: we sink back into anguish or we laugh. The knowledge that we are, in Kristeva's resonant phrase, *étrangers à nous-mêmes* can lead either to an ethics of self-repression governed by a taciturn 'spirit of seriousness' *or* to an ethics of imaginative play before the unnameable face of the other – a post-modern ethics where gaiety transfigures dread and love casts out fear.[70]

(e) Lyotard

Jean-François Lyotard, author of *The Postmodern Condition* (1979) and the thinker perhaps most responsible for giving the term 'post-modernity' its common currency in contemporary philosophy, also makes a significant contribution to a radical hermeneutics of imagination. Lyotard appeals to the notion of a 'narrative imagination' as a means of resisting the modern ideology of Total Theory. Any such Theory, no matter how ostensibly scientific or objective, is no more than a disguised narrative. Accordingly, we find that Lyotard's invocation of narrative imagination in a text such as *Instructions païennes* (1977) is motivated by a double desire: (1) to unmask Theory as Grand Narrative, and (2) to unmask Grand Narrative as a concealment, even suppression, of little narratives (*des petits récits*). He here argues that the ultimate reference of every narrative is not some totalizing reality but *other narratives*; and he thereby proposes to deflate the time-honoured metaphysical claim to a concept of *identity* subjugating *differences*.[71]

But the dissolution of Theory into a multiplicity of 'little stories' is not for Lyotard, as for many other proponents of a post-modern perspective, a slippage into a self-referential labyrinth of mirrors. Narrative play is never reducible to parody. On the contrary, one of the author's foremost concerns in his writings from the mid-seventies onwards – in particular *Instructions païennes*, *Just Gaming* (1977), *The Differend* (1983) and *L'Inhumain* (1988) – has been to establish a linkage between a post-modern model of narrative (as *petits récits*) and an ethical concept of justice. It is arguable, moreover, that Lyotard's preoccupation with narrative reference and historical justice still bears the hallmark of his early apprenticeship with the phenomenology of Merleau-Ponty (his first published work was entitled simply *La Phénoménologie*) and mark him off from many other post-structuralist theorists of the imaginary.

A recurring dilemma for Lyotard is how to reconcile a multiplicity of justices with a justice of multiplicity? Since he refuses a meta-narrative of narratives – which would seek to classify the *petits récits* in a conceptual hierarchy – Lyotard ultimately consigns imagination to a justice of *dissensus*. Where consensus seeks unity, dissensus cultivates difference. This is what Lyotard has in mind when he pleads at the end of *The Postmodern Condition* for a post-modern culture of diversity. 'Let us wage war on totality,' he declares. 'Let us activate the differences and save the honour of the name.'[72]

It comes as no surprise, therefore, to find him in *Instructions païennes* citing Solzhenitsyn's *Gulag Archipelago* as an exemplary fiction of *petits récits*, eroding the tyranny of Grand Narrative (in this instance, the Marxist Science of History). 'The efficacity of the *Gulag Archipelago*', he writes,

> resides in the fact that it is a work of literature. As a book, it is made up of scenes and tableaux which by their number and specific force, which is that of story, release the *narrative imagination* of the reader and make it conspire with the narrative imagination which is operative in the heroes of Solzhenitsyn. It is not an identification with their proper names which is at issue – we forget them all – but a continuity established with them by the inventions of short scenarios and rapid scenographies to which they have recourse in the very situation where such inventions are precisely forbidden.[73]

The *Gulag* is a medley of narratives, of which the author's own version is but one which contains and relates others. In addition to the author himself, the *referent* of the *Gulag* is a diversity of other narrators; and this crossing of narrator and referent in turn serves to remind us readers that we, too, are narrators in our own right. The democratic message of Solzhenitsyn's text is 'the power of the common, that anyone can narrate'.[74]

The narrative imagination, in other words, is committed to justice to the extent that it can relate the dissenting stories of the detainee in opposition to the Official Story of the Commissar (the latter Story masquerading, of course, as an objective Meta-Narrative and thereby concealing its own status as narrativity). The Official Story presents itself as *the* Official History. A narrative imagination introduces justice, by contrast, in that it deconstructs History into the plurality of stories that make it up. And this iconoclastic instance is particularly directed against the modern attempts at a totalizing Theory of History – in its secular, Marxist, Enlightenment or Christian versions – as an Onward March of inevitable progress towards the Kingdom of the Universal. Lyotard writes:

> Theories are no more than dissimulated narratives that should not be allowed to pose as omnitemporal. Therefore to have constructed

a narrative, at some point, which has come to assume the figure of a seamless system, in no way removes the task of starting all over again here and now. And this means that one has no reason to be immediately coherent, that is, sufficient unto oneself, but every reason to wish to be up to the task of narrating (*raconter*) what one believes one understands from what others are saying and doing.[75]

Lyotard describes this narrative imagination – committed to ethical judgements – as 'impious'. By this he means a refusal of the piety of absolutist politics: a piety embodied not just in tradition-bound monarchies but more subtly in the modern ideologies which legitimate the power of the Nation-State. In short, piety refers to those institutions and ideologies which totalize, and thereby suppress, differences. The disillusionment with Grand Narrative is not confined to the contemporary renunciation of the 'Communist Empire'; it is also widespread in the general disenchantment with the optimistic ideology of Progress which has informed the political rhetoric of most Western liberal states. Lyotard suggests, for his part, that the present (post-modern) multiplication of inconvenient 'little narratives' is by no means a bad augury.[76]

The terror of the camps and gulags, as extreme exemplifications of centralized power, aims to eliminate the *impious* potential of narrative imagination. The party only legitimates *free* citizens who conform to its Master Narrative (*Maître-Récit*). And this means subscribing to each of its three aspects (1) as supposed co-author of the Official Story, (2) as privileged recipient of the Official Story, and (3) as supposed agent who faithfully applies the implications of the Official Story to everyday life. 'One is thus officially commandeered in the three aspects of the Master-Narrative at once,' observes Lyotard. 'Your imagination as narrator, auditor and actor is completely shackled. And if you default on any of these duties, you forfeit all your qualities.'[77] This is the terror of the citizen in a totalitarian state. Otherwise stated: any lapse in the pre-established narrative duty of telling-listening-enacting means being deprived of the right to narrate altogether. You are censured. Silenced. Your designated role becomes that of hostage, *persona non grata et non dramatis* – that is, someone disempowered to recite or respond to a scenario. 'You are banished from the *scene*,' explains Lyotard, 'put outside the scenario, off-stage, even removed from the theatre wings. You are, in short, forbidden to narrate. And that is devastation.'[78]

The little narratives of dissensus are, in the totalitarian context, those stories which survive to tell the tale. But the dissenting imagination is also one whose last recourse is to 'narrate the fact that there is nothing left for it to narrate, no one to listen to its narration and no reality to invent in and through its narrative'.[79] One might legitimately ask, however, if this end-of-narrative nightmare is not also voiced by several post-modern authors in the West – Beckett, Pynchon, Duras and the *nouveau-romanciers*? And, if so, what distinguishes, finally, the apocalyptic fears of a 'wake of imagination' as described by such Western writers and similar fears expressed by *samizdat* writers such as Solzhenitsyn, Kundera or Gombrowicz? Surely there is a world of difference? Or has the post-modern problematic now assumed world proportions?

Against such a dramatic backdrop – where the author stages the alarming scene of the narrative imagination in straits – Lyotard appeals for the cultivation of 'impious fables'. Such fables refuse the tyranny of state blessings. Their non-piety is an affirmative token of their disrespect for the homogenizing consensus of power. It signals an insistence that the little stories of the narrative imagination also find a voice, an audience, a world. In this sense, narrative could be said to be an elementary ingredient of all genuinely civil societies – East and West. We are concerned here with more than a Manichaean opposition between the little narrative of the dissident and the Master-Narrative of the Commissar. That is an extreme instance of terror. But not the only one. Civil society exists there – anywhere – where little narratives circulate and remain unassimilable by the Master-Narrative of party or state. One such example cited by Lyotard in the West was the narrative of the student revolt in 1968 which resisted assimilation into the existing orthodox piety of the French Nation-State under de Gaulle, as well as resisting recuperation by the official narrative of the French Communist Party (primacy of proletarian class struggle, economic determinism, party centralism and so on). But there are many other less conspicuous examples. 'If the networks of uncertain and ephemeral narratives are capable of eroding the massive apparatus of institutionalised narrative,' writes Lyotard,

it is in multiplying the somewhat lateral skirmishes or disputes such as one finds in recent decades in the women's movement, prisoners' rights campaign, anti-draft revolt, prostitute rights groups, or farmer and student rebellions. Here one invents little histories-stories (*histoires*), even segments of stories, one listens to them, transmits them, puts them into play at the right moment. Why *little* stories? Because they are short, and consequently are not extracts from grand history (*la grande histoire*) and resist absorption into it.[80]

At this point in his own *petit récit* of pagan instructions, Lyotard compares his post-modern model of a narrative imagination with Kant's third *Critique*. In the *Critique of Judgement* imagination is presented as an end in itself, a *finality without end*, a power of play liberated from the universalizing constraints of law and knowledge. What interests Lyotard here is the Kant who has been cured of the 'malady of knowledge and rules', who has (in his third *Critique*) passed over to the 'paganism of art and nature'. And he adds: 'You will note that this discourse, if it is correct, cannot be *true* as a theory pretends to be: it is no longer a meta-narrative, even a critical one. It has itself become a work of art, one where imagination wants itself to be imagination.'[81]

Lyotard thus envisages an open culture based on a plurality of narratives. Here the State would yield to a civil society which continually puts itself in question, which acknowledges that it is not founded on any absolute bedrock of legitimation or exclusion. Such a social culture comprises a multifold history of narrative clusters – one where little stories are recounted, invented, heard, played out. It is a culture where 'the people does not exist as a Subject, but rather as an accumulation of thousands of little histories, futile and serious, and which permit themselves to be drawn together to constitute larger stories, sometimes to disperse again into wandering elements, but which on the whole hold more or less together to form what one calls the culture of a civil society'.[82] A just society is, accordingly, one which respects the *power of the common* – that is, the potentiality of each person to deploy his or her narrative imagination. And it must be conceded that we are always already engaged in some narrative or other, we have always been already told in some history and have in turn our own histories to retell.[83] This is not, of course, to say that all the little narratives are ultimately retraceable to some originating narrative. On the contrary, it means that the metaphysical privileging of a Transcendental Narrator – called Being, Arche, God, Truth or Party – is deconstructed in the name of a plurality of interdependent narrators operating in endless relay.

This is what Lyotard defines as a post-modern model of *paganism*. The piety of orthodox Theory is what seeks to deny this free interplay, to subject the impious post-modern interchanges between little narratives to some Master Narrative. But such subjection is the kiss of death to narrative imagination. The price paid for the return of narrative to a First or Final Narrator is exorbitant. It is nothing less than one's 'exclusion from the imagination of narratives'[84] – an exclusiveness paving the royal way to injustice.

In politics, as in literature or art, the implication is that justice is to be found by passing from *theory* to *narrative*, from transcendental piety to pragmatic impiety, from the dialectical opposition of reason and non-reason to a just (that is judging) imagination. But what is this just imagination? It is one which dispels the hegemony of Grand Narrative in favour of little narratives, without degenerating into the arbitrary or the cynical. Against the opportunism of anything-goes, Lyotard proposes the opportunity of a just narrative imagination – what he describes as a 'mistress without masters, the armoury of the disarmed, the power of the powerless'.[85] Here is a justice that cannot be grounded in canonical rules. It appeals rather to a 'perspective' of narrative pragmatics. Lyotard offers this account of such an appeal:

> Destroy all monopolies of narrative, destroy the exclusivist themes of parties and markets. Remove from the Narrator the privilege he gives himself and show there is just as much power in narrative listening and narrative action (in the socially narrated world) ... Struggle for the inclusion of all Master Narratives, of theories and doctrines, particularly political ones, within the (little) narratives. So that the intelligentsia may see its task not to proclaim the truth or save the world, but to seek the power of playing out, listening to, and telling stories. A power that is so common that peoples will never be deprived of it without riposte. And if you want an authority – that power is authority. Justice is wanting it.[86]

The virtue of a narrative imagination, committed to justice in this way, is that it resists what Lyotard calls in *The Postmodern Condition* the modern 'nostalgia for the whole and the one'.[87] As such, it exposes and renounces the demand to totalize the plurality of narratives into a so-called 'real unity' – a demand which is nothing other than a transcendental illusion; and whose price, as several events of the nineteenth and twentieth centuries tragically remind us, is *terror*.[88] The post-modern imagination – be it that of the writer, the artist or the thinking citizen – is one which invents and re-invents narratives without recourse to the unifying strategies of pre-ordained systems. 'A

201

postmodern artist or writer is in the position of a philosopher,' claims Lyotard, 'the text he writes, the work he produces are not in principle governed by pre-established rules, and they cannot be judged according to a determining judgment, by applying familiar categories to the text or the work. Those rules and categories are what the work of art itself is looking for. The artist and the writer, then, are working without rules in order to formulate the rules of what *will have been done*.'[89]

Justice, as envisaged by a post-modern imagination, is never simply a matter of conforming to a given law. It involves a responsibility to listen to *other narratives* (in the sense of alternative narratives and narratives of others). The justice of narrative imagination is, in short, a justice of multiplicity. Such justice, explains Lyotard, 'prescribes the observance of the singular justice of each game such as it has just been situated: formalism of the rules and imagination in the moves. It authorizes the "violence" that accompanies the work of the imagination. It prohibits terror, that is, the blackmail of death toward one's partners, the blackmail that a prescriptive system does not fail to make use of in order to become the majority in most of the games and over most of their pragmatic positions.'[90] The obvious paradox – and one readily adverted to by Lyotard himself – is that the prescription against universal prescriptivism can itself be taken as a universal prescription. And here we return to that ethical circle which seems to haunt Lyotard's post-modern hermeneutic of narrative imagination: How do you reconcile a justice of multiplicity with a multiplicity of justices? Whose justice are we talking about when we speak of the justice of imagination?

Notes

1 R. Kearney, *The Wake of Imagination* (London/Minneapolis, Minn.: Hutchinson/University of Minnesota Press, 1987).

2 The term 'post-modern' was used as early as 1938 by the historian Arnold Toynbee and in 1971 by the literary critic Ihab Hassan in a work entitled *The Dismemberment of Orpheus: Toward a Post-Modern Theory of Literature* (London: Oxford University Press, 1971). But it was in architectural theories of the mid-seventies that it first achieved international recognition as a critical term. Charles Jencks, along with Robert Venturi, Charles Moore, Michael Graves and Paulo Portoghesi became the most influential advocates of post-modern architecture. Jencks's first major study on the subject, *The Language of Postmodern Architecture* (London: Academy Editions) was published in 1977. This was followed by a more comprehensive comparative study, *Current Architecture* (London:

Academy Editions), in 1982. Here Jencks offered a useful definition of the term and a brief account of its genesis:

> Post-modern is a portmanteau concept covering several approaches to architecture which have evolved from Modernism. As this hybrid term suggests, its architects are still influenced by Modernism – in part because of their training and in part because of the impossibility of ignoring Modern methods of construction – and yet they have added other languages to it. A Post-Modern building is doubly coded – part Modern and part something else: vernacular, revivalist, local, commercial, metaphorical, or contextural. In several important instances it is also doubly coded in the sense that it seeks to speak on two levels at once: to a concerned minority of architects, an elite who recognize the subtle distinctions of a fast-changing language, and to the inhabitants, users, or passersby, who want only to understand and enjoy it. Thus one of the strong motivations of Post-Modernists is to break down the elitism inherent in Modern architecture and the architectural profession. Sometimes Post-Modernism is confused with Late-Modernism. Some architects practise both approaches, and there are also, inevitably, buildings which are transitional … (p. 111)

3   See Linda Hutcheon's lucid discussion of these characteristics of postmodernity in the opening chapter of *A Poetics of Postmodernism* (London: Routledge, 1988), pp. 3–21.

4   Italo Calvino, *The Literature Machine* (London: Picador, 1989), pp. 90–1.

5   *The Works of Jacques Lacan*, ed. B. Benvenuto and R. Kennedy (London: Free Association Books, 1986), p. 81. See also my more detailed commentary in 'Lacan: the dismantling of the imaginary', in *The Wake of Imagination*, pp. 256–61; and W. J. Richardson's excellent account of the 'mirror stage' in Lacan, 'The mirror inside: the problem of the self', in K. Hoeller (ed), *Heidegger and Psychology, Review of Existential Psychology and Psychiatry* (1988), pp. 98–9.

6   Louis Althusser, 'Freud and Lacan' in *Lenin and Philosophy and Other Essays*, NLB, London, 1971.

7   See my analysis of this question, 'Althusser: the imaginary as false consciousness', in *The Wake of Imagination*, pp. 261–5.

8   Roland Barthes, 'The death of the author', in *Image-Music-Text* (London: Fontana, 1977), p. 148.

9   ibid., pp. 146–7.

10 Barthes, 'Change the object itself: mythology today', in *Image-Music-Text*, p. 169.

11 Peter Washington, *Fraud: Literary History and the End of English* (London: Fontana, 1989), p. 163.

12 Michel Foucault, *The Order of Things* (New York: Vintage, 1973). For a comprehensive analysis of Foucault's celebration of this 'transgressive' potential of art (though it does not focus on the specific theme of the imaginary) see David Carroll, *Paraesthetics: Foucault, Lyotard, Derrida* (London: Methuen, 1987), pp. 53–80, 107–30. For a similar analysis

of the transgressive power of cinematic images see Gilles Deleuze, *Image-Movement, Cinema I* (Paris: Editions de Minuit, 1983), pp. 278 ff.; and my commentary on Deleuze's treatment of the cinematic imagination in *The Wake of Imagination*, pp. 329–32.

13 Michel Foucault, *This Is Not a Pipe* (Berkeley, Calif.: University of California Press, 1983), pp. 53–4.

14 ibid., p. 54. See also Foucault's analysis of Andy Warhol in 'Theatricum Philosophicum', in *Language, Counter-Memory, Practice* (New York: Cornell University Press, 1977).

15 Foucault, *Order of Things*, p. 387.

16 J. Derrida, 'The double session', in *Dissemination* (London: Athlone Press, 1981), p. 206.

17 ibid., p. 195.

18 ibid., p. 206.

19 ibid., p. 211. Derrida's deconstructive reading of the Romantic imagination focuses mainly on Kant and the German idealists. See ibid., pp. 192 ff., but also 'Economimesis' in *Mimésis: Desarticulations* (Paris: Éditions Philosophie en Gref,1981), pp. 62–73. In this latter text, Derrida argues that even the Kantian theory of the productive imagination is itself a mimetic activity, pp. 62, 67, 73. For example, p. 62:

> Mimesis occurs not only in the reproductive acts, as is self-evident, but also in the free and pure productivity of imagination. The latter only deploys the primitive power of its inventivity in *listening* to nature, its dictation, its edict .... Genius raises the liberty of play and the pure productivity of imagination to its highest point. It provides the rules, or at least the examples, but it has its rules dictated to it by nature: so much so that the very distinction between free art and mercenary art, with all the apparatus of hierarchical subordination which it commands, reproduces nature in its act of production, and so only breaks with *mimesis*, as the imitation of what is, in order to become one with the free unfolding and refolding of *physis*.

Another influential 'deconstructive' reading of imagination as imitation is to be found in Jean Baudrillard's *Simulations* (New York: Semiotext(e), 1983), pp. 4–5, 11, 23, 48.

20 David Tracy, *Plurality and Ambiguity* (New York: Harper & Row, 1987), p. 46.

21 ibid., p. 61.

22 ibid.

23 J. Lacan, *Ecrits* (Paris: Éditions du Seuil, 1966), p. 282; C. Lévi-Strauss, *La Pensée sauvage* (Paris: PLON, 1962), p. 326; J. Derrida, 'The ends of man', in *Margins of Philosophy* (Chicago, Ill.: University of Chicago Press, 1983).

24 Paul Ricoeur, 'Man and the foundation of humanism', in *Main Trends in Philosophy* (New York: Holmes & Meier, 1979), p. 369.

25 John Caputo, *Radical Hermeneutics: Repetition, Deconstruction and the Hermeneutic Project* (Bloomington and London: Indiana University Press, 1987).

26 ibid., p. 7. See also p. 119: 'Will the project of "radical" hermeneutics, which we are patiently staking out, turn out to be just another compromise, another insidious *"Aufhebung"*? ... Can there be a hermeneutics beyond "hermeneutics", beyond the "first essence" of hermeneutics, beyond the hermeneutics which looks for ... stability, a hermeneutics which wants to remain true to *kinesis*, which does not repress the fear and trembling?' I believe that the attempt by thinkers like Caputo and other 'post-modern' thinkers (such as Lyotard, Vattimo, Tracy and Kristeva) who seek to rework a post-Heideggerian hermeneutics in the direction of a radical critique of the metaphysics of identity, presence and totality indicate that the answer may be affirmative. I also believe that the later hermeneutic writings of Ricoeur – intent upon the elaboration of a 'critical hermeneutics' which surmounts the conservative limits of a Gadamerian hermeneutic of recollection in order to incorporate a 'critique of ideology' (that is, distorted dialogue and regressive fusion or identity), as formulated by Adorno and Habermas – also represents a significant opening in this direction. Regrettably, Caputo ignores Ricoeur's decisive contribution to this hermeneutic in his otherwise admirable *Radical Hermeneutics*. This omission is probably explicable in terms of Caputo's methodological intention to forge some kind of middle way between the conservative hermeneutics of Gadamer and the radical deconstruction of hermeneutics by Derrida. Ricoeur's medial position would no doubt have made this opposition less stark and less dramatic. See also David Carroll's model of paraesthetics and its relation to a radical hermeneutics (*Paraesthetics*). Though the role of imagination is never explicitly discussed by Carroll his discussion of the transgressive and critical power of the respective 'poetics' of Lyotard, Foucault and Derrida are most suggestive for our present reassessment of hermeneutic approaches to the imaginary. Caputo's evaluation of Derrida's variation on a 'radical hermeneutics' (*Radical Hermeneutics*, pp. 140 ff.), is also relevant here.

27 See my *The Wake of Imagination; Poétique du possible* (Paris: Beauchesne, 1984); and *Transitions* (Manchester: Manchester University Press, 1987).

28 Gianni Vattimo, in response to my paper 'Hermeneutics and myth' at the Turin Conference on Celtic Identity, May 1988; quoted by Paul Durcan in 'Passage to Utopia', in R. Kearney (ed.), *Across the Frontiers* (Dublin: Wolfhound Press, 1989), p. 192.

29 Gianni Vattimo, 'Myth and the fate of secularization', *Res*, vol. 9 (Spring 1985), p. 34.

30 ibid., p. 34.

31 ibid., p. 35.

32 ibid.

33 Gianni Vattimo, *The End of Modernity: Nihilism and Hermeneutics in Postmodern Culture*, trans. J. Snyder (Oxford: Polity, 1988); French edition, trans. C. Alunni (Paris: Éditions du Seuil, 1985), p. 111.

34 ibid., p. 112.

35 ibid.

36 ibid.

37 R. Kearney, *Poétique du possible*, subtitled *Vers une herméneutique de la figuration*, particularly the concluding section; see also *The Wake of Imagination*, pp. 359–97; and *Transitions*, subtitled *Narratives in Modern Irish Culture*, pp. 269–84.

38 Vattimo, *End of Modernity*, p. 181.

39 ibid., p. 183.

40 ibid., p. 184.

41 ibid., p. 185. For a more detailed treatment of imagination by Vattimo, see his monograph *L'Immaginazione: materiali per la Storia Del Concetto* (Turin: Giappichelli, 1980).

42 Julia Kristeva, 'On melancholic imagination', in *Postmodernism and Continental Philosophy*, Studies in Phenomenology and Existentialism 13, eds Hugh Silverman and Donn Welton (Albany, NY: State University of New York Press, 1989), pp. 12, 22–3; see also Kristeva's collection of essays, *The Language of Desire: A Semiotic Approach to Literature and Art*, ed. and trans., L. S. Roudiez (Oxford: Blackwell, 1981), pp. 6–7, 159 ff., 36 ff.

43 Kristeva, 'On melancholic imagination', p. 22.

44 ibid., p. 13.

45 ibid., p. 13 (my italics).

46 ibid., p. 13.

47 ibid., p. 14.

48 ibid.

49 ibid., p. 15.

50 ibid., pp. 15, 23.

51 ibid., p. 15. Kristeva adds: 'The father-figure of this symbolic triumph is not, however, the well known oedipal father but, indeed, that "imaginary father", father of personal pre-history that for Freud guaranteed so-called primary identification.'

52 ibid., p. 16.

53 ibid.

54 Julia Kristeva, *Soleil noir: dépression et mélancolie* (Paris: Gallimard, 1987), p. 200 (my italics). Kristeva elaborates on the implications of this process thus: L'imaginaire est cet étrange lieu où le sujet risque son identité, se perd jusqu'au seuil du mal, du crime ou de l'asymbolie, pour les traverser et en témoigner ... depuis un ailleurs. Espace dédoublé, il ne tient qu'à être solidement accroché à l'idéal qui autorise la violence destructrice à se *dire* au lieu de se *faire*. C'est la sublimation, elle a besoin du *par-don*. Le Pardon est anhistorique. Il brise l'enchaînement des effets et des causes, des châtiments et des crimes, il suspend le temps des actes. Un espace étrange s'ouvre dans cette temporalité qui n'est pas celui de l'inconscient sauvage, désirant et meutrier, mais sa contrepartie: sa sublimation en connaissance de cause, une harmonie amoureuse qui n'ignore pas ses violences mais les acceuille, ailleurs. (pp. 210–11)

55 ibid., pp. 194, 216.

56 ibid., pp. 216–17:

Ce pardon comporte au départ une volonté, postulat, ou schème: *le sens existe*. Il ne s'agit pas nécessairement d'un déni du non-sens ou d'une exaltation maniaque à l'encontre du désespoir (même si, dans nombre de cas, ce mouvement peut dominer). Ce geste d'affirmation et d'inscription du sens qu'est le pardon porte en soi, comme en doublure, l'érosion du sens, la mélancolie et l'abjection. En les comprenant il les déplace, en les absorbant il les transforme et les lie pour quelqu'un d'autre. 'Il y a un sens': geste éminemment transférentiel qui fait exister un tiers pour et par un autre. *Le pardon se manifeste d'abord comme la mise en place d'une forme. Elle a l'effet d'une mise en acte, d'un faire, d'une poïesis.* Mise en forme des relations entre les individus humiliés et offensés: harmonie du groupe. Mise en forme des signes: harmonie de l'œuvre, sans exégèse, sans explication, sans compréhension. Technique et art. L'aspect 'primaire' d'une telle action éclaire pourquoi elle a le pouvoir d'atteindre, en deçà des paroles et des intelligences, les émotions et les corps meurtris. Cependant, cette économie n'a rien de primitif. La possibilité logique de relève *(Aufhebung)* qu'elle implique *(non-sens et sens, sursaut positif intégrant son néant possible)* est consécutive à un accrochage solide du sujet à l'idéal oblatif. Celui qui est dans la sphère du pardon – qui le donne et qui l'accepte – est capable de s'identifier avec un père aimant, père imaginaire, avec lequel, en conséquence, il est prêt à se réconcilier en vue d'une nouvelle loi symbolique.

Le déni est partie prenante de cette opération de relève ou de réconciliation identificatoire. Il procure un plaisir pervers, masochique, dans la traversée de la souffrance vers cette affirmation de nouveaux liens que sont le pardon ainsi que l'œuvre. Cependant, contrairement au déni de la dénégation qui annule le significant et conduit à la parole creuse du mélancolique, un autre processus entre ici en jeu pour assurer *la vie imaginaire.*

Il s'agit du pardon essentiel à la sublimation, qui conduit le sujet à une identification complète (réelle, imaginaire et symbolique) avec l'instance même de l'idéal. C'est par l'artifice miraculeuz de cette identification toujours instable, inachevée, mais constamment triple (réelle, imaginaire et symbolique) que le corps souffrant du pardonnant – comme de l'artiste – subit une mutation: une 'transsubstantiation', dira Joyce. Elle lui permet de vivre une seconde vie, une vie de forme et de sens, quelque peu exaltée ou artificielle aux yeux de ceux qui n'y sont pas, mais qui est la seule condition pour la survie du sujet.

57 ibid., p. 226.
58 Kristeva, 'On melancholic imagination', p. 21.
59 ibid., p. 23.
60 Kristeva, 'Moderne et postmoderne', in *Soleil noir*, pp. 264–5.
61 Milan Kundera, *The Art of the Novel* (New York: Harper & Row, 1988), pp. 158, 160.
62 Julia Kristeva, *In the Beginning Was Love: Psychoanalysis and Faith* (New York: Columbia University Press, 1987), p. 51.
63 ibid., p. 52.
64 ibid., p. 18.

65   ibid., p. 19.
66   ibid., p. 58.
67   ibid., p. 60.
68   Julia Kristeva, 'Postmodernism?', in H. R. Garvin (ed.), *Romanticism, Modernism, Postmodernism* (Lewisburg, Pa: n.p. 1980), pp. 141 ff.
69   Julia Kristeva, *In the Beginning was Love*, pp. 61–2.
70   Julia Kristeva, *Étrangers à nous-mêmes* (Paris: Fayard, 1988), pp. 282, 284–5, 269.
71   J.-F. Lyotard, *Instructions païennes* (Paris: Galilée, 1977). All translations quoted are my own.
72   J.-F. Lyotard, *The Postmodern Condition* (Minneapolis, Minn.: University of Minnesota Press, 1984), p. 82. Lyotard's most sustained analysis of this post-modern problematic of multiple justice is to be found in the seventh part of *Just Gaming* (Minneapolis, Minn.: University of Minnesota Press, 1985), pp. 93–100. *Au juste* originally appeared in French (Paris: Éditions Bourgois, 1979).
73   Lyotard, *Instructions païennes*, p. 24.
74   ibid., p. 40.
75   ibid., p. 29.
76   ibid., p. 30.
77   ibid., p. 31.
78   ibid., p. 32.
79   ibid., p. 38.
80   ibid., p. 34.
81   ibid., p. 36. Lyotard expands on this Kantian model of imagination and art in *Au juste*, p. 126. See also David Carroll's instructive discussion of Lyotard's critical aesthetic in *Paraesthetics*, pp. 23–52, 155–84; and Geoffrey Bennington, *Lyotard* (Manchester: Manchester University Press, 1988), in particular the concluding discussion of 'Art and politics'.
82   Lyotard, *Instructions païennes*, p. 39.
83   ibid., p. 47.
84   ibid., p. 77. Lyotard describes paganism as 'an impious and just politics' (p. 44). The basic elements of such a politics are narratives (les récits) not knowledge (le savoir). And here Lyotard advocates a politics of the *Pagus* over that of the *Heim*, a policy of borderlands, frontalier, criss-crossing and transgressing regional boundaries, as opposed to the centralized and hegemonic politics of Homelands – be they Motherlands or Fatherlands or Nativelands. He writes: '*Pagus* se disait de la région des bornes aux confins des bourgs. *Pagus* a fait *pays*. Ce n'est pas le *Heim* ou le home, l'habitat, l'abri, mais des parages, des contrées, qui ne sont pas nécessairement incultes, qui sont les horizons de ces ballades au cours desquelles on voit du pays. On n'y est pas chez soi. On ne s'y attend pas a decouvrir la vérité, on y rencontre des entités en nombre, sujettes aux métamorphoses, aux mensonges, aux envies and aux colères: des dieux passibles' (p. 42–3). Is this nomadic politics not close to Seamus Heaney's version of a nomadic poetics as a 'journey work' of the émigré imagination – 'a migrant preoccupation with threshold and transit, passage and pilgrimage, with the crossing

over of frontiers and divisions ... whose chosen emblem is Terminus,
the god of boundaries'? (See my introduction, entitled 'The transitional
paradigm', to *Transitions*, p. 15, and also my chapter in the same work
entitled 'Heaney and homecoming', pp. 101–22.)

85 Lyotard, *Instructions païennes*, p. 84.
86 ibid., p. 87.
87 Lyotard, *The Postmodern Condition*, p. 81.
88 ibid.
89 ibid.
90 Lyotard, *Just Gaming*, p. 100. In his appendix to *The Postmodern Condition*
    and in several subsequent texts – in particular *Du sublime* (Paris: Belin,
    1988); *L'Enthousiasme* (Paris: Galilée, 1986); *Le Postmoderne expliqué
    aux Enfants* (Paris: Galilée, 1986); *L'Inhumain* (Paris: Galilée, 1988);
    and *Heidegger et les 'Juifs'* (Paris: Galilée, 1988) – Lyotard establishes
    a radical contrast between the 'imagination' which he now restricts to
    the limits of presentation (in the sense of Kantian representation or
    Husserlian intuition) and the 'sublime' which he elevates as that category
    of non-intuitive experience which deals with the 'unrepresentable' as such
    (Kant's *noumenal*, Husserl's unfulfilled signifying intention or *visée à vide*
    as it became known in French phenomenology). The sublime thus comes
    to represent the *mise-en-abîme* of narrative imagination, the terror of what
    cannot be presented, represented, recollected or retold – an anaesthesis
    preceding the aesthetic, an anamnesis preceding remembrance, a *pathos*
    preceding sensible experience, an *archi-écriture* preceding literature. For
    a lucid account of these distinctions, see Lyotard's *Heidegger et les 'Juifs'*,
    pp. 59–61, 78, 51, 128.

Suggestions for further reading

None of our three advocates of a post-modern hermeneutic of imagination – Vattimo, Kristeva, Lyotard – has yet devoted a book exclusively
to this subject. The most suggestive texts by these authors are isolated
essays such as Vattimo's 'Myth and the fate of secularisation', *Res*, vol. 9
(1985); Kristeva's 'On melancholic imagination', in *Postmodernism and
Continental Philosophy*, Studies in Phenomenology and Existentialism
13, eds H. Silverman and D. Welton (Albany, NY: State University of
New York Press, 1989); and Lyotard's short discursive text *Instructions
païennes* (Paris: Galilée, 1977). Although my analysis above of other
post-modern critics of imagination such as Lacan, Barthes, Foucault
and Derrida is necessarily cursory and condensed, I have developed
this analysis in more detail in chapter 7 of *The Wake of Imagination* (London/Minneapolis, Minn.: Hutchinson/University of Minnesota
Press, 1988).

Afterwords: Vive l'imagination

The post-modern philosophies of imagination we have been examining share at least one common question: How does the contemporary imaginary take account of the other? Whether we are concerned with Kristeva's *melancholic* imagination, Vattimo's *fragile* imagination or Lyotard's *narrative* imagination, we are in each case confronted with what appears to be an irreducibly ethical scruple. I am referring to that scruple of answerability to the other which cannot be dispelled in our Civilization of the Image. The other defies the limitless circularity of mirrors, the looking-glass play of blank parody, the echo-chamber of *imagos*. The other will not leave imagination be. It insists that our images remain insomniac, that the forgotten be recalled, that the pastiche of mirror reflections be penetrated until we reach to the other side, the other's side. Imagination is summoned to invigilate the dark night of the post-modern soul until the other comes, even if only and always in the come-back of a trace. After imagination there is still the trace of its passage, its wake – the impossibility of sleeping and forgetting. At the end of the day, imagination cannot take leave of the other.

Is this not what Lyotard is hinting at in his reflections on the efforts of narrators such as Adorno, Wiesel and Lanzmann to retell in images what cannot be represented and yet cannot be repressed from our history – the event of Auschwitz?[1] Is this not what Kristeva alludes to in her vacillation between melancholic and parodic imagination as symptoms of post-modern culture? And is it not what Vattimo gestures towards when he speaks of the need to elicit an alternative hermeneutics of myth: one more attentive to other narratives surpassing the modern opposition between rationalism and irrationalism?

Such at least has been the hermeneutic wager motivating my reading of the above thinkers. It is my conviction that these thinkers – and others besides – are gesturing towards an ethics of alterity by re-inscribing ways of imagining which elude both the prison-house of mirrors and the cheerless conformity of Grand Theory. Whether we take the path through a pre-linguistic semiotics (Kristeva), a narrative pragmatics (Lyotard) or an anti-foundationalist aesthetics (Vattimo), we end up confronting a common post-modern dilemma – how to acknowledge the ethical relation to the other? And this leads in turn to the corollary hermeneutic question – how to do justice to the other if, as most post-modernists claim, there is no concept of universal right or regulation to guide our interpretations?

What, in other words, is there to prevent the post-modern imagination from simply *forging* its own other, casting it as but one *imago* amongst others, the figment of its own paranoid fantasies? And what is there to preclude a justice of multiplicity from slipping into a free-wheeling multiplicity of justices – a relativism as arbitrary as it is anaemic, where so-called ethical judgement would be determined by nothing more than the rules of whatever particular language game you happen to be playing? Can a post-modern imagination of radical pluralism afford to abandon the modern project of universalism altogether and still remain *just*? How, if at all, are we to conduct a hermeneutic dialogue between the poetics and ethics of post-modernity?

(i)

A post-modern hermeneutics is not just a hermeneutics which is post-modern in its theoretical approach to its subject. It is also, and just as importantly, a hermeneutics *of* post-modernity: one that takes post-modern culture as the *object* of its inquiry. The 'of' linking hermeneutics and post-modernity, in other words, does double duty as both subjective and objective genitive. The two are inseparable.

The vexed character of the post-modern imaginary solicits a new hermeneutic perspective capable of (1) critically interpreting its 'terminal paradoxes' (the phrase is Milan Kundera's) and (2) responding to its threatened paralysis by inventing – in the sense of both creating and discovering – alternative ways of being in the world.

Here again we discover the hermeneutic circle which conjoins post-modern poetics and ethics. For as we pass from poetic theories to practices (the former makes no sense without the latter) we re-encounter, in heightened fashion, the incontrovertible dilemma – how to imagine a set of relations which will do justice to the post-modern imaginary? And do justice in both senses of that felicitous term: to render due account of the complexities of our civilization of images; *and* to judge it justly according to adequate ethical criteria. The first is a poetic task, the second a moral–political one. Both require a radical hermeneutic of interpretation.

How, then, are we to *interpret* our post-modern culture of images? How are we to judge the images of the electronic mass media (television, cinema, video, computer games) in addition to the literary media of fiction or poetry and the plastic media of painting and sculpture, all of which are today dependent on the technology of mass communications? This dependence relates to the fact that artistic form and content are increasingly influenced by the mass-media society we inhabit; and to the related fact that contemporary works of literary or plastic art almost invariably rely on communication networks of publicity and promotion to reach a large audience. Indeed, even those artists who seek to escape media exposure, refusing television and press interviews or turning down prestigious international awards, frequently end up being the most obsessional objects of media attention. One thinks of Salinger, Beckett, Pynchon – not to mention Greta Garbo, Jackie Onassis or Houdini, who made a media art of disappearance itself.

Paradoxically, the disappearing act often becomes the star act of a civilization, such as ours, obsessed with the appearance of images. This curious phenomenon has prompted a series of vivid descriptions from cultural commentators: Guy Debord refers to our *Société du Spectacle*, Jean Baudrillard to our Culture of the Simulacrum, Umberto Eco to our Kingdom of Fakes, and Dan Boorstin to our World of Pseudo-Events. These are all synonyms for a post-modern civilization where the image seems not only to have replaced reality but also to have become virtually indistinguishable from it. And to be cutely self-conscious that it is doing so.

The curious paradox of a post-modern imagination trying to imagine its own life-and-death story is perhaps most graphically evidenced in the electronic media themselves. I am thinking not only of the 'Candid Camera' series – where television takes television for a ride – but also of the increasing tendency in popular talk-shows to include shots of cameras, lighting and technicians within the spectator's frame of vision (something unthinkable in the early years of television). Not to mention the new fashion of 'critical' shows – ranging from the 'Did You See?' variety to the 'Television as Death of Culture' self-interrogations: here the medium of television becomes its own message, both the form and the content of its own representation. Indeed, so self-regarding does the television medium sometimes appear that one wonders if Walter Benjamin may have been correct when, in his famous essay on 'The work of art in an age of mechanical reproduction', he anticipated a time when human beings would become so anaesthetized with electronic images as to contemplate scenes of their own destruction with aesthetic pleasure! And is it not for similar reasons that university students on American campuses have been reported rescheduling their time-table so as to fit in the latest television soap showings – the sophistication of the camp being proportionate to the simplification of the image. Parody thus becomes a voyeur of parody itself: a typically post-modern phenomenon described by Milan Kundera as 'the kitsch-man's need for kitsch – the need to gaze into the mirror of the beautifying lie and be moved to tears of gratification at one's own reflection'.[2]

What is true of television is equally true of other media. Thus in cinema we find the post-modern paradox of parody exemplified in the *retro* craze for the images of earlier Hollywood periods – the thirties or the sixties became particularly popular in the eighties – as well as in a new spate of more subtle take-offs of earlier film genres. For example, David Lynch's *Blue Velvet* mixes mimicries of thirties thriller, forties heroism, fifties romance, sixties lyricism, seventies consumerism and eighties cynicism. And other examples might include Truffaut's *Day for Night*, Scorcese's *King of Comedy*, Pakula's *Network* or Fellini's *Ginger and Fred* – all attempts to parody the fakery of the silver screen by means of the silver screen. Even Hollywood has taken to sending up Hollywood, and with considerable commercial success, as the 1988 box-office hit *Who Framed Roger Rabbit?* demonstrated – a Hollywood production, *après* Disney, which parodied the history of Disney productions!

Similar post-modern parodies are to be found, as I argued at some length in *The Wake of Imagination*, in architecture, music and the visual arts. In painting we find artists such as Warhol, Lichtenstein and Ballagh mimetically reproducing images not only of the great classical masterpieces, but also of comic strips, television commercials, pop posters and other mass media representations. And the reverse is equally common, as is the familiar trend in advertising to package the 'image' of a commodity by associating it with visual 'quotations' from the works of celebrated artists – Rembrandt's Burgermeisters contemplate Henri Winterman cigars while Botticelli's Venus rises from the foam of the latest brand of bubble bath.

213

Contemporary music also features 'revivals' of earlier period styles. The practice of compositional parody, for instance, was made popular by the Beatles (*The White Album* and later records) whose own music, of course, itself became subject to multiple *retro* parodies in the popular music of the late eighties. These revivals can vary greatly from the hack 'oldies' cult groups to the ingenious double-takes of a self-proclaimed post-modern band like Scritti Politti. But there are other post-modern trends in popular music which merit attention. There is the increasingly common technique of double parody as exemplified in the Talking Heads song 'Mr Jones' which (as Mark Edmundson points out) sends up Bob Dylan's send-up of corporate Jones in 'Ballad of a Thin Man', creating levels of irony bordering on cynicism which it is virtually impossible to unravel. And there is Rap, a form of popular music which reached cult status in the eighties with NWA and Public Enemy, groups determined to subvert the accredited criteria of originality by composing music pieced together out of prerecorded sound-bites. Here post-modern music takes the form of a palimpsest of sound which makes a boast of its boundless plagiarism!

But it is no doubt in architecture – where the term 'post-modern' first entered critical and common currency in the seventies owing to the enormous influence of theorists like Venturi, Jencks and Portoghesi – that the phenomenon of imagistic quotation from earlier period styles became most prevalent. Under the rubric of 'radical eclecticism', Charles Jencks included a variety of post-modernist buildings – the common trait being a playful recoding and re-citing of multiple architectural styles, from past and present, in defiance of the homogenous International Style promoted by modernist masters like Mies van der Rohe and Le Corbusier.

(ii)

If the post-modern wake of imagination is to mark a passage to other ways of imagining, rather than a dead end, our culture must devise means of reaching through the labyrinth of depthless images to the other. This is where poetics re-aligns itself with a certain ethical concern – a concern evident in an author like Kundera when he calls for radical forms of fiction capable of leading us beyond the contemporary 'labyrinth where man loses his way'. So saying, he endorses a 'legacy of anti-modernism' typified by such figures as Beckett, Gombrowicz and Fellini. Might this definition not be read as a critical version of post-modernism – the kind intended by our own project for a radical hermeneutic of imagination? Does not Kundera's indictment of the modern cult of the New (as epitomized by both the American Way of Life, based on endless consumerism, and the Communist Way of Life, based on the slogan 'New, New, New is the star of Communism, and there is no modernity outside it');[3] does this not bear striking resemblance to the post-modern denunciations of modernity's idolatry of progress by thinkers like Lyotard and Vattimo?

Not all advocates of the modernity-gone-wrong thesis wish to reject modernity *per se*. Many, in fact, would deny the possibility of occupying some transcendental space *after* or *outside* the modern, preferring to diagnose its terminal paradoxes from within. From this point of view the task is to reinvent what is most enabling in modernity's latent if hitherto deflected potencies. And this is perhaps what Lyotard has in mind when he insists that post-modernity – in the critical sense – is not something that comes when modernity is *over* (in a succession of historical periods) but rather the imaginative struggle by thinkers, writers and artists to formulate the rules of *what will have been done*. This supposition requires that we understand the post-modern according to the paradox of the future (post) anterior (modo).[4] Or we could say (again with Lyotard) that if modernity is an attitude ruled by the prefix of *pro* – pro-gress, pro-ject, pro-duction – post-modernity designates an attitude governed by the prefix *ana* – *ana*mnesis (to re-collect and re-create what has been eclipsed by history) or *ana*logy (to re-say one thing in terms of another). We might thus postulate that, where 'bad' post-modernity refers to modernity in its terminal condition of amnesia, paralysis and conformity, 'good' post-modernity refers to the ongoing struggle to reanimate what is nascent in modernity by reinscribing its betrayed promises.

But how retrieve the betrayed stories of history if not through a critical redeployment of imagination? Here we find that a critical hermeneutics of imagination – guided by thinkers like Ricoeur, Lyotard, Vattimo or Caputo – rejoins the utopian theory of 'anticipatory memory' outlined by the Frankfurt School. Herbert Marcuse's version of imagining-as-remembering offers a suggestive version:

Utopia in great art is never the simple negation of the reality principle, but its transcending preservation in which past and present cast

215

their shadow on fulfilment. The authentic utopia is grounded in recollection. 'All reification is forgetting' (Adorno) ... Forgetting past suffering and past joy alleviates life under a repressive reality principle. In contrast, remembrance spurs the drive for the conquest of suffering and the permanence of joy ... The horizon of history is still open. If remembrance of things past would become a motive power in the struggle for changing the world, the struggle would be waged for a revolution hitherto suppressed in the previous historical revolutions.[5]

Not to wager on such historically motivated utopias is to condemn imagination to the circles of mirror-play. Kundera realizes as much when he derides the perilous equation of fiction and reality in our time and appeals to a hermeneutic imagination able to discriminate between reality as *fact* and existence as *possibility*. 'In Europe we are living the end of the Modern Era,' writes Kundera, 'the end of art conceived as an irreplaceable expression of personal originality; the end that heralds an era of unparalleled uniformity.'[6] And if we do not develop a critical hermeneutics capable of discerning differences and making judgements we will find ourselves helpless before the malign post-modern view that culture is but an anthology of indifferent images, a bric-à-brac of imitations where nothing means anything because everything is the same as everything else. 'If we reject the question of value and settle for a description (thematic, sociological, formalist) of a work ... if we equate all cultures and all cultural activities (Bach and rock, comic strips and Proust); if the criticism of art (or meditation on value) can no longer find room for expression, then the historical evolution of art will lose its meaning, will crumble, will turn into a vast and absurd storehouse of works.'[7]

One riposte to such a regime of sameness is to advance a model of judgement motivated by a poetics of the possible. And this Kundera hints at when he promotes a form of fiction committed to the hermeneutic wager that 'existence is not what has occurred [but] the realm of human possibilities, everything that man can become, everything he is capable of ... being-in-the-world understood as *possibilities*'.[8]

The challenge of the post-modern imaginary is to chart a course leading beyond both the Idolatry of the New and the Tyranny of the Same.

(iii)

But how feasible is it to discriminate between good and bad post-modernity? The message of bad post-modernity is that such hermeneutic discernment is impossible. Why? Because the very hermeneutic act of imagining new possibilities beyond the givens of reality is precluded, we are told, by the post-modern syndrome of 'simulation'. The age of simulation, as defined by Jean Baudrillard, 'begins with the liquidation of all referentials . . . Simulation threatens the difference between "true" and "false", between "real" and "imaginary".'9 The option of critique is thereby annulled since the capacity to unmask 'false consciousness', or promote a 'liberating consciousness', is predicated upon the belief that the imaginary does refer to some order of meaning *other* than itself, an order which already exists or might exist in the future. Devoid of this distinction between the imaginary and its referent (actual or possible), we are deprived of the capacity to make value judgements about the revealing and concealing power of images, we are unable to ask the hermeneutic question – is this particular image augmenting or distorting meaning?

Such questioning is rendered null and void by the 'irreference' of simulation. The imaginary is no longer said to reflect, negate, deform or transform reality. 'It bears no relation to any reality whatsoever: it is its own pure simulacrum.'10 A graphic illustration of this is to be found in the phenomenon of Disneyland, which seeks to hide its own simulating activity. 'Disneyland is there to conceal the fact that it is all of "real" America which *is* Disneyland. Disneyland is presented as imaginary in order to make us believe that the rest is real, when in fact all of Los Angeles and the America surrounding it are no longer real, but of the order of the hyperreal and of simulation. It is no longer a question of a false representation of reality (ideology), but of concealing the fact that the real is no longer real . . .'11 In stating as much, of course, Baudrillard appears to be accepting a *de facto* equation of the imaginary and the real.

Such acceptance in turn implies the end of ideology and the end of art. Both theses of termination have been given serious hearings in contemporary critical debate. The critique of ideology presupposes the betrayal of truth by images, just as the celebration of art presupposes the revelation of truth by images. But the post-modern practice of simulation nullifies both presuppositions, affirming that there is no ulterior meaning to ideology or art: nothing to conceal or reveal, only the simulacrum. For simulation there is nothing other than simulation. And this is why someone like Habermas sees such 'bad' post-modernity – it is the only kind he acknowledges – as the abrogation of all ethical critique. The denial of the principle of individuation which separates the self from the other, the real from the imaginary, the true from the false, is also a denial of the *moral* distinction between just and unjust.

Is imagination, then, to take this threat of simulation lying down? The stakes, I believe, are too high for such acquiescence. To permit the replacement of imagination by simulation would be to abandon not only imagination's poetic powers – recognized through the centuries – but also its crucial ethical powers. These latter powers I here summarize under three main headings: the *utopian*; the *testimonial*; and the *empathic*.

As the utopian potential of imagination has already been sketched out above, I will confine myself to a few supplementary remarks.

The utopian function discussed in several of the above chapters was seen to derive from the imaginative ability to disclose the possible in the actual, the other in the same, the new in the old. All these acts of utopian disclosure are expressions of the basic power of imagination to discern the *dissimilar in the similar*. But the utopian function is not complete without the corollary power to discern the *similar in the dissimilar*. While Aristotle identified this with the poetic trope of metaphor, Kant and later Ricoeur extended it to embrace the schematizing power of the productive imagination which transforms the manifold of experience into a certain temporal/spatial unity. Thus each person, thing or event can be identified as *this* or *that*. If there was no imagination to provide this sense of identity in and through temporal difference (by synthesizing our past, present and future horizons of experience in terms of certain recurring features), there would be (a) no sense of a perduring 'I' which could be expected to remain faithful to the promises and pledges it makes to a perduring 'other', and therefore no possibility of individuated moral agents with individual responsibility; and (b) there would be no sense, either, as Husserl and Ricoeur both realized, of a commonly shared goal (telos) to guide our historical actions. Deprived of the possibility of a commonly identifiable sense of persons and goals, moral agents would be delivered over to the most malign scenario of post-modern irreference and indifference.

It is the schematizing power of imagination which opens the possibility of some kind of unified horizon for our diverse actions. So doing it provides a sense of common purpose for meaningful social practices. This common purpose is a utopian horizon of history. But the fact that it is a *u-topos* which is always never-yet realized should itself be a guarantee against dogmatism. The utopian horizons of social imagination are open-ended goals which motivate a free variation of possible worlds. They are not pre-established or predetermined. They are tentative, provisional, fragile. The universality of the *u-topos* derives from the fact that it is the possession of no one and the possibility of everyone.

The *u-topos* is where differences may converge without fusing. Once we recognize imagination as the source of this communal character of utopian projects, the totalitarian ideologies of the Commissar or Caesar are resisted; for such ideologies can only totalize reality because they mask the fact that they are constructs of imagination – and constructs, moreover, which seek to deny the open-ended and metaphorizing character of imagination. To forswear all utopias because of the pathological nature of ideological utopianism is to renounce the possibility of a commonly shared horizon of history which never reaches its end but perpetually motivates moral agents to bring it nearer. Without this utopian function of imagination it is difficult to provide a historical motivation for moral solidarity – a point to which I will return below. Suffice it to say for now that it is the imaginative capacity to see unity-in-difference and difference-in-unity which opens up the possibility of a genuine utopian horizon of shared aspirations mobilizing human beings to action. All goal-oriented social praxis strives to attain some kind of utopian image. Or, as Ricoeur puts it in his analysis of the social imaginary, 'without imagination, no action'.

If we totally abandon the utopian potential of imagination we will be submerged in bad post-modernity – a labyrinth of mirror images devoid of paths to a future. E. Ann Kaplan makes this point forcefully in her introduction to *Postmodernism and Its Discontents* (1988) when she warns of the emergence of a 'co-optive postmodernism' where the collapse of the distinction between the imaginary and the real, brought about by omnipresent consumer technologies, suggests there is no way out – no possibility of critical transcendence – because no power to imagine things existing *otherwise*. 'This postmodernism', she explains, 'is described as radically transforming the subject through its blanketing of culture. Inside is no longer separate from outside; private cannot be opposed to public space; high or avant-garde culture no longer stands in stark contrast to the all-consuming popular. Technologies, marketing and consumption have created a new, unidimensional universe from which there is no escape and inside which no critical position is possible. There is no "outside", no space from which to mount a critical perspective. We inhabit, on this account, a world where the television screen has become the only reality, where the human body and the televisual machine are all but indistinguishable.'[12]

The only answer to such a 'co-optive' post-modernism is, Kaplan argues, a 'utopian' post-modernism capable of moving beyond the oppressive binary oppositions of gender, race or class 'in search of a liberating position'.[13] This remedial option implies, of course, the operative existence of imagination – the power to unrealize repressive realities in favour of emancipatory possibilities. Deprived of this utopian perspective, post-modernity would indeed appear to be condemned to that paralysis of 'neo-conservatism' of which it has sometimes been accused. And, as Hilary Lawson observes in *Dismantling Truth: Reality in the Postmodern World* (1988), if post-modernists simply 'destroy all authority and propose a permanent revolution from within, they are thereby denied authority themselves and it is precisely for this reason that they risk having nowhere to lead us. And without goals, without direction, is it not easier to stay where we are?'[14] The status quo reigns supreme for as long as we refuse our utopian capacity to imagine things being other than they are.

This capacity to project future possibilities itself requires to be supplemented by the capacity to ground such projections on examples drawn from the past. And here the utopian imagination looks to the *testimonial* imagination – that is, the power to bear witness to 'exemplary' narratives legacied by our cultural memories and traditions. Without such witness the utopian imagination risks degenerating into empty fantasy; it forfeits all purchase on historical experience.

The post-modern scruple of undecidability (implicit in Jacques Derrida's deconstruction and explicit in John Caputo's radical hermeneutics) is doubtless salutary in liberating us from the false securities of metaphysical absolutes. But can we really take seriously a scruple devoid of exemplary criteria to discriminate between one act and another? Caputo offers the following formula for what he calls a post-modern ethic of dissemination: 'We act, but we act with a heightened sense of the delimitations of subjectivity, not sure of this "we" or of who or what acts within us or what deeper impulses are at work on us. We act with fear and trembling, with a deep sense of *ébranler*, whose tremors are all around us.'[15] Caputo is surely correct when he argues that such post-modern ethics serves to remind us that, when it comes to the good as to the true, we lack a master key and do not hold the master name. And such an ethics is also to be commended for its resolve to 'give what is other as big a break as possible ... displacing oppositional arrangements in favour of the open and the non-exclusionary'.[16] Where this approach is lacking, however, is in its reluctance, even refusal, to decide the ethical difference between one view and another, to cut through the 'fair play' of multiple language-games and make a commitment to the 'better' argument and the 'better' action. It is simply not good enough to be content – like Richard Rorty ÷ to keep the conversation going on the assumption that the conversation is itself the good. Civilized chat for its own civilized sake is post-modernism not only laid back but laid low.

One must ask, at some point, what guides our evaluation of conflicting interpretations? What standards form or inform our judgements? And a post-modern ethic of dissemination which dismisses such questions as 'futile and wrong-headed' is itself futile and wrong-headed.[17] If it is true that we cannot possess knowledge of what is good in any absolute sense, it is equally true that we have an ethical duty to decide between what is better and what is worse. To promote the 'political ambidexterity of the postmodern' as Linda Hutcheon does in *A Poetics of Postmodernism* (1988) is ultimately, I believe, to shirk the challenge of ethical responsibility.[18] In every lived situation the ludic undecidabilities of imagination are answerable, in the first and last analysis, to the *exemplary* narratives of imagination. It is imagination that tells the difference between good and bad imaginations. Its hermeneutic readiness to listen and respond to others' stories is inextricably linked to its ethical function of recalling what has been silenced and projecting what has not yet been spoken. Without this dual focus of the testimonial and utopian, there can be no historical criteria for our judgements.

This is, I suspect, what the post-modern novelist Italo Calvino has in mind when he recommends literature's vocation to project exemplary 'patterns of language, of vision, of imagination ... in short, of the creation of a model of values that is *at the same time aesthetic and ethical*, essential to any plan of action, especially in political life'.[19] But Calvino treads carefully. He insists that his support for a certain literary pedagogy is not to be confused with propaganda. Educating in and through the exemplary imagination can yield results, he adds, 'only if it is difficult and indirect, if it implies the arduous attainment of

221

literary stringency'.[20] In other words, he refuses any political use of art for the purposes of mass instruction. The appropriate image here is not that of literature as the 'hammer of a benevolent propagandist' (Lenin) nor as the 'loaded pistol' of the committed revolutionary (Sartre). One of the most important ethical functions of the literary imagination is to teach politics to distrust itself – to remind it that its words are not always what they seem, and that what it takes to be scientific fact and doctrine is often no more than a verbal construction. But perhaps the most useful ethical value imparted by the artistic imagination is, paradoxically, the awareness of its own poetic uselessness. Socrates exemplified this when he insisted on learning a new tune on the flute as his enemies prepared his hemlock. 'What good will it do you', they asked, 'to know this tune before you die?'[21]. His answer was to play on. The good was in the playing itself.

How does the exemplary role of the imagination work? In the *Critique of Judgement*, Kant describes how the schematizing power of imagination can function to provide criteria of 'exemplary validity' for moral judgement. Morality could not work effectively without the imagination's ability to narrate particular stories which exemplify an otherwise abstract rule. The moral law is thus communicated intuitively. And in making the law answerable to *particular* persons and circumstances the exemplary role of imagination refuses the option of some absolute vantage-point; instead it privileges the capacity to identify with 'the others in whose place the judging person has put himself for his consideration'.[22] This power of identification stems directly from Kant's definition of imagination, taken up again by Husserl and the phenomenologists, as the 'faculty of representing a person or thing that is not itself present'.[23] Without this imaginative ability to invoke exemplary figures and narratives, to put oneself in others' shoes, to identify oneself with their actions, thoughts or feelings, it is difficult to see how moral sentiment or reason could operate at all.

At its simplest, imagination provides moral judgements with 'exemplary validity' to the extent that it recounts stories of others whose example might guide us. The exemplary imagination works by witness not by dogmatism, by intuition rather than by abstraction. Just as the Greeks had the image of Achilles in their mind's eye when they spoke of courage, Christians the image of Christ or St Francis when they spoke of love, every concept of the good needs to be exemplified in particular narratives. And not simply by way of illustrating or *reproducing* a principle. The narratives and parables can actually produce the doctrine. This central role of exemplary imagination would seem to suggest a priority of moral testament over moral theory, reminding us that the latter is founded on the former.

The testimonial imagination plays a moral role, however, not only in recalling the exemplary figures of our cultural memories and traditions, but also in recalling the forgotten victims of history. This power to remember the repressed, to represent the unrepresented, to put a name on the unnameable crime by recounting it in images, is perhaps nowhere more evident than in the case of Auschwitz.

There are at least two ways in which imagination serves the ethical role of commemorating the victims of evil. One is by opting for a 'writing of disaster', as Blanchot calls it, where narrative deconstructs itself, cancels itself out until it leaves a void, a silence which bears witness to the fact that the unspeakable is quite literally a death of words, the impossibility of speaking for the dead. But there is also an argument which says that to renounce narrative is to run the risk of forgetfulness. Even in the case of the most unrepresentable of all horrors, Auschwitz, one is ethically compelled to tell and retell the story, 'to utter the words without creating the illusion of a violently coherent discourse; to go on invoking the images without any desire to fill up the voids of evil, to cover the holes of horror'.[24] Narrating the story of man's inhumanity to man is affirming that the power of human witness can reach beyond silence to others who in remembering the dead are, at the same time, recalled to the moral responsibility of never allowing it to happen again. As Primo Levi, one of the most articulate survivors of the Nazi camps, has written: 'The need to recount to "others", to make the "others" participate, acquired in us before and after our liberation the vehemence of an immediate impulse, just as imperious as all the other elementary needs; and it was in response to such a need that I wrote my book.'[25] In such a manner, the testimonial imagination puts itself into the service of the unforgettable, not in the manner of the exemplary model which recalls the noble deeds of saints and heroes, but in the manner of a rememoration which refuses to allow moral evil, no matter how unspeakable, to silence the voice of narrative imagination. Indeed, as the Jewish philosopher Emmanuel Levinas has suggested, to refuse to recount the narratives of Israel and its covenants, because of Auschwitz, would be to complete the criminal enterprise of national socialism.[26] To those post-modern connoisseurs who celebrate the 'sublime' unrepresentability of certain experiences of terror, one is compelled to reply that if the silence imposed on imagination in such circumstances can be described as aesthetically *sublime* it is morally *suspect*.

But there is a third sense in which imagination is indispensable to ethics – I refer to its *emphatic* powers of receptivity to the other. Can we be responsible for the other if we are not first receptive to the other? Can we answer to and for the other if we cannot hear its call, if we cannot empathize? Since Kant we have recognized that imagination is the common root of both sensibility and understanding.[27] While the role of imagination in understanding pertains to its productive and projective powers, its role in sensible intuition expresses its ability to remain open to what is given from beyond itself. Kant, at least as interpreted by Heidegger in *Kant and the Problem of Metaphysics*, identifies the intuitive dimension of imagination with its receptivity to the law, that is, its capacity for ethical *respect*. By extension, one could argue that the receptive power of imagination lies at the very root of our moral capacity to respect the otherness of the other person, to treat the other as an end rather than a means, to *empathize*. So that if we cannot be *free* without the projective capacity of imagination we cannot be *moral* without its receptive capacity. We find an arresting expression of this in the conclusion to John Banville's post-modern fiction *The Book of Evidence* (1989). The narrator, a murderer, confesses to the unforgivable crime of having failed to *imagine* what it was like to be his victim: 'This is the worst, the essential sin, I think, the one for which there will be no forgiveness: that I never imagined her vividly enough, that I never made her be there sufficiently, that I did not make her live. Yes, that failure of imagination is my real crime, the one that made the others possible ... I could kill her because for me she was not alive.'[28] Claudio Magris makes a similar point on a larger scale in his book *Danube* (1989), when he attributes one of the reasons for the holocaust to a *lack of imagination* on the part of the Nazis:

> Fascism is also the attitude of someone who knows himself to be a good friend to his next-door neighbour, but fails to realize that other people can be equally good friends to their next-door neighbours. Eichmann was sincere when, as a prisoner in Jerusalem, he expressed horror at discovering that the father of Captain Less, the Israeli officer who had been interrogating him for months, and whom he felt profound respect, had died in Auschwitz. He was horrified because his lack of imagination had prevented him

from seeing the faces, the features, the expressions of real people behind the statistical lists of victims. (p. 45)

Imagination is ethical to the extent that it suffers the other to be other while suffering with (*com-patire*) the other as other. Its power of reception becomes compassion. The ethical imagination allows the other to exist 'without why' – not for *my* sake, or because it conforms to *my* scheme of things, but for its own sake. Imaginative receptivity or *Gelassenheit* is, as Meister Eckhart knew, the possibility of *caritas* and the impossibility of murder.[29]

Milan Kundera also has a phrase for this: 'the imaginative act of tolerance'. While acknowledging the threat of a kitsch culture of global uniformity, he refuses to disavow that art of fiction 'which creates the fascinating imaginative province where no one owns the truth and everyone has the right to be understood'. Hailing the power of fiction as the 'echo of God's laughter' when He first created the world, Kundera makes an act of faith in Western culture's ability to revive its art of imagining and thereby unite its peoples in a 'fraternity that stretches far beyond the little European continent'.[30]

In conclusion, we may postulate that the three ethical functions of imagination – *utopian, testimonial* and *empathic* – are intimately linked to the poetic activity of imagining otherwise. How could we commit ourselves to utopian possibilities of existence, recount the stories of past heroes and victims, or respond to the ethical call of fellow-humans, without the imaginative ability to *listen* to other voices from other times and places? And is it not this aesthetic acoustic which enables us to record a new voice for those others here and now?

Deprived of the fundamental ability to imagine otherwise, it is difficult to see how any ethics worthy of the name could operate. Imagining otherwise lies at the root of the two main principles of human value – *freedom* and *solidarity*. The freedom to transcend the world as given and choose which values to realize in one's existence is a recurring feature of the philosophies of imagination discussed in this book. But alongside the value of freedom – lacking which no credible notion of choice could exist – there is the equally significant value of solidarity. Where liberal philosophies have tended to emphasize individual liberties and rights, socialist and communitarian philosophies have often sought to redress the balance in favour of fraternity. The imaginative power of sympathy is doubtless the origin of our capacity to identify with the other, to welcome the stranger, to expose oneself, in Lear's words, 'to feel what wretches feel'. This is a *sine qua non* of all ethics, explicitly acknowledged by moral theorists as diverse as David Hume and Martin Buber.[31] But it is not confined to a liberal ethic of I–Thou intimacy. The empathic power of imagination breaks beyond the charmed circle of the *face-à-face* extending the range of compassion from the private to the public. It introduces the other as *third* alongside the other as *thou*. It is here, moreover, that the ethical imagination also takes on a political role: that of envisaging the needs of others not immediately present to us; and of envisaging the most effective social means of meeting them. It is surely the case that the deepest motivational springs of political involvement are located in the capacity to *feel* needs for others beyond our immediate circle of family and friendship.[32]

But if imagining others' needs is the first task of a political imagination – transforming abstract needs into felt ones – its ultimate task is reconciling the ostensibly conflicting needs for freedom, on the one hand, and solidarity, on the other. In fact the two tasks are inseparable; for the conflict of needs cannot be resolved in *principle* alone, it requires the emphatic experience of imaginative *practice*. Thus may the old clichés of fraternity, belonging and community be revivified, empty slogans transmuted into lived convictions. And, if it is true that post-modern society has altered the possibilities of civic solidarity, it is equally true that imagination can re-create a new language of poetry, painting, television and cinema – forging new images of belonging adequate to our times. As Michael Ignatieff reminds us in *The Needs of Strangers*: 'It is the painters and writers, not the politicians or the social scientists, who have been able to find a language for the joy of (contemporary) life, its fleeting and transient solidarity. It is Hopper's images of New York, Joyce's Dublin, Musil's Vienna, Bellow's Chicago, Kundera's Prague, which have enabled us to find a language for the new pleasures of living as we do.'[33] But I would want to add that it is the new language of the artistic imagination which, in turn, can summon politicians to envision our society in new ways. If it is indeed the business of imagination to make politics distrust itself – reminding it that its principles are not literal facts but constructs of imagination – it is also its business to encourage politics to remake itself by remaking its images of the good life.[34]

Poetic imagining, I am arguing finally, is the most redemptive power of mind. Yet, as Ihab Hassan who first launched the term post-modern in literary theory in the sixties, rightly concedes in *The Postmodern Turn*

(1971), 'The imagination of postmodern criticism is a disestablished imagination'.[35] It lacks authority and belief. This can lead to a certain confusion, or even disillusion. It can also lead to a salutary humility. The challenge is to work from the basis of such humility to revive imagination: to re-establish its former poetic prowess without reinstating its egotistical role as sovereign subjectivity. If there exists one poetic impulse to set up imagination as master and possessor of all things other than itself, there is another which renounces such a claim for the sake of the other. Hassan proposes, for his part, that we 'remythify the imagination, at least locally, and bring back the reign of wonder into our lives'.[36] To which end, he invokes Emerson's eloquent dictum: 'Orpheus is no fable: you have only to sing, and the rocks will crystallize; sing, and the plants will organize; sing, and the animals will be born.'

Such a re-empowered imagination would take as starting-point the post-modern deflation of the sovereign subject. Building from the ground up, it would invoke as blueprint not the imperious plans of self-sufficient consciousness but those other voices which reach us through the post-modern night of the soul. Is this sense of openness to others-beyond-the-self not what Joyce had in mind when he said of *Finnegans Wake*, the prototypical post-modern text: 'This book is being written by the people I have met or known.'[37] It is the work, as he himself confessed, of 'Allmen'. Such self-effacement of the authorial imagination invites the auditory imagination to come into its own. It solicits a re-creative response from the listener. It lends its ear to the other.

The deflation of the authorial imagination is not just a matter of humility. It is also a matter of humour. At best, the nightbook of the post-modern imagination achieves a comic wakefulness, a readiness to invigilate the advent of the other, a fidelity to its vocation as 'gracehoper always jigging ajog, hoppy on akkant of his joyicity' (*Finnegans Wake*). The other comes to imagination sometimes as laughter from a utopian future, sometimes as playback of the forgotten voices of history – as if reciting the final refrain of the *Wake*, 'mememormee, mememormee'. Here, once again, the imagination's poetic vocation to sing rejoins its ethical vocation to remember.

(iv)

In the various *exposés* of the post-modern imaginary we have discerned a recurring scruple to re-invent the art of imagining. After all the

227

apocalyptic accounts of the End of the Story in our age – from Benjamin's sober caveat in 'The Storyteller' to the recent post-structuralist 'prophets of extremity' – there are still stories being told. We are still being summoned by the hermeneutic task of inventing and re-inventing history. Indeed, if pre-modernity could be caricatured as merely discovering history, and modernity as merely creating it, *good* post-modernity, at least, might be characterized as an invention of history in the double sense of creation-and-discovery: a hermeneutic replay of history on the stage of what is yet to come.

A post-modern hermeneutics of imagining might thus be in a position to conjoin, without confusing, the often opposed claims of poetics and ethics.[38] The poetic commitment to *story-telling* may well prove indispensable to the ethical commitment to *history-making*. Ethics without poetics leads to the censuring of imagination; poetics without ethics leads to dangerous play. But if a poetics of imagining is ever to respond to the ethical crisis of our Civilization of the Image, I suspect it will not be by beating a retreat to the modernist sanctuary of High Art. The votaries of poetical imagination can no longer afford to hold the so-called 'mass media' in contempt. It is not only in novels and paintings that the crisis of imagination is to be addressed but also in television, video and cinema – those media which most dramatically epitomize the post-modern paradox of the image. The labyrinth must be confronted from within as well as from without.

Today we rely more than ever on the power of imagining to recast other ways of being in the world, other possibilities of existence. Perhaps it is time for the dismembering of Orpheus to be supplemented by a re-membering. Perhaps it is time to put Humpty Dumpty – and other childhood images – back together again. To reimagine, with Joyce, the old Irish dream of Finn-again-awake. To wager once again that imagination lives on in the wake of imagination, that the best response to the post-modern news that 'l'imagination est morte' is: 'Vive l'imagination!'

Notes

1 J.-F. Lyotard, *Heidegger et les 'Juifs'* (Paris: Galilée, 1988), p. 51. See in particular his comments on Claude Lanzmann's film of the holocaust, *Shoah*, p. 51; on Elie Wiesel's autobiographical writings on the concentration-camps, p. 128; and on Theodore Adorno's philosophy as a 'writing of ruins' in testimony to his haunting question to the contemporary imagination

- 'after Auschwitz who can write poetry?' See also Olivier Mongin's discussion of this same problematic, 'La Shoah, comment se souvenir, comment raconter?', in *Esprit*, January 1988.

2   Milan Kundera, 'Sixty-three words', in *The Art of the Novel* (New York: Harper & Row, 1988), p. 135. See also A. Kroker and D. Cook, 'Television and the triumph of culture', in *The Postmodern Scene* (London: Macmillan, 1988), pp. 267–79.

3   Kundera, 'Sixty-three words', p. 141. Kundera's verdict on the fate of the poetic imagination in our post-modern world of communications is not optimistic. The following extracts are typical of his mordant irony: 'The unification of the planet's history, that humanist dream which God has spitefully allowed to come true, has been accompanied by a process of dizzying reduction ... Man is caught in a veritable *whirlpool of reduction* where Husserl's "world of life" is fatally obscured and being is forgotten ... Like all of culture, the novel is more and more in the hands of the mass media; as agents of the unification of the planet's history, the media amplify and channel the reduction process; they distribute throughout the world the same amplifications and stereotypes easily acceptable by the greatest number, by all mankind'; ibid., pp. 17–18. This common 'spirit of the mass media', camouflaged by political diversity, is the 'spirit of our time', affirms Kundera. And he opposes this to what he calls 'the spirit of the novel' which he defines as the 'spirit of complexity', a perpetual reminder to the reader that things are not as simple as they seem.

Another term that Kundera assigns to the post-modern imaginary of mass-media culture is – as mentioned – *kitsch*. Kitsch is defined as the 'translation of the stupidity of received ideas (*idées reçues*) into the language of beauty and feeling'. It represents, for Kundera, one of the most pervasive and perverse symptoms of the death of modernity – exemplifying some of its most uncanny 'terminal paradoxes'. Kitsch represents beauty as what *looks good*, weight as levity, experience as sentimentality, complexity as cliché, universal culture as the lowest-common-denominator of sameness, truth as media opinion. Invoking Hermann Broch's somewhat apocalyptic vision of a forthcoming and ineluctable 'tide of kitsch', Kundera fears for what he sees as the global dominion of a fake mass-media culture, based on conformity and an absence of creative imagination. If fiction is, as Kundera argues, that echo of God's laughter which attended the birth of the modern 'wisdom of uncertainty and ambiguity', the threat to fiction spells the demise of the modern dream. Modernity in its present terminal condition is a modernity which has betrayed its own best images, reducing the poetic imagination of individual human beings to the collectivist imaginary of a pre-programmed mass media. The following is Kundera's uncompromising version of the *end of modernity* thesis:

The irresistible flood of received ideas, programmed into computers, propagated by the mass media, threaten soon to become a force that will crush all original and individual thought and thus will smother the very essence of the European culture of the Modern Era ... however heroically the modern novel may struggle against the tide of kitsch, it ends up being overwhelmed by it. The word 'Kitsch' describes the attitude of those who want to please the greatest number, at any cost. To please, one must confirm what everyone wants to hear, put oneself at the service of received ideas ... Given the imperative necessity to please and thereby to gain the attention of the greatest number, the aesthetic of the mass media is inevitably that of kitsch; and as the mass media come to embrace and to infiltrate more and more our life, kitsch becomes our everyday aesthetic and moral code. ('Jerusalem address: the novel and europe', in *The Art of the Novel*, p. 163)

Kundera notes accordingly that, while modernism originally meant a revolt against conformist ideas and images, its current terminal phase represents an alarming reverse of its initial project. Today, Kundera observes, 'modernity is fused with the enormous virtuality of the mass media' – to such a degree that to be modern means a relentless struggle to be up-to-date, *au courant* with everything just as it happens, to conform to the very imperatives of conformity itself. 'Modernity has put on kitsch's clothing,' surmises Kundera ruefully. It has become post-modern.

The consequences of this fashion-ware of images for the future of imagination are considerable. Above all, the threat to imagination manifests itself in a threat to the spirit of laughter and *poiesis*. The terminal phase of modernity – now turned against its own best intentions – is typified by the reign of a new breed of persons, whom Kundera (borrowing a phrase from Rabelais) calls the *agélastes*, those cheerless masters of sameness who take their own kitsch imaginary so seriously that they have forgotten that the art of fiction was born as an echo of God's laughter.

There is an ethical *cri de coeur* in Kundera's plea for the survival of the poetical imagination. He knows that the 'imaginative world of the novel' is both fragile and perishable. But the very acknowledgement of this terminal threat to fiction is surely a refusal to allow the story to end, and therefore a commitment to the ongoing recreation of imagining. See my essay on the crisis of the post-modern novel, 'Rushdie, Kundera, Wolfe' in *Irish Review*, no. 7 (1989), pp. 32–40; French version 'La crise de L'imagination, in *Lettre internationale* (Paris, 1990). See also Mark Edmundson, 'Prophet of a new postmodernism: the greater challenge of Salman Rushdie', *Harper's Magazine*, December 1989, where the author distinguishes between 'negative' and 'positive' post-modernism, citing Rushdie's work as an example of the latter.

4 Lyotard, 'What is postmodernism', in *The Postmodern Condition* (Minneapolis, Minn.: University of Minnesota Press, 1984), p. 81.
5 Herbert Marcuse, *The Aesthetic Dimension* (Boston, Mass.: Beacon Press, 1978), p. 73.
6 Kundera, 'Sixty-three words', p. 150.
7 ibid., p. 150.
8 ibid., pp. 42–3.
9 Jean Baudrillard, *Simulations* (New York: Semiotext(e), 1983), p. 45.

10 ibid., p. 11. See Thomas Docherty's analysis of the post-modern impli-cations of Baudrillard's theory of simulation in *After Theory* (London: Routledge, 1990), pp. 100-5.
11 Baudrillard, *Simulations*, p. 25.
12 E. Ann Kaplan, *Postmodernism and Its Discontents* (London: Verso, 1988), pp. 4–5.
13 ibid., p. 5.
14 Hilary Lawson (ed.), *Dismantling Truth: Reality in the Postmodern World* (London: Weidenfeld & Nicolson, 1988), p. xxvi.
15 John Caputo, *Radical Hermeneutics* (Bloomington, Ind.: Indiana University Press, 1987), pp. 239–40.
16 ibid., p. 260.
17 ibid., p. 261.
18 Linda Hutcheon, *A Poetics of Postmodernism* (London: Routledge, 1988), p. xiii.
19 Italo Calvino, *The Literature Machine* (London: Picador, 1988), p. 99.
20 ibid., p. 99.
21 ibid., p. 134.
22 Hannah Arendt, *Between Past and Future* (New York: Viking, 1968), p. 221; and also her essay on 'Imagination' in *Lectures on Kant's Political Philosophy* (Sussex: Harvester Press, 1982), pp. 79–165.
23 Kant, *Critique of Pure Reason*, trans. N. Smith (New York: St Martins Press, 1965) B 151.
24 Olivier Mongin, 'La Shoah'.
25 Primo Levi, *Si c'est un homme* (Paris: Julliard, 1987).
26 Emmanuel Levinas, *Les Nouveaux Cahiers*, no. 85 (Summer 1989).
27 See, in particular, Martin Heidegger's phenomenological reading of Kant's claim that imagination is the 'common root' of the two stems of our knowledge, understanding and sensation: M. Heidegger, *Kant and the Problem of Metaphysics* (Bloomington, Ind.: Indiana University Press, 1962). See also my commentaries on this reading in the chapter on 'The hermeneutic imagination' above and the section 'Heidegger and the Kantian imagination' in *The Wake of Imagination* (London/Minneapolis: Hutchinson/University of Minnesota Press, 1988), pp. 189–96.
28 John Banville, *The Book of Evidence* (London: Secker & Warburg, 1988), p. 215.
29 See John Caputo, *Radical Hermeneutics: Repetition, Deconstruction and the Hermeneutic Project* (Bloomington, Ind.: Indiana University Press, 1987), p. 267: 'In our post-metaphysical ethics we want to think *Gelassenheit* toward others, the sense of respect or reverence the other commands, which arises from the fact that we know we are dealing with deep waters.' For a similar perspective, see A. De Nicholas, *Powers of Imagining: Ignatius de Loyola* (Albany, NY: State University of New York Press, 1986), pp. 31–75.
30 Kundera, 'Sixty-three words', p. 164.
31 See David Hume on 'sympathy' as a moral quality engendered by imagination, *A Treatise of Human Nature* (London: Oxford University Press, 1976); and Martin Buber's phenomenological account of the ethical

act of imagining the other in *The Knowledge of Man*, trans. M. Friedman (London: Allen & Unwin, 1965), p. 81: 'Applied to intercourse between men, "imagining the real" means that I imagine to myself what another man is at this very moment wishing, feeling, perceiving, thinking, and not as a detached content but in his very reality, that is, as a living process in this man'. See my NUI Studentship thesis, 'The Phenomenology of Imagination', University College Dublin, 1977, pp. 192–5.

32   M. Ignatieff, *The Needs of Strangers* (London: The Hogarth Press, 1990), p. 17.

33   ibid., p. 137.

34   Ignatieff sees this major shift of image or language model as corresponding to a transition from the nation-state as a permanent home of identity and belonging to a more cosmopolitan and ecological sense of belonging to the 'earth'. I would agree with the inclination towards a post-nationalist imagination but would argue that the movement outwards to the global needs to be complemented by a movement inwards from the centre as nation-state to the regions. Here I would endorse Kenneth Frampton's post-modern project of 'critical regionalism' (in *Postmodernism*, ICA Documents 4 (1986), pp. 26–7). See my discussion of the post-modern model of a global–local dialectic in 'Postmodern Ireland', in M. Hederman (ed.), *The Clash of Ideas* (Dublin: Gill & Macmillan, 1988), pp. 112–41; and 'Thinking otherwise' in R. Kearney (ed.), *Across the Frontiers* (Dublin: Wolfhound Press, 1989), pp. 7–28; and 'The fifth province: between the local and the global', in R. Kearney (ed.), *Migrations* (Dublin: Wolfhound Press, 1990).

35   I. Hassan, *The Postmodern Turn* (Colombus, Ohio: Ohio State University Press, 1987), p. 180.

36   ibid., p. 182.

37   Quoted by Hassan in 'Finnegans Wake and the postmodern imagination', in ibid., p. 103.

38   On the critical relationship between post-modern aesthetics and ethics, see R. Shusterman, 'Postmodernist Aestheticism: A New Moral Philosophy', in *Theory, Culture and Society*, vol. 5, nos 2–5 (London: Sage Publications, 1988), pp. 337–57.